On Clausewitz

Also by Hugh Smith

NAVAL POWER IN THE PACIFIC (*co-editor with Anthony Bergin*)
THE STRATEGISTS (*editor*)

On Clausewitz

A Study of Military and Political Ideas

Hugh Smith
School of Humanities and Social Science,
University College,
University of New South Wales,
Australian Defence Force Academy

macmillan

First published 2005 by
PALGRAVE MACMILLAN
Houndmills, Basingstoke, Hampshire RG21 6XS and
175 Fifth Avenue, New York, N. Y. 10010
Companies and representatives throughout the world

PALGRAVE MACMILLAN is the global academic imprint of the Palgrave Macmillan division of St. Martin's Press, LLC and of Palgrave Macmillan Ltd. Macmillan® is a registered trademark in the United States, United Kingdom and other countries. Palgrave is a registered trademark in the European Union and other countries.

ISBN 1–4039–3586–6 hardback
ISBN 1–4039–3587–4 paperback

This book is printed on paper suitable for recycling and made from fully managed and sustained forest sources.

A catalogue record for this book is available from the British Library.

Library of Congress Cataloging-in-Publication Data
Smith, Hugh, 1943–
    On Clausewitz : a study of military and political ideas / Hugh Smith.
        p. cm.
    Includes bibliographical references and index.
    ISBN 1–4039–3586–6 – ISBN 1–4039–3587–4 (paperback)
        1. Clausewitz, Carl von, 1780–1831. Vom Kriege. 2. Military art and science. 3. Politics and war. I. Title.

U102.C6643S63 2004
355.02–dc22   2004052588

10   9   8   7   6   5   4   3   2   1
14   13   12   11   10   09   08   07   06   05

Printed and bound in Great Britain by
Antony Rowe Ltd, Chippenham and Eastbourne

Contents

Part VI   Theory and Practice

*Two chapters analyse Clausewitz's approach to strategic theory
and his ideas about the practice of strategy.*

Part VII   The Political Context

*Three chapters describe Clausewitz's ideas about the political context
of war: politics within the state, the nature of external policy, and the
character of international politics.*

Part VIII   The Relevance of *On War*

*Five chapters look at Clausewitz's ideas as they relate to
developments in war since his death in 1831 and to arguments
that war has had its day.*

Acknowledgements

All those who study international relations have at least a passing interest in Clausewitz. I was prompted into a more enduring analysis of his ideas by the late John Vincent, then of the Australian National University and subsequently Montague Burton Professor of International Relations at the London School of Economics. To John, to colleagues at the Australian Defence Force Academy, and to successive classes of postgraduate and honours students with whom I have discussed Clausewitz at length, go my sincere thanks. To my family for their interest and patience over many years goes my deep appreciation.

I am grateful to Princeton University Press for permission to use the following publications:

Carl von Clausewitz, *On War*
Michael Howard and Peter Paret (editors and translators)
© 1976 Princeton University Press, 2004 renewed PUP
Reprinted by permission of Princeton University Press

Carl von Clausewitz, *Historical and Political Writings*
Peter Paret and Daniel Moran (editors and translators)
© 1992 Princeton University Press
Reprinted by permission of Princeton University Press

Preface

On War – the lengthy and somewhat disjointed *magnum opus* of an otherwise obscure Prussian general of the Napoleonic era, Carl Philipp Gottlieb von Clausewitz – has occupied a critical place in Western thinking about war for over a century and a half. It has been both vilified and venerated. Detractors have dismissed it as the work of a pseudo-philosophical pedant, a narrow-minded Prussian, or an unabashed militarist committed to war as an instrument of policy. Clausewitz, others suggest, has been made redundant by successive revolutions in military technology that began shortly after his death and still continue to transform war. The most radical critics argue that he makes the fundamental mistake of treating war as a rational act.

Supporters of Clausewitz have also made extravagant claims. For Bernard Brodie *On War* is 'not simply the greatest book on war but the one truly great book on that subject yet written'.[1] Only Sun Tzu's *The Art of War* might be mentioned in the same breath.[2] Though the latter is often cited for its emphasis on winning by diplomatic rather than military means, *On War* is placed in a class of its own. Comparisons are found only in quite different fields. Amos Perlmutter likens *On War* to Adam Smith's *Wealth of Nations* in offering a theory of human behaviour in an important area of human life.[3] *The Origin of Species* is another parallel: 'What Darwin accomplished for Biology generally Clausewitz did for the Life-History of Nations nearly half a century before him'.[4] General J.F.C. Fuller critically compared him to both Darwin and Marx, claiming that all three based their theories on '*mass struggle*, whether in war, in life, or in economics'.[5]

On War has attracted interest for many reasons. It offers a view of the place of war in human affairs. It has provided ideas about all-out war and 'absolute war' but also about limited war, the importance of political direction and control, the role of chance and friction, the impact of psychological factors, the conduct of campaigns, and the prospects for a theory of war. Written after Prussia's humiliation at the hands of Napoleon and the country's eventual liberation, *On War* speaks about national revival and mobilisation of the people. Political and military leaders have thus looked to Clausewitz at times of defeat – Britain after the Boer War, the United States after Vietnam – and also at times of challenge – the Soviet Union in World War II and both superpowers during the Cold War.

On War was a product of its time. For Clausewitz Prussia's survival as an independent nation was at stake. Napoleon threatened the entire European balance of power, while doctrines of revolution, individual rights, cosmopolitanism and the like threatened order at home. Napoleon also injected a new dynamism into war by enlisting the enthusiasm of the population at large and waging campaigns with unprecedented skill and vigour. Prussia and its army, Clausewitz believed, must reform to counter the threat. Intellectually, too, strategy was in dispute. Was it, as the High Enlightenment thought, a field which could yield analytical propositions like other areas of science; or was it, as the Romantic movement claimed, a human endeavour that was at heart creative and beyond rational analysis?

Clausewitz sought to understand war and strategy as phenomena in themselves and to provide an analysis of practical value to commanders. Given its historical context the shelf-life of *On War* might have been a few decades at best. Whatever their subject most classic texts are soon superseded as their ideas are either absorbed or rejected.[6] Yet *On War* is still read by both practitioners and professors, remaining a constant reference point in Western thinking about war. If there are rivals in longevity in this field the most apt comparison is Machiavelli's *The Prince* which – significantly – also deals with the security of states.

Writers after Clausewitz have explored the subject of war in greater detail, even with greater sophistication – for example, the application of technology to warfare and the intricacies of nuclear strategy. But no-one, to use Isaac Newton's metaphor, has stood on Clausewitz's shoulders? Have later writers allowed themselves to be dominated by Clausewitz's interpretation of war, failing to realise the narrow assumptions on which it is based?[7] Is the continuing preeminence of *On War* 'one of the greatest condemnations of the quality of military studies'.[8] Or is it simply that *On War* raises questions about war and politics that, once raised, remain perennial issues for all who think about war and peace?

For various reasons Clausewitz has been more open to misunderstanding than many other writers – the fact that *On War* remained unfinished and largely unrevised, the ambivalence surrounding his views on the conduct of war, his advocacy of political control over the military, the diverse reactions which war elicits in people, and his political stance which was both conservative and radical. All of these have prompted diverse and sometimes dangerous misinterpretations. Giving *On War* to the military, one later German general said, is like 'allowing a child to play with a razor blade'.[9] On occasions, indeed, Clausewitz has had 'less cause to fear his critics than to be wary of his professed admirers'.[10] Raymond Aron suggests there is less danger of misunderstanding now that he has found his 'natural home' in the universities.[11] While Aron's confidence in the academic world might be justified, one doubts the ivory tower would satisfy Clausewitz.

This study does not claim to present the 'real' or 'definitive' Clausewitz. For one thing, he is a moving target. Clausewitz changed his understanding of the nature of war in a fundamental way in 1827 and his ideas were only partially incorporated into the collection of his writings published as *On War* in 1832, the year after his death. The book contains contradictions and inconsistencies; it mixes the analytical and the normative; and it neglects important aspects of war such as seapower while including trivial matters such as moving cavalry across marshes. Its language is at times brilliant and incisive, at times turgid and obscure.

Even where authors have been clear and consistent in their views, intractable problems arise in analysing a work written by another person in another age for another audience.[12] No writer's ideas can be taken out of their historical, social and intellectual context and pickled for posterity. Interpretations of Clausewitz are liable to say as much – if not more – about the reader's view of war and politics as about the original author.[13] As Michael Howard has warned, '[t]oo much should not be read into Clausewitz, nor should more be expected of him than he intended to give'.[14]

In re-presenting Clausewitz I have tried to do the least amount of violence to the understanding of war he had developed at the time of his death. I focus primarily on *On War* although other works are cited where they add to an understanding of Clausewitz's ideas. Most references are to the reliable and readable translation of *On War* by Michael Howard and Peter Paret, published by Princeton University Press in 1976. Page references to this edition are given in square brackets in the body of the text. Where I have used the German text, I have relied on the 19th edition of *On War*, edited by Werner Hahlweg and published by Dümmler in Bonn in 1980. These citations are also in square brackets. For Clausewitz's other works an English translation is used where available. On occasions I suggest my preferred translations into English which are given in brackets with the German original.

My debt to Peter Paret, Azar Gat and Raymond Aron will be apparent.[15] Paret's study sets Clausewitz in his historical and political context while Gat focuses on his place in the world of ideas. Aron's work is a detailed explication of Clausewitz's thought. Their works have been of major importance in the contemporary understanding of Clausewitz but much of this scholarship is intended for specialist audiences. The most accessible introduction to Clausewitz – by Michael Howard – is eminently lucid but is necessarily short and does not claim to be comprehensive.[16] There remains, I believe, a need for a straightforward and extended exposition of Clausewitz's ideas about war and politics.

The present work is not intended to replace a reading of *On War*. This is partly because the lucidity of Clausewitz's mind can only be appreciated at first hand (albeit in translation), but principally because Clausewitz's work is suggestive rather than definitive, as he himself insisted. *On War* was intended to stimulate readers to work out their own response to the problems posed by war not to serve as a ready-reckoner for commanders in the field or as a manual for statesmen. To paraphrase General Douglas MacArthur, there is no substitute for Clausewitz.

Part I
Clausewitz's Life and Personality

1
Soldier

'war alone can lead me to my happy goal'.[1]

Carl von Clausewitz was a soldier from the age of 12 until his death in 1831. In combat before he was 13, he fought in five campaigns against France by the age of 35. After 1815 he took part in no more battles but began writing a work that became the best known study of war in the Western world. His background did not suggest such potential.

Clausewitz's father, Friedrich Gabriel, had fought without distinction as a lieutenant in the Seven Years War (1756–63) under Frederick the Great but, unable to authenticate his claim to nobility, was pensioned off in 1767. Appointed collector of taxes in Burg about 70 miles from Berlin, he married Friederike Schmidt who bore him six children. Carl was the second youngest, born on 1 June 1780.[2] The local school taught grammar, arithmetic and a little Latin but a major influence were the ex-soldiers who frequented the family home. As Clausewitz later wrote of himself:

> He grew up in the Prussian army. His father was an officer in the Seven Years' War, filled with the prejudices of his class. In his parents' house he saw almost no one but officers, and not the best educated and versatile at that.[3]

Unsurprisingly, three of the four brothers were anxious to enlist in the army. Carl's two older brothers – Friedrich and Wilhelm – were permitted to join the year after the king's death in 1786. Carl followed in May 1792 when his father took him to Prince Ferdinand's 34th Infantry Regiment in Potsdam. Though 12 was not unusually young for enlistment, the pain of leaving his family always remained.

War soon occupied his mind. As a *Fahnenjunker* (ensign and officer candidate) Clausewitz marched out with his regiment in January 1793 to face the armies of revolutionary France. He first saw action when his regiment shelled a village near Mainz held by the French. The siege to recapture Mainz itself began in earnest in June. When incendiary bombs set fire to the city Clausewitz cheered along with his fellow-soldiers – for which he later felt a sense of shame.[4]

Though Prussia's army performed well enough against France's citizen soldiers, the campaigns of those years were strategically inde-cisive. France, hampered by internal divisions, and Prussia, con-cerned to consolidate gains from the partitions of Poland in 1793 and 1795, concluded a separate treaty in April 1795. Clausewitz moved with his regiment to the small garrison town of Neuruppin some 40 miles from Berlin where he spent six years in the routine of peacetime barrack life of drill and exercises. By good fortune, his commanding officer was an enthusiast for education and encouraged junior officers to discuss and read widely in history, literature and military affairs.[5]

Clausewitz began a lengthy period of self-education, attending classes in mathematics, history and French. A growing capacity for self-reflection and self-analysis made him aware of his talents and his ambi-tion. But prospects for realising either seemed minimal. As he later wrote of his limited horizons at this time:

> until 1800, he was suckled on no other opinions than those prevail-ing in the service: that the Prussian army and its methods were of surpassing excellence. In short, from the beginning, *national* feeling and even *caste* sentiment were as pronounced and firmly rooted in the author as the lessons of life can make them.[6]

Nonetheless, he took trouble to exercise his troops in skirmishing tactics which were relatively new and hotly debated in military circles. He noted the mechanical nature of the regiment's annual manoeuvres and the

> mock battles, arranged long in advance, thoroughly discussed and prescribed in every detail [which] were carried out by the most dis-tinguished men of the army ... with an all-absorbing seriousness and intensity that bordered on weakness.[7]

The young lieutenant was acquiring a capacity for independent thinking.

Good reports and the patronage of senior officers ensured Clausewitz's selection for the three year course at the Institute for Young Officers (later the War College) in Berlin in the autumn of 1801. Its director was Gerhard von Scharnhorst (1755–1813), an artillery officer of humble origins who had recently transferred from the Hanoverian to the Prussian army. Though unmilitary in bearing, Scharnhorst had demonstrated his military talents in the Belgian wars and his intellectual acuity through numerous studies of warfare. Prussia had entrusted him with reorganising the moribund college.[8] A member of the first intake under the new regime, Clausewitz was initially depressed by his lack of education and money. But Scharnhorst, who believed in encouraging talented officers, soon perceived the potential of this diffident student. In turn, Clausewitz developed a deep affection and respect for his mentor who, 25 years his senior, became a father figure to him, especially after his own father died in 1802. Scharnhorst, in turn, held a deep affection for and trust in his protégé.

Clausewitz was invited to join the exclusive Military Society which Scharnhorst founded in January 1802 to promote discussion of all aspects of the art of war.[9] Several noblemen were members, including the young Prince August, nephew of Frederick William III. This connection assisted in Clausewitz's appointment as adjutant to August's battalion in Berlin with a substantially increased income in 1803. He also came into contact with court circles and in December 1803 met his future wife, Countess Marie von Brühl, a lady-in-waiting to the queen mother. Marie's English-born mother, however, opposed an engagement because of Clausewitz's uncertain aristocratic status. His self-doubt was somewhat diminished when, along with his friend Karl von Tiedemann, he headed the 40 students in the graduating class of the Institute in 1804.

Clausewitz now participated in serious debates about professional military issues such as the need for changes in tactics and strategy and for organisational reform. He began to write notes and comments on Prussian security, strategy, military history and international politics. His first published work was an anonymous essay in 1805 which criticised in highly polemical language the abstract military theory propounded by Heinrich von Bülow.[10] It was misguided and dangerous, Clausewitz argued, to reduce war to a formal system based on measurable quantities. Another essay, written in French in 1805, argued that Prussia could defend itself against French attack but that an offensive war would require allies who would inevitably have clashing political interests.[11]

Promoted brevet captain in November 1805 at the age of 25, Clausewitz could look forward to opportunities to shine in the looming war against France. Napoleon's decisive victory over combined Russian and Austrian armies at Austerlitz in December 1805 meant that France again threatened to dominate Europe. At risk of losing territory, Prussia signed the Treaty of Paris with France in February 1806 and agreed to close its ports to British shipping. Clausewitz was angered by Prussia's acquiescence, but there were good reasons for it. The army still clung to traditional tactics and had done little to promote reform. Promotion by seniority filled the highest positions with those Clausewitz called 'worn-out old men'.[12] Of 142 Prussian generals more than half were aged over 60, while over 90 per cent of the 8,000 strong officer corps were drawn from the nobility.[13]

Prussia's political leadership vacillated between appeasement of France and ineffectual resistance. Frederick William seemed bewildered by the mass of conflicting and disorganised advice from officials and generals. Slowly, however, Prussian opinion turned against Napoleon's demands, and a spirit of nationalism in the court, led by Queen Louise, persuaded the king to order partial mobilisation in August 1806. War was now inevitable but Prussia and its army were ill-prepared. In a letter to Marie on 29 September 1806 Clausewitz deplored the lack of leadership, the complex decision-making and the fractious opinions that surrounded the king – prompting his first known use of the term 'friction'.[14] By no means confident of victory, Clausewitz still believed that energy and national pride could give Prussia a fighting chance. In eager anticipation of war, he wrote to Marie, by now his fiancée, on 12 October 1806:

> In two or three days there will be a great battle which the entire army is eagerly awaiting. I myself anticipate this day with the same joy as I would my own wedding day.[15]

Clausewitz had totally identified his own future with that of Prussia. But the occasion for glory turned into what he later called 'the great catastrophe'.

On 14 October Napoleon sought out the Prussian armies at Jena and Auerstädt in Saxony. Clausewitz acquitted himself well in fierce fighting, assuming command of the battalion when August took over other forces – the largest command he held in battle.[16] Other units displayed great bravery but the army as a whole suffered from indecisive leadership, inadequate tactics and poor equipment. Losing the will to fight, it disintegrated before Napoleon's onslaught. At Jena with 53,000 men against France's 96,000 (of whom 54,000 saw action), Prussia suffered 25,000 killed, wounded and prisoners against France's 5,000. At Auerstädt, 13 miles to the north, the main Prussian army of 63,000 men faced only 27,000 but suffered 21,000 casualties against 8,000 French losses.[17]

For Prussia worse was to come. In characteristically ruthless fashion Napoleon pursued the defeated army, driving it into Prussia and taking nearly 150,000 prisoners. French cavalry forced August's battalion into an exhausting retreat that lasted 14 days until both Clausewitz and the Prince were captured on 28 October. Most of Prussia's seemingly strong fortresses surrendered meekly and civil officials greeted Napoleon with abject servility.[18] French forces occupied most of Prussia, including the capital, Berlin, on 26 October.

Though Frederick William avoided capture and Prussian forces continued to resist in the east with Russian support, the utter defeat of the army at Jena-Auerstädt was both a national disaster and a personal humiliation for Clausewitz. He and August were taken to Berlin where Napoleon interviewed the Prince. Clausewitz waited uncomfortably in an ante-room wearing a dirty, dishevelled uniform among scornful and finely-dressed imperial adjutants.[19] Once August had recovered from wounds, he and Clausewitz were ordered to France as prisoners of war. Leaving Berlin on 30 December, they made their way unescorted.

Between December and February Clausewitz wrote three letters on Prussia's defeat which were published in the journal *Minerva* in early 1807.[20] His view remained unchanged: victory would have been possible if Prussia had risen to the occasion with inspired leadership and total determination. In February Clausewitz and August reached Soissons where they spent most of their 'captivity' in comfortable lodgings. Enjoying considerable freedom of movement, Clausewitz made a three-week visit to Paris, read widely and improved his fluency in French. Inspection of an institute for the deaf and dumb in Paris impressed on him the potential of education.[21] Though Clausewitz's sojourn in France was pleasant enough, it brought home both Prussia's weakness and the importance of reform and education in revitalising Prussia.

When France made peace with Russia in July 1807, the Treaty of Tilsit deprived Prussia of its richest provinces and nearly halved its population from 9.7 million to 4.9 million. Napoleon also required Prussia to pay the costs of French occupation. At least, August and Clausewitz could now be released. Travelling first to Switzerland in

July, they stayed with the French literary figure in exile, Madame de Stäel. Here Clausewitz pursued his growing interest in education, visiting a school run by the Swiss educationist, Johann Pestalozzi. Convinced of the benefit of education both to individuals and the nation, Clausewitz shared Pestalozzi's belief that social background was of no relevance in the classroom.[22] This progressive view of education, unpopular in conservative circles, was to underlie his approach to military and political reform.

Returning to occupied Berlin in November 1807, Clausewitz wrote a study of French and German national characteristics.[23] Replete with simplistic generalisations, it criticised French artificiality and fickleness while praising German seriousness and originality. Though given to philosophical wrangling, Germans had soldierly qualities and the potential to create a warlike spirit in order to regain their independence. As Clausewitz wrote later, the nation had only itself to blame for the disaster of 1806. After the death of Frederick the Great in 1786, Prussia had lapsed into lethargy and indecision, failing to show the energy and vigour necessary to keep a small nation with limited resources in the front rank.[24] In the words of Queen Louise a generation of Prussians had fallen asleep on the laurels of Frederick the Great.[25]

Now nothing less than radical reform of the army and other institutions could restore Prussia's place in European affairs. It must follow France by placing war on a national footing and harnessing the talents of all citizens. Clausewitz threw himself into the push for reform, working under Scharnhorst as chairman of the Military Reorganisation Commission and August von Gneisenau who had been another of the heroes of 1806, defending the fortress at Kolberg against all odds. Initially, the shock of defeat allowed significant reforms.[26] In August 1808 the king proclaimed a law ending the requirement for noble status for entry into the officer corps. Social origins were now disconnected from military competence. Promotion by seniority was dropped, military discipline made less harsh and corporal punishment limited to serious offences. A full Ministry of War with overall control of military affairs was created in 1808–9.

One of the youngest and most junior figures among the group of military and civilian reformers at this time, Clausewitz was impatient for action. On several occasions he called for extreme measures, even war, against France.[27] His letters more than once declared that it was better to die fighting honourably than yield to Napoleon's demands.[28] When Austria renewed its struggle against France in April 1809

Clausewitz and other officers made moves to join the Austrian or British army in order to fight Napoleon. To this end Clausewitz took up learning English with a degree of success.[29]

If the reformers had a clear vision of Prussia's interests and the need for vigorous policy, this was not necessarily true of their fellow-citizens. Before 1806 most Prussians had been anxious to avoid war albeit for very different reasons: as Clausewitz put it, one party admired France, the other feared her.[30] After 1806 Prussia seemed to Clausewitz again divided – between those who saw resistance to France as hopeless and therefore regarded cooperation as the only means of salvation, and those who put their faith in popular resistance and a new war for independence.[31] Universal military service was another divisive issue. While reformers like Clausewitz thought the needs of the state overrode class and factional interests, the king feared conscription would diminish his control over the army, while the nobility saw it as a step towards loss of privileges. Only when these internal struggles were resolved could Prussia regain the freedom of action and national will essential to secure its liberation.

By 1809 the reform process had lost its head of steam as France tightened its grip on Prussia. The leading reformist minister, Baron vom Stein, had been forced to resign in 1808 after a letter dealing with plans for an uprising fell into French hands, and he fled to Prague in early 1809. Among the continental powers only Austria stood against Napoleon. It proved unequal to the task. After defeat, albeit narrowly, at the battle of Wagram in July 1809, Emperor Francis I sued for peace and the Treaty of Schönbrunn reduced Austria to a second-rate power.

In Prussia Napoleon presented the king with new demands for financial subsidies and insisted that Scharnhorst leave the War Department. The early death of Queen Louise in July 1810 removed a strong influence at court for reform and national independence.[32] To Clausewitz Prussia's fortunes seemed at their lowest ebb. But his own career and personal life had progressed rather more smoothly. In 1809 he was promoted to captain (first class) and became aide to Scharnhorst in the new ministry where he contributed to crucial reforms in personnel, weapons, training, officer education and fortifications. Reluctantly Clausewitz began to accept his lot as a staff officer rather than a commander.[33]

Promotion to major came in August 1810 together with appointment as instructor in tactics at the revitalised War College in Berlin. 'Half against my will', Clausewitz wrote to Gneisenau, 'I have become a professor ... my activities are nearly as peaceful as planting cabbage'.[34]

His lectures at the College were written out at length but his style was conversational, witty and animated.[35] Of particular importance were his presentations on *Kleinkrieg* or 'little war', the innovative use of small detachments to skirmish, harass and gather information, and the integration of these activities with traditional tactics and formations.[36] Clausewitz also served as tutor on military subjects to the 15 year old Crown Prince (later Frederick William IV in 1840) from October 1810 to March 1812.

On 17 December 1810, after a long courtship and many lengthy separations, Clausewitz and Marie von Brühl were married. Marie's mother had reluctantly consented in the face of Clausewitz's advancement and good connections. The couple were well-matched. Marie was intelligent and knowledgeable about politics, art and literature, and often assisted Clausewitz in his writing. They were also prolific correspondents – due in large measure to extended separations – and some 239 letters on topics of all kinds survive.[37] Their relationship proved deep and lasting and was a source of great emotional and intellectual support for Clausewitz.

Towards the end of 1811 political events once more intruded. War between France and Russia seemed imminent and the king was torn between aligning with the Tsar and accommodating Napoleon. He solved the dilemma by avoiding a decision and refusing to prepare for war. This was too much for Clausewitz. In February 1812 he wrote a long, anguished, rather self-important memorandum [*Bekenntnisdenkschrift*] in which he analysed the threat to Prussian security after 1806, condemned the dishonourable policy of submission to France, and outlined Prussia's capacity for war, including an irregular force drawn from the people. The tone was one of unrestrained, emotional commitment to the nation:

> It does not matter at all whether we have more or less means with which to save ourselves; the decision should arise from the need for salvation, not from the ease of gaining it. There is no help for us but ourselves.[38]

The king saw matters differently, finally agreeing to provide a Prussian Corps of 20,000 to support Napoleon's invasion of Russia. In March French troops again entered Berlin.

Clausewitz, along with 25–30 fellow officers, felt driven to resign his commission and seek military service with the Tsar.[39] With strong recommendations from Scharnhorst and Gneisenau he was commissioned as lieutenant colonel in the Russian army. Staying with

Scharnhorst en route to Russia Clausewitz found time to write an essay for the Crown Prince on the principles covered in his course of instruction.[40] This work anticipated certain of the ideas later developed (some heavily qualified) in *On War* – for example, the importance of decisiveness and daring, the wisdom of maximum effort, the inevitability of friction and the difficulty of adhering to military plans. The essay may also have given him the idea of writing a larger work on war of value to all officers.

Clausewitz reached the Tsar's headquarters at Vilna in May but a series of posts as staff officer left him frustrated. He could see faults in Russia's plans to counter Napoleon's 450,000-strong army but was unable to influence them. Speaking virtually no Russian did not help and he likened himself to a deaf-mute.[41] Nor was he impressed with Russian leadership, later describing the Tsar's headquarters as 'overrun with distinguished idlers'.[42] Clausewitz played no useful part when the Russians at last took a stand before Moscow at the equally-matched battle of Borodino on 7 September 1812. In one day's fighting Russia lost 44,000 men and Napoleon 30,000. It was a victory of sorts for the French who went on to occupy Moscow a week later. But the Tsar had left the city and refused to sue for peace. To Clausewitz it was a clear lesson that military success does not always bring desired political results.

Without a peace treaty and with much of Moscow destroyed by fire (possibly by accident rather than design), Napoleon had no choice but to leave the city as winter approached. Clausewitz campaigned with the forces harassing the French whose losses were magnified by cold, hunger and exhaustion. In November during the French army's crossing of the Berezina river Clausewitz witnessed a ghastly scene as 10,000 French soldiers were killed or drowned or simply froze to death. He wrote to Marie of seeing the dead and the dying in their hundreds, and ghost-like figures screaming for help:

> If my feelings had not been hardened it would have sent me mad. Even so, it will take many years before I can remember what I have seen without feeling a shuddering horror.[43]

Nonetheless, Clausewitz later wrote in criticism of the Russian general closest to the scene, that if Wittgenstein had attacked more vigorously 'he might have made the French loss much greater'.[44]

Clausewitz's contribution to Napoleon's defeat was diplomatic rather than military. As an emissary for Russia he played a critical role in persuading his fellow countryman, General von Yorck, to withdraw the Prussian Corps from Napoleon's retreating army by an agreement known as the Convention of Tauroggen. Negotiated in late December 1812, it was in clear disobedience to the King's orders and raised the possibility that Yorck might be brought to trial.[45] For Clausewitz, at least, it ended the fearful prospect of fighting against his two brothers serving under General Yorck.[46] Napoleon's retreat from Russia, however, did not resolve the dilemmas facing Prussia in early 1813. Scharnhorst was vigorously building up Prussian forces and pressed for immediate action against France which still occupied Berlin. The upper and middle classes also came to favour active resistance and in March 1813 the king finally declared war on France. Prussia's struggle for independence had begun.

Returning to Berlin in March 1813 with Wittgenstein's corps, Clausewitz attempted to re-enter the Prussian army. The king remained adamant despite appeals from influential supporters. Members of the court called him 'Lausewitz' behind his back.[47] Of all officers who served with Russia Clausewitz was treated most harshly.[48] The king never understood and never forgave what he regarded as his abandonment of Prussia. With the help of friends Clausewitz nonetheless succeeded in gaining appointment as a Russian liaison officer with the Prussian army, enabling him to work alongside Scharnhorst.

A surge of patriotism among the community, especially in East Prussia, helped produce large numbers of volunteers for the army. Despite deep suspicion by the court and active resistance in some quarters, Prussia built up its army from less than 60,000 in December 1812 into a force of about 130,000 by spring 1813 and 270,000 by autumn. A nation in arms was created. In May 1813 Prussian and Russian forces combined in a first attempt to expel the French from Prussia. At the battle of Lützen Napoleon drove the allied armies from the field in what was for Clausewitz the fiercest and most intense battle of his career. Though he distinguished himself in action and received a gash to the head, the recommended award for bravery was rejected by the king. Another casualty of Lützen was Scharnhorst whose wounds became infected, leading to his death a few weeks later. Clausewitz felt the loss deeply, especially as the king paid inadequate tribute to his close friend.

In mid-1813, hoping for another chance to fight the French, Clausewitz secured a post with the Russo-German legion, an all-German force of 6,000 men raised by the Duke of Oldenburg. Hostilities were renewed in the autumn and Clausewitz acquitted himself well in the minor battle of Göhrde and was promoted colonel. But he fretted at being unable to take part in the main campaign. The combined Prussian, Austrian, Russian and Swedish armies at last had superior numbers – over 340,000 facing nearly 200,000 – and their vast and bloody encounter at Leipzig on 16–19 October 1813 – the 'Battle of the Nations' – made inevitable both Napoleon's defeat and Prussia's independence. Apart from minor engagements Clausewitz did little more than observe the campaign which drove Napoleon back to Paris by March 1814. Though failing to find the glory he sought, he was finally permitted to re-join the Prussian army in the rank of full colonel in April 1814.

In the same month allied armies entered Paris and Napoleon was exiled to Elba. Clausewitz could at last enjoy a respite from war, spending several weeks at Aachen where he visited the spa in an attempt to restore his health that had suffered during the Russian campaign. A last opportunity for glory came with Napoleon's escape from Elba and triumphant return to France on 1 March 1815. Clausewitz was appointed chief of staff to the third Prussian Corps under General Thielmann which numbered around 20,000 men. But again he was disappointed. In the campaign leading to the battle of Waterloo in June the role of his Corps turned out to be crucial in the battle of Wavre – preventing two French corps under General Grouchy from reinforcing Napoleon at the decisive battle – but it was not one in which he was able to shine. Clausewitz was little pleased with the Iron Cross Second Class, the lowest Prussian decoration.[49]

There followed a period in occupied Paris during which Clausewitz argued for a more generous attitude towards the defeated enemy than many Prussians. Some were keen to exact revenge by blowing up the Pont d'Iéna which commemorated France's victory at Jena, but the Duke of Wellington posted guards to prevent this. Clausewitz believed the English would gain most politically from victory because they lacked the short-sighted passion for retaliation. A punitive policy would simply increase hostility against the allies, and could provoke open military resistance.[50] Now, Clausewitz believed, attention had to be directed towards Prussia's long-term interests in the peace. This had been the true purpose of the war.

2
Scholar

'I am one of those people who is much concerned with the future and thus rarely content with the present'.[1]

By 1815 Clausewitz had fought in five campaigns against the most powerful army in Europe. Aged 35, he had proved his courage and was recognised as a highly competent and intelligent staff officer, but he had not had the opportunity to exercise high command. He had gained social standing and married well and happily, but his nobility remained unconfirmed. He had seen his fatherland at last victorious but the disaster of 1806 had wounded his confidence in the state he served and his temporary abandonment of Prussia had deeply angered the king. Clausewitz's future was by no means certain.

The settlement of 1815 marked a transition to more stable international politics and Clausewitz's life reverted to routine when he was appointed chief of staff to the army based in Coblenz. Some variation came through a month-long tour of the Rhineland with the Crown Prince in April 1817. Travelling on horseback through the Eifel Mountains, Clausewitz saw at first hand the 'heart-rending' effects of famine:

> wasted figures, scarcely human in appearance, creeping around the fields trying to glean some nourishment from unharvested, immature, and already half-rotten potatoes.

Observing that starvation is always felt 'only by the *lowest* class', his pity was mixed with anger against the Prussian government for its failure to relieve widespread distress.[2]

In mid-1817 Clausewitz completed an essay on Scharnhorst designed both to secure the reputation of his late friend and mentor and to criticise opponents of reform for their lack of courage.[3] It proved impolitic to publish the study. The following year he was nominated for appointment as Superintendent of the War College in Berlin in the rank of major general. The king still doubted his loyalty but Clausewitz was eventually approved and promoted at the relatively young age of 38 in September 1818. Taking up the appointment in early 1819, Clausewitz rightly feared the position would prove a military backwater. His duties were largely administrative, such as approving leave or granting advances in pay to impecunious students. The curriculum was controlled by a Committee of Studies and Clausewitz had less opportunity to impart his military knowledge than as a junior instructor in 1811.[4]

Clausewitz also watched in despair as reformers were steadily eased out of positions of influence in Berlin. Many Prussians believed reform was unnecessary once national independence had been achieved. The position of the *Landwehr*, a conscript force of men between 17 and 40 organised in local units, was typical. It came under attack on both political and military grounds, and Clausewitz, one of the few reformers still in the army, responded with three memoranda in its defence. Each pointed to external threats that demanded a strong military stance. Each claimed the *Landwehr* would enhance rather than diminish Prussia's strength by bringing government and people closer together. One even suggested a representative government along the lines of the English Parliament.[5] The most polemical argued that to stay in the first rank Prussia should arm its entire population.[6] Unsurprisingly it failed to secure publication. In December 1819 over the objections of Gneisenau and Boyen, the minister for war, the king ordered reorganisation of the *Landwehr* to subordinate it to the regular army.[7]

Clausewitz himself considered more rewarding employment, including diplomatic service.[8] In spring 1818 he travelled to London, apparently with a view to securing nomination as ambassador to the Court of St James. Eventually political machinations at home – from which he held aloof out of a dislike of intrigue – deprived him of the appointment. The king also blocked his nomination for several lesser diplomatic posts. Clausewitz did give some thought, not for the first time, to becoming a civilian scholar but lacked the means to do so.[9] If there was a positive side to his career at this time, it was that undemanding duties at the War College gave him the opportunity to absorb the flourishing intellectual and artistic atmosphere of Berlin and to spend more time writing. To his satisfaction he was now free to engage in more inward, intellectual activity.

Political and military questions drew his attention. He saw that the European balance depended on states with differing political systems and social structures and with diverse concerns and ambitions. Prussia's security had to be understood in a much wider context than simply opposition to France and its policy had to accommodate many complex interests. A somewhat disjointed study of social change within states entitled *Agitation* was completed by 1823. It included an objective study of the historical decline of the nobility and the rise of the middle classes, a critical discussion of the unrealistic political demands of contemporary university students, and a distancing from his earlier support for constitutional government. Clausewitz may have written this essay in part to allay suspicion about his presumed radical views.[10]

In his first years in Berlin Clausewitz also wrote *The Campaigns of Frederick the Great* and *The Campaigns of Gustavus Adolphus 1630–1632*, the latter unusual for its focus on leadership and psychological factors rather than battles and sieges.[11] By 1825 he finished *Observations on Prussia in her Great Catastrophe*. Too critical and hyperbolic to be published in his lifetime, the study developed his theme of poor leadership in 1806 and contained biting comments on Prussian policies and personalities involved in the disaster: 'Like a loafer who consumes but earns nothing, the government vegetated and gambled on a lucky card in the lottery of fate'.[12] Clausewitz also completed *The Campaign of 1812 in Russia* which he had started in 1814.

Between these histories he continued work on a lengthy study of war and strategy which he had conceived in 1816. By 1827 a draft of the first six Books of *On War* was complete – about one thousand pages of manuscript.[13] That year also brought long-awaited recognition of the Clausewitz family's noble status, an advancement attributable more to social connections and service to the state than to genealogy.[14] The fact that two elder brothers were well-respected and courageous soldiers – Friedrich a major general and Wilhelm about to become one – no doubt influenced the king's decision. Though he never doubted his nobility Clausewitz welcomed formal and public confirmation.

From 1827 Clausewitz resumed his work on military history, while beginning a revision of the manuscript of *On War*.[15] One reason for his return to history may have been a desire to re-examine campaigns in the light of his new perspective on war.[16] In December 1827 two letters commenting on strategic exercises his friend Roeder was undertaking set out new themes that needed to be incorporated into his manuscript on war – war as a continuation of policy with different means, and the idea of two types of war, limited and unlimited.[17] The planned revision of his major work was never completed. Following a request in December 1829 to return to active duty, Clausewitz was appointed to the Inspectorate of Artillery in February 1830. While familiarising himself with his new post to be taken up later in the year, Clausewitz put aside the manuscript of *On War*.

In the course of 1830 turmoil erupted across Europe – the overthrow of Charles X in France, a civil war in Spain, an uprising by the Belgians against the Dutch, disturbances in several German states and an insurrection in Poland. The European order again seemed in jeopardy. Clausewitz thought France likely to initiate hostilities early the following year and prepared several studies of Prussia's options in such a war. Following rebellion in Warsaw and collapse of Russian authority in Poland at the end of November 1830, Clausewitz was summoned to serve as chief of staff to Gneisenau. His old friend, now aged 70, commanded a corps responsible for observing and containing the Polish disturbance.

Returning to Berlin in early 1831 to prepare for his new post, Clausewitz wrote an essay, *Europe since the Polish Partitions*, in which he complained of those who supported Polish independence out of sentiment rather than concentrating on the demands of Prussian security and the European balance. To him Polish nationalism was an exercise in futility and a constant source of instability. Another essay, *On the Basic Question of Germany's Existence*, criticised cosmopolitan sympathy for the national rebellions in Belgium, Italy and Poland, and pointed to the danger that independence for Poland, a friend of France, would present to Prussia's security. The real need, Clausewitz argued, was to focus on the continuing threat from France. Though intended for publication, this study was rejected by a cautious publisher who perhaps found it too hard-headed for the times.[18]

Clausewitz welcomed the opportunity to serve again under Gneisenau. The two left Berlin in March for Posen from where Prussian forces could monitor developments in Poland. If war came, Clausewitz expected that it would be against the real enemy – France – and that he would be sent to the west. He became frustrated with Prussian indecision and anxious about the future, both Prussia's and his own. Several letters to Marie complained of the stupidity of the world and contemplated the prospect of his own death. By mid-1831 the cholera that was sweeping Poland approached the Prussian frontier and efforts were made to establish a *cordon sanitaire*. In August Gneisenau fell victim to the disease, and Clausewitz's depression was made worse by the scant recognition the king paid to his friend. Hope for permanent command in Gneisenau's place proved in vain.

During October Russian forces regained control in Poland and on 7 November Clausewitz returned to Breslau where Marie joined him two days later. On 16 November Clausewitz was struck down by a mild attack of cholera that appears to have precipitated a heart attack from which he died that evening. He was buried at the military cemetery in Breslau without ceremony in accord with laws designed to contain the cholera epidemic. Family and friends were prohibited from attending though Marie's brother bribed the gravediggers to allow him be present.[19] Frederick William sent a message which came close to sympathy: 'The news of the sudden death of Major General Clausewitz ... is as unexpected as it is painful. The army has suffered a loss which will be difficult to remedy, which greatly saddens me'.[20]

Assisted by her brother and two family friends, Marie von Clausewitz set about the task of putting her husband's manuscripts in order for publication. Three volumes which constituted *On War* appeared between 1832 and 1834. A further five volumes had been completed by January 1836 when Marie died and was buried next to her husband. Clausewitz's friends attended to the final two volumes of his intellectual legacy. In 1971, the 140th anniversary of his death, his physical remains were returned to the cemetery at Burg, his birthplace, for interment with full military honours, and a simple monument was erected.[21]

Clausewitz's life alternated between action and reflection, achievement and frustration, happiness and melancholy, romantic ideals and scientific analysis, ardent patriotism and disillusionment with Prussia. It offers scope for diverse interpretations. Was he at heart unstable, depressive, ill at ease with himself and the world; or was he a man who reconciled himself with reality and found a measure of contentment? Both views have won favour.[22]

For the young Clausewitz war and the state promised personal fulfilment and social recognition. My path takes me across 'a great battlefield', he wrote to Marie, and 'unless I enter upon it, no lasting happiness can be mine'.[23] Position and prospects, including marriage, depended on service to the army and the nation. Selection for the Institute in 1801, for example, was critical to his career and left him indebted to the army. Identification with the state, however, led to permanent tension between his aspirations for Prussia and the reality of mediocre leadership and blinkered conservatism. In 1812 his frustration led him to abandon Prussia itself. Transfer to foreign armies was common at this time but rarely accompanied by explicit denunciation of national policy. Risking one's career for the interests of the state can be admirable – later German history showed the need for such people – but raises profound questions about who should determine those interests. Clausewitz seems never to have doubted the rightness of his decision, nor to have understood why the king found it difficult to accept his return.

Lacking confidence in his talents, Clausewitz constantly sought reassurance through external measures of his worth, not least in the progress of his career. In a letter to Marie in 1807 he wrote that nature had perhaps endowed him 'too richly with that vanity we call ambition'.[24] He set his aims very high but never found the rewards and respect he received to be quite enough. While several positions he sought were denied, his advancement in the army was very competitive and he was not ill done by overall. In similar vein he pursued recognition of his noble ancestry over many years, partly out of a sense of obligation to his father, partly to establish his place in society. Again, the state provided the reassurance he needed, albeit later than he wished.

In social relations Clausewitz was self-effacing and reserved, lacking the ease and confidence most of his fellow officers enjoyed. Many thought him standoffish, over-critical of others, and something of a pedant who took life too seriously. Even in more mature years, he was fearful of being scorned and reluctant to give a spontaneous opinion, often expressing his views with undue modesty. Putting arguments in writing came more easily. Among soldiers, too, according to General von Brandt who saw him at close quarters in 1831, Clausewitz seemed ill at ease and lacked the ability to inspire troops; though a brilliant staff officer, he never acquired the habits of command in the field.[25] This inability to fit in easily was something Clausewitz was aware of and regretted.

Yet for all his anxieties and obsessions, and his difficult and sometimes melancholic character, Clausewitz showed a capacity for human relationships, a sense of fairness and an intellectual honesty which do not point to a fundamentally disturbed personality. Throughout his life Clausewitz always had a small number of close friends and colleagues whom he loved and respected and who in return genuinely admired and loved him. In the right company he was engaging, warm, even exuberant and liable to uncontrollable fits of laughter.[26] Few saw this side of his character. Above all, his marriage to Marie, an intelligent, sensitive and sophisticated woman with whom he constantly shared feelings and ideas, was a remarkably close relationship that brought deep happiness and contentment.

Clausewitz's response to constant physical ailments is also revealing. He suffered from arthritis, violent headaches, gout, toothache, haemorrhoids, as well as frostbite caused by his time in Russia; and in 1822 he suffered an apparent stroke that temporarily paralysed his right arm and in 1827 a severe illness of an unknown nature.[27] Yet these sufferings never undermined his mental robustness. Like many contemporaries, he used opium to relieve pain but was determined not to become over-reliant on it.[28] Despite occasional complaints in letters, physical afflictions were met with a determination to overcome them and were never more than temporary sources of depression.

Immediately after Clausewitz's death Marie wrote to a friend that he had died 'as though he pushed life away like a heavy burden' – a life that 'had consisted of an almost unbroken chain of effort, sorrow, and vexation'.[29] This was true in part but has to be weighed against more positive factors. Clausewitz's gloomy ruminations were often balanced by comments on more fortunate aspects of his life and by his determination to be active.[30] He recognised his own weaknesses and was perhaps more absorbed with them than most, but introspection and self-criticism were often a spur to greater effort. If his determination to achieve and to be recognised bordered on the obsessive, this is perhaps a measure of the obstacles he faced and the strength of character he brought to overcoming them. Clausewitz was a complex personality but intellectually honest and – with rare exceptions such as his scorn for the Poles – humanly decent. His personality was, in short, 'sadly over-strained yet curiously winning'.[31]

In retrospect the events of 1812 were a turning-point. Clausewitz's rejection of Prussian policy prefigured – after three more years of war – a less idealistic view of the state. His stance towards Prussia's destiny and the nation's honour was more disillusioned and fatalistic, but also more objective and realistic. The extended peace after 1815 allowed him time to consider questions of war and politics more deeply. War had a certain purity about it: clear objectives could be set and pursued with total commitment and maximum effort. Peace involved compromise and uncertain aims. But even war, Clausewitz came to recognise, had its ambiguities. Understanding the relationship between military action and policy became his overriding interest.

A man from a narrow background with a limited education, committed to the Prussian army through its most desperate years, might have produced a narrowly militarist and nationalist analysis. Yet his study of war proved remarkable for its balance and objectivity. For Clausewitz was above all an intellectual in the sense that he desired and had the ability to understand the phenomena around him. Not an original thinker in philosophical terms, he nonetheless produced a work that spoke to succeeding generations. *On War* was marked by acceptance of the elements of reason, chance and passion which Clausewitz saw at the heart of war and which in the form of intellect, the fortunes of war and commitment to the state had also governed his own life.

Part II

War in the Napoleonic Era

3
On Warfare

'war itself ... stood at the lectern and every day offered practical instruction to its students'.[1]

On War must be seen against the dramatic transformation of warfare that occurred in Clausewitz's lifetime. His first campaign in 1793 typified eighteenth century warfare as armies manoeuvred for limited objectives and favoured skirmishes over major battles. Neither the traditional armies of Prussia and Austria nor the 'citizen armies' of France emerged victorious. His second campaign in 1806, by contrast, demonstrated all too clearly Napoleon's strategy of actively seeking out an opponent, forcing a decisive encounter and vigorously pursuing a defeated army. In the space of a few years war had taken on radically new characteristics and an explanation had to be found. Clausewitz's hypothesis was that war reflected 'the nature of states and societies as they are determined by their times and prevailing conditions'. [586] In remarkably few years, he concluded, 'the transformation of the art of war resulted from the transformation of politics'. [610]

The transformation of warfare

Prior to 1789 war was an enterprise of monarchs aimed at promoting dynastic interests and securing territorial possessions. Both royal ambition and military capability were usually limited:

> The enemy's cash resources, his treasury and his credit, were all approximately known; so was the size of his fighting forces. No great expansion was feasible at the outbreak of war. Knowing the limits of the enemy's strength, men knew they were reasonably safe

from total ruin; and being aware of their limitations, they were compelled to restrict their own aims in turn. Safe from the threat of extremes, it was no longer necessary to go to extremes. [590]

Even the Seven Years War, despite intense actions, ended in accustomed fashion as diplomats agreed on a settlement at the negotiating table.

The general state of equilibrium, Clausewitz argued, 'transformed most wars into mongrel affairs, in which the original hostilities have to twist and turn among conflicting interests to such a degree that they emerge very much attenuated'. [387] It was not that states were unable to fight wars with vigour. Eighteenth century battles had a higher ratio of casualties than those of the Napoleonic era.[2] Rather, war was based on a limited segment of society. The danger was that an army could be 'pulverized' and another could not be raised, for 'behind the army there was nothing'. [590] Armies were a royal possession with officers drawn from the nobility owing personal allegiance to the monarch. Governments, Clausewitz observed, had 'parted company with their peoples' so that 'the people's part [in war] had been extinguished'. [589] Most wars touched the bulk of the population hardly at all.

Primitive communications and logistics also made armies unwieldy. Campaigns were mostly confined to the period May to September when grass could feed horses and crops nourish soldiers. Plunder and despoliation of enemy territory were out of fashion. [590] Ceremony and etiquette, much valued in society, transferred to armies and warfare itself.[3] Chivalry and courtesy befitted noble officers. The art of war had become 'a half-and-half affair and often ... downright make-believe'. [609] These constraints, Clausewitz noted, were not caused by the spirit of progress and enlightenment in the eighteenth century, merely consistent with it. [591] Once political and social circumstances changed, war itself would change.

The French Revolution and Napoleon's leadership demonstrated a power and dynamism in war previously unimaginable. For France war became 'the business of the people – a people of thirty millions, all of whom considered themselves to be citizens'. [592] Frenchmen identified themselves with the nation and could be called to arms in great numbers. Before 1789 an army in the field rarely exceeded 50,000 men. Within a decade or so conscription and militia systems were able to raise forces of over 100,000, and in 1812 France could assemble 600,000 men for its Russian adventure. Even with these larger forces

Napoleon showed that flexible and aggressive strategies were possible, pushing soldiers to the limits of endurance and manoeuvring rapidly to launch enveloping attacks. With a continuing supply of troops generals could risk major battles. Between 1790 and 1820 Europe saw 713 battles – an average of 23 a year compared with eight or nine a year over the previous three centuries.[4]

War could also pursue greater ambitions. Under Napoleon war brought France an empire stretching at times from Madrid to Moscow, from Copenhagen to Cairo. States were occupied and driven into subservience, national boundaries re-drawn, puppet monarchies created and the Holy Roman Empire brought down. Once Napoleon overcame the technical and organisational imperfections of France's army,

> this juggernaut of war, based on the strength of the entire people, began its pulverising course through Europe ... all limits disappeared in the vigor and enthusiasm shown by governments and their subjects. ... War, untrammeled by any conventional restraints, had broken loose in all its elemental fury. [592–3]

War was no longer a matter of 'one king against another, one army against another, but one people against another'.[5]

> [After 1793] a force appeared that beggared all imagination ... The people became a participant in war; instead of governments and armies as heretofore, the full weight of the nation was thrown into the balance ... nothing now impeded the vigor with which war could be waged. [591–2]

The underlying cause, Clausewitz believed, lay in social and political changes within France and their inevitable impact on France's neighbours:

> Very few of the new manifestations in war can be ascribed to new inventions or new departures in ideas. They result mainly from the transformation of society and new social conditions. [515]

It was not the doctrines propounded by the French Revolution that impressed Clausewitz, but its political and military energy.[6] Conscription, militia forces and guerrilla war all demonstrated new possibilities while governments also learned to harness the economy to war.

Conscripting the population

The idea that armies might rely on popular participation was not new. Montesquieu (1689–1755) and Rousseau (1712–78) both advocated armies of volunteer citizen-soldiers, the former seeing them as a bulwark against tyranny, the latter as an expression of civic virtue. Both believed in the fighting qualities of such a force. Before 1789, however, volunteers provided the majority of troops though various forms of compulsory service existed. In France the king periodically called on local authorities to provide a specified number of men by means of their own choosing – for example, a levy of one in 24 adult males.[7] In Prussia Frederick the Great forced prisoners to serve in the army.[8] Compulsion, however, was regarded with scepticism on account of its cost and practical difficulties.

France demonstrated the new potential of conscription. Having recruited over 100,000 volunteers in 1791, the government found the supply of 'active citizens' drying up.[9] A *levée en masse* to raise troops was the only solution and the Convention passed its famous decree on 23 August 1793:

> From this moment until that in which our enemies shall have been driven from the territory of the Republic, all Frenchmen are permanently requisitioned for service in the armies.[10]

With a larger population than any country save Russia, France began to unlock its military potential. By 1794 three quarters of a million men were under arms, a combination of new conscripts, volunteers and experienced soldiers from the *ancien régime*. Not merely an army of citizens but a nation of soldiers was being created.[11]

The opening skirmish of the Revolutionary Wars at Valmy in 1792 was little more than an indecisive artillery duel with few casualties and no strategic import. But it took on historic significance for a different reason. France's citizen-soldiers held up against well-trained Prussian infantry and remained calm under fire. The mass of the population could evidently be relied on to fight with spirit and discipline. In Clausewitz's judgement, therefore, '[t]he cannonade of Valmy decided more than the battle of Hochkirch'. [222][12] Goethe, who was present at Valmy, observed that '[f]rom this place and from this day begins a new era in the history of the world'.[13]

The *levée* worked initially not only because of popular enthusiasm for war but also because poor harvests, high inflation and unemployment were active recruiters. Yet the system suffered many defects. Peasants resented being taken from home and family, and valuable rural labour was lost.[14] Ardent Catholics were reluctant to fight for an atheist republic. Some citizens resorted to self-mutilation to evade service or exploited exemptions for married men. Substitution, bribery and token service in guards of honour were other escape routes.[15] Local officials disliked administering unpopular laws and dealing with frequent disturbances.

Despite these problems conscription got large numbers into the field and ensured that numbers could be sustained in the face of heavy losses from enemy action, disease and desertion. The 600,000 French soldiers who died between 1792–99 could be replaced.[16] And when Napoleon's run of easy victories ended after 1807, the system could be pushed still harder.[17] Punishments were instituted for assisting evaders and missing men hunted down.[18] While a prisoner in France Clausewitz was shocked to see reluctant conscripts in the streets shackled to a rope and led by police.[19] Up to 1812 the annual average rose from 78,000 to 127,000 recruits though quality fell. Even after the retreat from Moscow a further 840,000 men could be called to the colours.[20] The supply of French soldiers seemed endless. Napoleon's boast to Metternich that he could 'spend' 30,000 soldiers per month was not idle.[21]

None of France's opponents escaped their pre-1789 systems to the same degree. Some, notably Britain and Russia, made only minimal changes. In Prussia conscription remained controversial because political and social conditions had not yet changed. The king feared compulsory service would bring in soldiers more loyal to country than to crown. The nobility believed it would lead to greater egalitarianism in the officer corps, and the bourgeoisie were reluctant to spend time in uniform. The common people saw obvious drawbacks in compulsory service in an army renowned for harsh discipline and poor conditions. But for Clausewitz and the reformers conscription was the only way to match France's power. Not simply the citizen-soldier but the patriot-soldier had to be created.

Militia forces

The significance of militia forces based on part-time military training is often overshadowed by the attention given to conscription for full-time service. Common in Europe before 1789 these forces supplemented a nation's military capability and provided a flow of volunteers to the regular army. Clausewitz was eloquent on their value:

> the concept of a militia embodies the idea of an extraordinary and largely voluntary participation in the war by the whole population ... [Compared with the regular army, it constitutes] a reservoir of strength that is much more extensive, much more flexible, and whose spirit and loyalty are much easier to arouse. [372]

The primary purpose of a well-organised militia, in Clausewitz's view, was to strengthen the state by promoting a military spirit among the population.

The militia took on greater importance in Prussia after 1808 when France limited the Prussian army to 42,000 men under the Convention of Paris. Only widespread use of militia forces could increase the number of men in uniform with any rapidity. The most ambitious militia organisation was the *Landwehr* which was based on provincial governments and enlisted men between the ages of 17 and 40. *Jäger* formations were aimed at middle and upper class patriots with reasonable education who did not wish to serve in the ranks and could afford their own uniforms and equipment.[22] The *Landsturm*, which was least well equipped and often lacked arms and uniforms, picked up the rest.

An opportunity to employ the militia came in early 1813 with Napoleon in retreat from Russia but still occupying Prussian territory. Universal conscription was introduced with the aim of creating a *Landwehr* of 120,000 men. In March the king made his resounding 'Appeal to my People', calling for 'every son of the fatherland [to participate] ... in this battle for ... freedom'.[23] In April all remaining men were required to serve in the *Landsturm* though it was so tightly regulated its purpose was undermined.[24] By mid-1813 Prussia had about 270,000 men or 6 per cent of its total population in the field – a proportion twice as high as in 1806 when many more foreigners served.[25] In the war of liberation the *Jäger* and *Landwehr* did tolerably well. With more civilians in uniform than regulars, the myth – partly true – was born of the victorious nation in arms.

Following the defeat of France, the *Landwehr* again became a matter of contention. Though it had proved its value in war, many thought it less necessary in time of peace. Clausewitz continued to press for a strong *Landwehr*, favouring three continuous years of service rather than one month each year for 24 years since this would make it 'easier to impart a martial character to the soldier's mind, habits, and values'.[26] Objections to the mixing of classes in the militia, he argued, were based on prejudice; in any case mixing was unlikely in practice.[27] The important thing was to ensure that all sections of society shared the burden. But in reality, Clausewitz observed in letters to Gneisenau, the militia is marked by 'graft, unimaginable arbitrariness, and injustice'; and '[t]he end result of our miserable system is always that the poor man becomes a soldier, the rich man remains free'.[28]

More difficult were objections that the *Landwehr*, by arming the people, would become 'a means of revolution, a state of legalized anarchy that is as much of a threat to the social order at home as it is to the enemy'. [479] Clausewitz, first, challenged the supposed political reliability of the regular army, pointing out that in all recent revolutions, especially 'the mother of them all', the standing army had failed to actively defend the monarchy.[29] Popular attitudes inevitably penetrate any standing forces. Louis XIV's army had thus melted away 'under the rays of the revolutionary spirit, like snow in springtime'.[30] Second, Clausewitz argued that even if a political risk existed retention of the *Landwehr* was advantageous.

> The *Landwehr* increases the danger of revolution; disarming the *Landwehr* increases the danger of invasion and enslavement. On the historical evidence which is the greater danger?[31]

> *Prussia has need to arm her entire people so that she can withstand the two giants who will always threaten her from east and west.* Should she fear her own people more than these two giants?[32]

By December 1819, however, the battle was lost and leading reformers resigned. Their nation in arms of 1813 had been designed not only to increase numbers and rouse popular feeling but also to make waging war 'less dependent on the weak will of the monarch'.[33] Now, the king might reluctantly accept conscription to strengthen the regular army, but could not support the militia save in the direst circumstances.[34] Later Prussian governments never fully trusted citizens armed and in uniform and the *Landwehr* lost much of its significance.

Guerrilla war

The most dramatic form of popular involvement in warfare was manifest in Spain where irregular fighters took on Napoleon's army after 1807 in a campaign of harassment or small war (*guerrilla*).

Guerrillas, as these fighters came to be called, excelled at marauding, banditry, massacres, maiming, torture and murder, often attacking isolated French detachments, messengers and those fallen behind marching columns. A German veteran referred grimly to 'the incessant molestations of an invisible enemy'.[35] Such warfare was not new but in Spain it served as a means of national defence alongside or in place of a standing army. Antoine Jomini (1779–1869), who served with Marshal Ney in Spain, was impressed by this 'most formidable' type of war.[36]

Clausewitz also saw it as a significant development. For him the idea of people's war [*Volkskrieg*] referred to a wide range of popular involvement in war.[37] At one extreme, it meant the extensive use of militia in support of the regular army as in Prussia in 1813–14. At the other, it referred to the irregular and often ill-disciplined activities of non-uniformed guerrillas harassing regular armies. The common element was popular participation in fighting an invader. Clausewitz identified several necessary conditions for guerrilla war: war on one's own territory; a series of engagements rather than a single battle; a large theatre of operations with terrain that is rough and inaccessible because of mountains, forests or marshes; and a people whose temperament is suited to irregular war. [480]

For Clausewitz the great advantages of guerrillas were flexibility, surprise, and their ability to concentrate forces like 'a dark and menacing cloud out of which a bolt of lightning may strike at any time'. [481] Their tactics, however, did not appeal to professional soldiers and reports of atrocities in Spain were received with horror throughout Europe. The Duke of Wellington had as little to do with the guerrillas as possible.[38] Efforts were made to bring them under control but with limited success. Their real contribution lay in preventing the French army from concentrating its forces in order to defeat the British and Spanish armies; the presence of these regular forces also meant that the French could not devote enough effort to eliminate the guerrillas.[39] What Napoleon called his 'Spanish ulcer' was never cured. The medicine existed – large numbers of regular troops – but these could not be spared in sufficient doses. Successful suppression of popular uprisings in Calabria and Tyrol showed what the French army could achieve.[40] Even so, French forces remained in control of much of Spain until 1811–12 when troops were withdrawn for the invasion of Russia.

For Clausewitz the great contribution of irregular forces was to inspire national resistance. It did not matter too much why people joined the guerrilla effort – whether patriotism, private ambition, economic gain, pro-church sentiment – or that guerrillas often lived off the country, making them unpopular with local communities and sometimes more hated than the French.[41] Once the flames of national resistance are lit, Clausewitz argued, they will spread like a brushfire, endangering the enemy's communications and eventually his entire force. 'Like smoldering embers, [people's war] consumes the basic foundations of the enemy forces'. [480] The methods may be unpleasant but results count.

There were echoes of Spain during Napoleon's invasion of Russia. Tsar Alexander called on the Russian people to undertake 'a general rising against the universal tyrant'.[42] Peasants exacted violent and brutal revenge against retreating soldiers who shortly before had marched heedlessly across their land. Clausewitz believed that Russia had emulated Spain in making war a concern of the people, and thought the result 'brilliant'. [592] But he recognised that guerrilla tactics did not win the day. Napoleon was defeated by the Russian army, Russian strategy (improvised as it was), Russian weather and his own logistic failures. In Prussia the king was finally persuaded to authorise limited irregular operations in 1813. Contrary to the traditions of war, he declared that members of the *Landwehr* need not wear uniform and remained lawful combatants if taken prisoner.[43]

Spain was an inspiration, not a model.[44] For Prussia and Clausewitz guerrilla war was a last resort, employed only when all else failed:

> like a drowning man who will clutch instinctively at a straw, it is the natural law of the moral world that a nation that finds itself on the brink of an abyss will try to save itself by any means. [483]

It was no alternative to professional forces and should be pursued 'within the framework of a war conducted by the regular army, and coordinated in one all-encompassing plan'. [480] Command must be retained over scattered forces, particularly in mountainous country. Militia and armed civilians should not be used against sizeable enemy forces since their role is not 'to pulverise the core but to nibble ... around the edges', to operate just outside the theatre of war and deny those areas to the invader. [480–1] Overall it is 'a slow, persistent, calculated business, entailing a definite risk' [482].

Guerrilla war was a politically sensitive topic that Clausewitz treated with caution. *On War* makes only one direct reference to the insurgents in Spain [350] but the message is clear. People's war in all its facets is 'simply another means of war' in principle available to all countries. In general terms it is

> an outgrowth of the way in which conventional barriers have been swept away in our lifetime by the elemental violence of war. It is, in fact, a broadening of the fermentation process known as war. [479]

No nation could afford to ignore the value of armed civilians in desperate times.

The economic dimension

Most eighteenth century monarchs paid little attention to economic measures in warfare.[45] After 1789, however, governments at war faced unprecedented financial burdens and looked for ways of extracting economic as well as human resources from the population. Regulations, price-fixing and taxation were common responses. Britain introduced income tax in 1799 enabling it to supply weapons, materiel, uniforms, munitions and funds (mostly to be spent on British goods) to any country that opposed Napoleon. One of the principal beneficiaries, Prussia obtained most of its new arms from Britain by 1813. Just as armies required soldiers, the war economy required artisans. Governments set up or expanded factories to produce the numerous items of equipment every army needs. In the early 1790s, for example, France established 15 arms factories and 20 others to manufacture swords and bayonets.[46]

Blockade was another critical economic dimension of war. Napoleon made extensive use of this strategy together with prohibitions on commerce. In 1806 he proclaimed the so-called 'continental system', requiring Prussia to close its ports to British shipping and forbidding all trade with or via Britain. In retaliation the Royal Navy cleared what little shipping Prussia had from the high seas and imposed a blockade on all neutral trade with continental Europe except that passing through British ports.

On War seemingly ignores the economic dimension of war. But Clausewitz was not indifferent to such matters. He recognised that adequate funds were essential to an effective military campaign: '[t]oday money can compensate for everything, and for this reason it is the measure, or rather the multiplier, of all active forces'.[47] Indeed, '[m]oney can be thought of as acting like oil, which reduces natural friction and permits all forces to operate with much greater independence and flexibility'.[48] His historical and political writings emphasise the importance of financial constraints in the conduct of war, not least for Frederick the Great. Prussia's current military budget also attracted his interest. It was wrong for the government to spend proportionately less on the army than in Frederick's time despite needed improvements in weapons, equipment, soldiers' conditions, care for invalids and payment for requisitions.[49]

> It has become fashionable among writers to heap scorn on the fact that the military consumes half of a state's income. They seem to regard the army as a kind of incidental expense.[50]

Clausewitz also calculated the cost of one Prussian soldier lost, taking into account all the expenses of arming, equipping and transporting troops[51]; and, like many soldiers, he criticised increases in the budget for civil administration.

Nor did the impact of blockades escape his attention. The French 'system' undermined credit in national economies, brought higher interest rates, stimulated inflation, encouraged corruption and caused resources to lie fallow. 'The emperor of France blocks trade, and the whole continent languishes in misery'.[52] Clausewitz was certainly familiar with some of the ideas of Adam Smith and with the importance of national wealth and trade as a source of military power. But his subject was war and economic factors, while important, could be left aside in *On War*.

War, politics and society

The revolution of 1789 opened up new dimensions of warfare and new sources of power for the state. In France government reached more deeply into citizens' lives and not just through conscription. In the 1790s price controls, censorship and repression of religion were used to boost popular support for war. Under Napoleon cheap newspapers disseminated government propaganda, state authorities monitored teachers, and high school students were compelled to wear uniform and adopt martial practices. Passports and identity papers were introduced.[53] Even painting, music and architecture were appropriated for the glory of the Emperor.[54]

The people increasingly identified themselves with their country; war and the army came to symbolise the strength and spirit of the nation. But the process was complex, incomplete and variable from nation to nation. Both traditionalists and reformers supported central control by the state, but differed over how far and how fast change might progress. Provincial authorities, the clergy, craft associations and village communities often resisted the centralising thrust of the state, sometimes violently. Feudalism and parochialism also remained formidable. Nor should cosmopolitanism be overlooked. Turning to France for culture and enlightenment, it ran against both provincialism and nationalism.

Prussia's survival, the reformers believed, depended on maximising the energies and talents of its people without undermining the established social order. The nobility had to be persuaded of the need for reform while remaining willing to serve the state. The middle class – essential to the development of national bureaucracy, expansion of trade and industry, and growth of the professions, not least the armed forces – had to be accommodated.[55] The masses were needed in the army for their numbers and their patriotism – one of the most powerful passions ever harnessed for the purpose of war. But while Napoleon, a usurper, could welcome the mass army, traditional monarchs feared the duty of the citizen to the nation would replace the loyalty of the subject.

To Clausewitz it was clear that the old political, social and administrative structures had collapsed – overtaken by 'a broadening and intensification of the fermentation process known as war'. [479]

> War was returned to the people, who to some extent had been separated from it by the professional standing armies; war cast off its shackles and crossed the bounds of what once seemed possible.[56]

The new sources of power, Clausewitz believed, would inevitably be exploited. Discussing Russia's reliance on the people in 1812 and Prussia's militia forces in 1813, he concluded:

> Now that governments have become conscious of these resources, we cannot expect them to remain unused in the future, whether the war is fought in self-defense or in order to satisfy ambition. [220]

There would be no going back:

> the reader will agree with us when we say that once barriers – which in a sense consist only in man's ignorance of what is possible – are torn down, they are not so easily set up again. [593]

This did not mean that all future wars would follow the same pattern. Only major wars would stimulate governments sufficiently to engage a nation's entire resources. [488] But the new possibilities could never be ignored. For Clausewitz 'the question only remains whether mankind at large will gain by this expansion of the element of war'. It was a question he sensibly chose to leave 'to the philosophers'. [479]

4
On Armies

'The true nature of war will break through again and again with overwhelming force, and must, therefore, be the basis of any permanent military arrangements'. [313]

If the people were now participants in war, could old military structures carry the weight? Most eighteenth century armies were small, consisting of long-term soldiers together with foreigners and mercenaries. In the ranks, often drawn from the lowest elements of society, there was little loyalty and much desertion. Soldiers needed to be highly-trained to operate cumbersome weapons and move in tight formations.[1] Generals were reluctant to hazard them in pitched battles that might bring 25 per cent casualties in a morning's fighting.[2] Manoeuvring for position or cutting an opponent's supply lines seemed preferable. It was relatively easy to avoid or break off battle, relatively hard to compel an opponent to fight or pursue a defeated opponent. Static fortifications, cumbersome logistics and the need to defend long lines of communication further constrained operations. These armies, Clausewitz observed, 'with their fortresses and prepared positions, came to form a state within a state, in which violence gradually faded away'. [591]

Changes were already under way before 1789. Military professionalism was emerging among the officer corps and some countries established military academies. Here and there progressive armies adopted new forms of organisation and control, more flexible tactics and better methods of supply. More humane treatment of the common soldier, some argued, would encourage recruitment and increase effectiveness. Reform of armies was everywhere proposed and almost everywhere resisted, since it was bound up with social and political change. But until the 1790s there seemed little need for urgency.

Military professionalism

Clausewitz believed the officer corps had to break with its past. The nobility had come to regard the profession of arms not as 'an honorable *corporate duty*, but rather a corporate prerogative', a source of privilege and patronage.[3] After the Seven Years War, for example, Frederick the Great systematically excluded commoners, including Clausewitz's father, from the officer corps, deeply distrusting 'the calculating spirit that he associated with men of a bourgeois background'.[4] France was more progressive. The purchase of commissions was phased out, public and uniform rules for promotion applied, and some non-aristocratic officers accepted.[5] But armies, like society, remained deeply divided by class, and new policies were sometimes ignored or reforms reversed.[6]

Slowly and unevenly military professionalism challenged old assumptions. More officers saw themselves as members of a profession requiring specialised knowledge. The need for expertise in artillery, supply, maintenance, transport, fortifications, pontoons, roads, bridge-building, mapping and topography was recognised.[7] From around the middle of the eighteenth century several countries established schools for training officers in artillery and military engineering. (Napoleon attended France's artillery school.) Books on military topics were published, specialist journals founded and earnest debate took place over tactics and doctrine.

Warfare, the progressives argued, was too serious to be left to the aristocrat or the amateur. The key criterion was professional competence: all those meeting required standards should qualify for officership regardless of social origins, an approach readily adopted by the French armies of the 1790s which also commissioned competent NCOs. Napoleon further opened the way for experience and talent. France's junior officers were mostly youthful, energetic and competent and many generals were 'young, dynamic, ambitious and in a hurry'.[8] Even so, fewer than 10 per cent of professional officers came from the poorest classes; the required level of education was still confined to the middle and upper classes.[9]

Napoleon also nurtured professional pride among his diverse army of enthusiastic citizen-soldiers, willing and unwilling conscripts and seasoned regulars. They were flogged less often than their counterparts and enjoyed more initiative and self-respect. Standard terms of service such as length of enlistment, pay and conditions were set.[10] Among NCOs literacy became more common as reliance on written orders and the practice of record-keeping grew. (Literate NCOs could also read revolutionary and nationalist propaganda.[11]) Distinct uniforms developed group cohesion, usually focused on the regiment or battalion which became a soldier's primary loyalty.[12] Within such units élite companies were often created. Public parades and ceremonies permitted soldiers to show off splendid uniforms.[13] In 1802 Napoleon introduced the Legion of Honour award, open to all ranks and carrying a substantial pension.[14] The Emperor also made a point of appearing among his men at times of danger; 'the little corporal' was accepted as one of them.[15] Desertion remained a problem everywhere, but French armies suffered least.

Prussia's army failed to meet the challenge. In 1789 it boasted 170,000 men in a population of less than six million – a far higher proportion under arms than France whose army numbered 181,000 out of more than 26 million. More efficient and more ready to promote on merit than other armies, the Prussian army set an example in discipline and tactics copied by the rest of Europe. It performed well enough up to 1795, but learned no lessons. In 1800 only 13 of 142 generals were under 50 while more than half were over 60; non-Germans still filled one-third of the ranks.[16] Fortresses were neglected and Prussian soldiers lacked winter coats.[17] As Clausewitz later described the army prior to 1806:

> The senior commanders were without spirit; the higher ranks down to staff captain as a group were old and decrepit. Many of the soldiers were also too old. ... equipment was the worst in Europe ... the soldier's food and clothing were beneath contempt. ... the spirit of the army was unwarlike to the highest degree.[18]

Prussia's defeat in 1806 was only to be expected.

After Jena the Prussian army became a battleground for reform driven by the Military Reorganisation Commission. Some 208 officers were cashiered for poor performance and of 142 generals, 120 were retired or placed on the inactive list.[19] Changes in organisation and tactics were pushed through, including a flexible mix of skirmishers, lines and columns in 1809. Drill was simplified, training improved, and corporal and capital punishment reduced.[20] Of great symbolic importance was the order issued by Frederick William III on 6 August 1808 opening the officer corps to merit:

> From now on a claim to officer rank shall in peacetime be warranted only by knowledge and education, in time of war by exceptional

bravery and quickness of perception ... All social preference which has hitherto existed ceases completely in the army.[21]

In principle, at least, the link between social status and military rank was broken. But the tight control over new commissions exercised by each regiment ensured the officer corps retained its aristocratic character.[22]

Nonetheless, greater attention was given to educating the officer corps. The reformers advocated learning as a 'prerequisite for advancement into the upper echelons of the army'.[23] Following the practice in Prussia's civil service, exams were introduced for appointment and promotion.[24] Two schools for officer cadets were established and the War College (later the War Academy) set up in 1810. There was to be no danger of the army becoming an 'object of derision for the educated'.[25] In Prussia learning and military professionalism marched in step.

Military organisation and control

As early as 1763, following the humiliating peace at the end of the Seven Years War, the French army began to change its basic structure from the traditional battalion or regiment in response to the seemingly intractable problem of exercising command over a single army larger than about 50,000 men.[26] A distinctly larger formation known as a division began to be adopted. Numbering up to 10–12,000 men under independent command, it consisted of infantry, cavalry and artillery supported by engineering, medical and communications personnel. As conscription raised ever greater numbers of soldiers, the division became indispensable, allowing large forces to be organised in a way that retained effective control.[27]

There were other benefits. Napoleon put divisions together to create corps of up to 30,000 soldiers and put corps together to create separate armies. With a wide range of capabilities a corps could operate independently and enjoy tactical flexibility lacking in smaller formations. A corps of 20–30,000 men, it was said, could not be eliminated in an afternoon, being able to resist long enough for relief to arrive.[28] Skilful and energetic commanders could more easily pursue an opponent and compel him to give battle. Striking power was increased by concentrating cavalry into independent divisions, while concentration of artillery allowed massive bombardments.[29] Logistics also became easier as formations could safely be divided between different roads for movement or widely spread to more readily exploit the countryside.[30]

Military organisation became a vital component of military effectiveness. Yet only on the eve of war in 1806 did Prussia establish permanent divisions.

Control of the new formations was still no easy task, especially given the vast geographical range of Napoleon's campaigns. His inability to gain rapid victories in the extremes of empire – Spain and Russia – was due in part to command failure.[31] Communications were still limited to the speed of messengers on horseback. Staff work in support of commanders – detailed planning, use of reliable topographical maps, accurate transmission of orders, constant monitoring of events, and coordination between formations – was probably more advanced in France than elsewhere but still underdeveloped. The benefits of a permanent corps of staff officers attached to formations (not to individual commanders as first happened) became apparent, as did the need for specialist training. Less happily, mutual suspicion between staff and line officers inevitably appeared. Intelligence was another problem. Napoleon understood the importance of gathering all manner of relevant information but he still lacked sufficient dedicated officers and a central analytical organisation.[32] If everything came together at one point, it was in the mind of the commander.[33]

Unlike Jomini, Clausewitz fought on the wrong side to be aware of the attention which Napoleon paid to the collection of data of strategic significance.[34] From his own experience Clausewitz's belief that information was mainly unreliable was correct enough. At Auerstädt, for example, Prussia's reconnaissance was unenterprising and failed to discover how Napoleon was massing his forces. This helps explain the disparaging comments in *On War*: 'Many intelligence reports in war are contradictory; even more are false, and most are uncertain'. [117] Reports of battle casualties are 'never accurate, seldom truthful, and in most cases deliberately falsified'. [234] Clausewitz did not draw the now familiar distinction between raw information and processed intelligence, using the term *Nachrichten* only in the former sense. Translating *Nachrichten* as 'intelligence' rather than 'reports' is thus misleading – especially in such generalisations as 'most intelligence is false'. [117].[35] His concern was to emphasise that most information is 'unreliable and transient' and that a plan in war constitutes 'a flimsy structure that can easily collapse and bury us in its ruins'. [117] Wherever possible, of course, patrols, feints and other methods should be used to gain as much accurate information about an enemy as possible. [236, 258, 302]

The wars in which Clausewitz fought were a transitional stage 'between the age-old tradition of oral operational command and the new system of written staff work'.[36] Commanders such as Blücher came to respect and rely on staff expertise; the staff officer slowly became a recognised and invaluable specialist, occupying a central role in campaigns. The collection and organisation of intelligence was also in the early stages of development. Recognising the need for training and education in these and other areas of expertise, the Prussian army laid the foundations for the Great General Staff that later became its 'collective brain'.[37] In the longer term Prussia rather than France institutionalised the 'genius for war'.[38]

Tactics and strategy

Until 1792 the standard order for battle in all European armies was the line of infantry, three men deep, designed to maximise the volume of fire from inaccurate muskets. Re-loading these cumbersome weapons was a lengthy business that could be improved only by many hours of drill. Effective fire also demanded tight discipline. For such reasons the soldiers of Frederick the Great required between two and six years of harsh training.[39]

The line also made it easier for officers to control their men on the battlefield. But linear tactics began to run into problems. Rapid advance was always difficult and penetration of enemy lines even more so. Enclosure of Europe's open landscape by fences, hedgerows and ditches added to the problem.[40] Moreover, the very effectiveness of pre-war drill, some increase in the accuracy of firearms and improved battlefield leadership, made combat 'almost too costly to sustain'.[41] In the Seven Years War battle casualties of 20 per cent and more became common. Infantry could not quickly be replaced because of the intensive drill required, while substituting artillery greatly hampered logistics and manoeuvre.[42]

More flexible tactics seemed essential. France, where serious debate about tactics began as early as the 1720s, adopted the infantry column, some 50 men wide and 12 deep (*ordre profond*). Easier to manoeuvre and to keep moving than the long line (*ordre mince*), it was designed to be thrown against an enemy and to use shock to maximum effect.[43] With fewer firing in the front rows less musket training was needed.[44] Esprit de corps, it was argued, could hold the column together. England, by contrast, stuck resolutely and successfully to the linear formation.

Another problem with the old armies was that infantry could hardly be trusted to fight in small detachments, even less as skirmishers.[45] Officers feared loss of control and desertion. Reform-minded tacticians, however, advocated use of skirmishers to harass and disrupt enemy forces before and during an attack, to conduct reconnaissance and patrolling, and to operate in smaller detachments in rough country or behind enemy lines. The effect was to entrust the conduct of engagements to more junior personnel, even individual soldiers. With better morale and discipline French troops proved up to the task.

A third major change came after the battle. Earlier generals were often reluctant to pursue a defeated force, sometimes providing a 'golden bridge' for their escape. They preferred to bring regiments back to order while their soldiers were anxious to plunder the dead and wounded.[46] Napoleon, by contrast, regularly undertook aggressive pursuit of a retreating enemy, often greatly magnifying the scale of his original victory. Cavalry came into its own, disrupting efforts at orderly withdrawal and hunting down fleeing enemy units. Clausewitz experienced French cavalry in this role at first hand after Jena.

More flexible tactics and new military structures offered scope for a different style of campaigning. In a way never matched by his opponents Napoleon brought speed, energy, flexibility, logistic freedom and imagination as well as large numbers of troops to the campaign. He could disperse formations and bring them together rapidly for battle. A favourite stratagem was the *manoeuvre sur les derrières* – moving troops behind an enemy force and cutting its lines of supply and communication prior to attacking from the rear or flank. Napoleon used it 30 times between 1796 and 1815, mostly to good effect.[47]

The older style of warfare was proven inadequate. It still had admirers but Clausewitz dismissed them as both narrow-minded and high-minded:

> More recent wars appear to them as crude brawls that can teach nothing and that are to be considered as relapses into barbarism. This view is as petty as its subject. [218]

New military forms had made possible new and more dangerous forms of campaign. 'The revolutionary methods of the French', as Clausewitz put it, 'had attacked the traditional ways of warfare like acid'.

> Now war stepped forth in all its raw violence, dragging along an immense accumulation of power; and nothing met the eye but ruins

of the traditional art of war on the one hand, and incredible successes on the other. [48]

For Clausewitz war had opened up unprecedented possibilities.

Supplying armies

If armies were growing in size and had to move further and faster, how were they to be provided with food, shelter, equipment and munitions? Clausewitz's picture of eighteenth century logistics emphasised its limitations and stressed the advances adopted in the new manner of campaigning – in both cases more than the facts warranted. Certainly, armies had found living off the countryside difficult, requiring dispersal over large areas with its strategic disadvantages and increased desertion. They therefore aimed to be as independent as possible, taking with them extensive baggage trains and relying also on depots and a flow of supplies from the rear. Yet armies routinely drew supplies from the land; and efforts were made to ensure orderly provisioning through purchase from local sources. [49]

The new system, in Clausewitz's view, threw off the old shackles. Napoleon cared little for depots and supply systems: troops and generals alike were driven into the field and left to 'procure, steal, and loot everything they needed'. [332] French armies travelled fast, living off the land as they went and using bivouacs for shelter wherever they halted. Billets ceased to be necessary. Soldiers were trusted to disperse to secure supplies. In turn, this minimised the danger of supply lines being cut and bold generals with good troops, Clausewitz concluded, enjoyed unprecedented scope for strategic innovation. [330]

Logistics could not be ignored altogether. As Clausewitz acknowledged, considerations of supply commonly affect 'the strategic lines of a campaign and a war'. [131]

> An army is like a tree that draws its sustenance from the ground in which it grows. A mere sapling is easy to transplant, but the taller it grows, the harder this will become. [343]

Ensuring supplies, for example, could be one reason for moving into large towns and agricultural areas [298–9] or dividing one's forces during an advance. [622–3] Billets were often indispensable for the health of soldiers. [325] Napoleon's campaign in Russia demonstrated the cost of failure to heed logistics – 'the unprecedented wastage of his army on the advance, and ... its wholly calamitous retreat'. [339]

Clausewitz identified three main approaches to supply drawn from the land: (i) living off local households or community resources; (ii) requisitioning supplies on the spot by troops themselves; and (iii) organising requisitions through local authorities. [332–7] The last-mentioned is to be preferred as 'the simplest and most efficient way of feeding troops' which has constituted 'the basic method in all recent wars'. [335] While there are disadvantages, this 'modern way of provisioning ... allows the army to use 'everything available in the locality, no matter to whom it belongs'. [332] It 'knows no limits other than the complete exhaustion, impoverishment and devastation of the country'. [336] Payment, Clausewitz assumes, will not normally be necessary. Fear of punishment or maltreatment will serve as a 'collective burden that weighs on the whole population'. [335] The idea that the old methods of supply were more humane is irrelevant. 'War itself is anything but humane'. [338] His concern was efficiency, not ethics.[50]

Clausewitz dealt with logistics only because it influences the campaign. He shared the natural prejudice of fighting soldiers against those who merely supply war, while recognising the vital importance of operational skill as opposed to sound logistical planning in the campaigns of the era.[51] Too often, he claims, problems of supply are used as excuses by commanders for inactivity or opportunities missed. Too great a concern with supply risks making the quarter-master-general into the supreme commander. [339]

Weapons and technology

Though well under way by the beginning of the nineteenth century, the industrial revolution had produced no major advances in weaponry. Some development occurred in muskets – greater rate of fire and improved accuracy – and in artillery – barrels bored from solid metal rather than castings, and more accurate elevation and sighting devices. But in essence firearms remained similar to those of a hundred years earlier, while transport and communications were unchanged over a thousand years.[52] Differences in technology between armies thus did not matter much:

> Today armies are so much alike in weapons, training and equipment that there is little difference in such matters between the best and the worst of them. [282]

Besides, any significant technological imbalance would be readily corrected:

> Education may still make a considerable difference between technical corps, but what it usually comes down to is that one side invents improvements and first puts them to use, and the other side promptly copies them. [282]

In reality, most armies were slow to embrace change because of natural conservatism and shortage of technical skills.

That *On War* seldom mentions artillery is somewhat surprising since both Scharnhorst and Napoleon had been an artillery officers.[53] Though dismissing fortified garrisons and strong points because they can be 'mechanically flattened' by artillery [393], Clausewitz argues that in the field only infantry is essential, whereas artillery is ultimately dispensable. [285] [54] For him technology can never be at the heart of war. Technical matters stand 'in about the same relationship to combat as the craft of the swordsmith to the art of fencing'. [133]

In Clausewitz's time advances in weaponry produced only marginal effects while new inventions were usually treated as curiosities. Napoleon disbanded the balloon corps established by the French Army in 1793 for observing enemy positions; the Duke of Wellington dismissed the new 'Congreve' rockets out of hand.[55] Not until the 1820s when industrialists in Europe proposed a railway system able to deploy troops rapidly was there any inkling that technology could radically change war.[56] Clausewitz can hardly be criticised for failing to anticipate the extraordinary advances in military technology that began almost immediately after his death. Whether they challenge his understanding of war will be considered later.

Maritime warfare

If Clausewitz sought to understand war as a whole, it seems inexplicable that he virtually ignored warfare at sea. *On War* mentions neither economic blockades enforced by navies nor any of the Royal Navy's unbroken run of victories from 1794 to Trafalgar in 1805, a battle that put England's mastery of the seas beyond doubt. Clausewitz seems indifferent to the fact that seapower allowed Britain to seize French colonies, force the surrender of Napoleon's army in Egypt by destroying his fleet at the battle of the Nile in 1798, launch surprise attacks in Spain in 1804 and Denmark in 1807, land forces in Naples in 1805 and at Walcheren in 1809, and supply its armies in Portugal and Spain. Above all, perhaps, seapower prevented Napoleon from attempting his boldest ambition – invasion of England.

Why this 'astounding ... insularity of mind' on Clausewitz's part?[57] No British or American writer on war would dare omit all discussion of seapower. The Prussian perspective accounts for much. Lacking overseas possessions and taking little interest in questions of colonies, trade and empire, Prussia was vitally concerned with land borders and threatening neighbours. War on land was both the principal threat and the primary means of security. Clausewitz was an army officer of a continental power who naturally thought 'from the land outwards'.[58] Can anything be said in his defence?

First, Clausewitz does make a limited number of observations on seapower.[59] In *On War* a chapter on diversions (Book VII, 20) deals with the sea-borne landings by the British in North Holland in 1799 and Walcheren Island in the Scheldt estuary in 1809 (the latter proving a disaster due to bad weather, sickness, poor planning and bad leadership). Such operations were only warranted because 'British troops could not be used in any other way'. [563] Landings in force, moreover, may be justified if the local population can be counted on for support. [563] The most useful function of such threats against a coast is to immobilise enemy forces, possibly tying up two or three times as many of his troops and guns compared with the potential attacker. [634].[60] In an article written in 1831 Clausewitz also recognised that up to 1812 England's naval power had effectively substituted for putting large armies on European soil.[61]

Second, it can be argued that major wars are won on land not at sea, that Napoleon was ultimately defeated not by fleets but by armies. British dominance of the seas after Trafalgar would have been of little value if Napoleon had secured undisputed control of continental Europe.[62] An important proponent of this thesis was the maritime strategist, Sir Julian Corbett (1854–1922), whose 'discovery' of Clausewitz led him to claim that command of the sea is only a means to an end and that a genuinely great power cannot be defeated at sea alone.[63] Clausewitz was neither first nor last to believe that war is ultimately about gaining and holding territory and controlling its population, that in the final analysis navies exist to support and supply armies on land.

The key to Clausewitz's view of naval warfare, however, lies in his second reference in *On War* which draws a parallel between navies and standing armies of earlier times: 'Fighting on land therefore had something in common with naval tactics, a quality which has now completely disappeared'. [220] Formerly, neither were closely linked to the people or able to draw on the full range of national resources. Armies changed radically, navies remained in the eighteenth century – expensive to create and maintain, limited in size and carrying their own supplies. Navies also ranged beyond political control due to time and distance while at home they could not do what armies often did, namely prop up royal despotism.[64] Though Nelson took English nationalism to sea, maritime warfare in Clausewitz's time remained bound to its historical origins, unable to incorporate the energy and dynamism of war on land.

Armies and change

The greater involvement of the people allowed war on land to take on a more dynamic, destructive and decisive form. Changes already under way before 1789 were accelerated by the demands of warfare on a scale that was unprecedented in European history. Armies needed to become less amateur and aristocratic, more proficient and professional. Change was in the air and armies had better learn quickly. Only the technology of war remained substantially unchanged – like the navies of the day.

After 1815 governments began winding back the military reforms made necessary by war. Victory (and defeat) had been complete and there seemed little reason for winners or losers to invest in large armies at great expense. In the end the war had been won and lost by regular armies, not citizen volunteers or peasants taking up arms. Britain and Russia had come through the war with armies fundamentally unchanged. Conservative elements in Prussia and elsewhere reduced or eliminated the egalitarian and democratic compromises necessary during war. Yet there could be no simple return to 1789. Political and social reforms such as reduction of aristocratic privilege, held firm. Debate on organisation, strategy and tactics continued.

Governments also placed greater emphasis on nationals serving in national armies. Napoleon had raised troops in many countries – Belgium, Switzerland, Poland, Ireland, the Italian and German states among others – a grand total of 720,000 foreigners.[65] About half of his force for the invasion of Russia were not French citizens. After 1815 reliance on large numbers of foreign troops became less acceptable, as did the practice of officers changing armies. National loyalties were coming to provide the motive power for mass armies, encouraging volunteers, and making conscription more workable.[66] In turn, armies contributed to the flourishing of nationalism by breaking down parochial ties and promoting patriotism.[67]

What kind of force would be needed in future? Jomini advocated small, highly-trained, professional armies, while condemning Napoleon's unrealistic ambitions and arguing, not altogether soundly, that the key to his success was manoeuvre, speed and concentration.[68] Clausewitz, on the other hand, had his eye on the likely major threat to Prussia. Large armies with extensive reserves relying on the people's role in war were the safest bet. For the rest of the nineteenth century conservatives and most professional soldiers found Jomini's conclusion more amenable since, contra Clausewitz, it explained Napoleon's triumphs without reference to the social and political upheavals of the French Revolution.

Part III
On War

5
The Intellectual Provenance of
On War

'the theories [of war] we possess ... are stuffed with commonplaces, truisms, and nonsense of every kind'. [1]

Clausewitz's view of war was shaped not only by social, political and military developments but also by the intellectual climate of his time. In the eighteenth century and into the nineteenth ideas of the Enlightenment and Counter-Enlightenment swept through Europe. While France and England were epicentres of the Enlightenment, the German states experienced both movements in abundance. Intellectual and artistic creativity flourished through writers such as Schiller, Goethe, Heine and Kleist, composers such as Beethoven, philosophers such as Kant, Fichte, Schelling and Hegel, and historians such as Ranke. Familiar with many of their ideas and artistic achievements, Clausewitz entered a wider debate about what could and could not be understood about human and social behaviour. The question for him was how war fitted in to the scheme of things.

Enlightenment and Counter-Enlightenment

The Enlightenment saw the application of reason and scientific method as a means of understanding both the external world – planets, tides, geology, animals and the like – and the internal world of human thought and action. Throughout Europe works of scientific analysis, empirical study and philosophy abounded. This knowledge, it was believed, could and should be communicated to others. New journals were founded on all manner of subjects, encyclopedias compiled, public libraries established, and societies created for the discussion of scientific, artistic and political ideas. Public education through schools, universities and training institutions promised enlightenment for the masses and elimination of ignorance and superstition. Reformers such as Wilhelm von Humboldt, Prussia's first minister of education from 1808, also believed a better educated populace would strengthen the nation's economic, political and military capacity. Universal education became an issue for governments and an interest of armies.

A key assumption of the Enlightenment was a degree of uniformity in time, place and human nature. Though overlaid by historical detail, local culture and unique characteristics of individuals, human behaviour reveals continuities and regularities. Hence general principles can be discovered that hold true regardless of time or place. Historical events are not unique in their essentials but manifestations of universal rules or tendencies. Systematic knowledge of human behaviour and interactions could be envisaged. Better understanding of the human mind and human societies might also yield practical results. Adam Smith's *The Wealth of Nations* (1776), for example, had identified the 'moral sentiments' that govern behaviour in the market place and suggested rules that might be used by rational actors to maximise their interests.[2] More radical still, the power of reason might allow mankind to control its destiny. Progress in human affairs became thinkable.

Some hoped the application of reason to politics would eliminate war itself. Following earlier writers like William Penn (*Essay towards the Present and Future Peace of Europe*, 1693) and the Abbé de Saint Pierre (*Perpetual Peace*, 1712), philosophers such as Rousseau (*Jugement sur la Paix Perpétuelle*, 1782) and Kant (*On Eternal Peace*, 1795) seriously contemplated the possibility of ridding mankind of this scourge.[3] Rather less ambitiously, other thinkers believed war could be subjected to rational analysis and its conduct made more scientific. What Smith had done for economics might also be done for warfare – practical understanding that could be taught in military academies and passed on through instruction.

The Enlightenment met with inevitable reaction. The advance of reason challenged established certainties: tradition, doctrine, the word of authority. Opponents doubted science could deliver on its promise, especially in the human world. Actions and motives, the Counter-Enlightenment claimed, can be known only through personal experience since they derive from such imponderables as emotion, genius and fortune. The passions driving human beings are too powerful and human affairs too complex to be subjugated to rational theorising. At some point reason must give way to intuition, empiricism to faith.

Great art and achievement derive not from study and practice but from inspiration and genius. Playwrights thus took for their subjects human emotions and the psychological struggles of great men and women. Schiller, for example, whose plays Clausewitz admired, wrote of heroic figures like General Wallenstein, Mary Stuart and William Tell.[4] War above all was a matter of passion, and its conduct could not be made the slave of reason.

Worse still in the view of the Counter-Enlightenment, materialist and empiricist approaches drive out faith and moral values. The human condition is unique so that people need to cling to their history, their traditions, their emotions. Within the Counter-Enlightenment a distinctively 'German School' saw a resurgence of romanticism and of faith in national culture. Interest grew in the study of diverse cultures throughout the world, each seen to have its own values and worth that could not be measured against others. Historians also looked back to the Middle Ages and emphasised the unique nature of events and historical eras, a view that fed into Clausewitz's understanding of war.[5]

The German School also reflected and encouraged the nationalism that emerged after 1789. Some citizens of German states, as in other lands occupied by Napoleon, began to feel a common bond and a desire to be rid of the invader. Writers and artists 'discovered' a single German nation. The education of Germans in their own language took on special significance. In his celebrated *Addresses to the German Nation* of 1807–8 the philosopher Fichte, with whom Clausewitz corresponded, spoke of the patriotic duty and the destiny of the German people (*Volk*). Appointed first rector of the new University of Berlin in 1810, Fichte believed the state should compel citizens to enter a national system of education, just as it conscripted them for military service.[6] People had started to think in terms of a *German* identity and of *national* liberation.

Contemporary theorists of war

War itself was caught in this intellectual cross-fire. Was it an activity based on deep emotions, heroic effort and natural genius to be understood by empathy and experience? Or was it sufficiently enduring and distinct in its nature to yield to analysis like economics or even physics and mathematics? Around the middle of the eighteenth century a wave of theorising about war began, notably in France and Germany, that continued well into the following century. Individual writers – generals and junior officers, theorists and historians – began offering interpretations of 'the art of war'. More than one hundred such works were published between 1756 and 1789.[7] In Germany 16 new journals devoted to military science appeared between 1766 and 1790.[8]

For much of the second half of the eighteenth century Enlightenment thinking prevailed, including the Marquis de Puységur's *Art of War by Principles and Rules* in 1748 and Maurice de Saxe's popular *Reveries on the Art of War* in 1756. These and other French authors were promptly translated into German and English. German theorists in the Enlightenment tradition mostly emphasised education rather than building systems.[9] Frederick the Great completed *Military Instruction for his Generals* in 1746, and Scharnhorst *Handbook for Officers* in 1787. But others put their faith in scientific analysis of the campaign, encouraged by the routine character of much military activity, especially tactics, fortification and siegecraft. Developments in artillery also depended on precise calculation. Perhaps the spatial relationships between opposing forces, their bases and their supply lines – all capable of being represented on a map – could yield general theorems about the conduct of the campaign.

The prolific and provocative Heinrich von Bülow (1757–1807) pursued this line, publishing *Principles of Modern War* in 1805.[10] Clausewitz published a hostile anonymous review, criticising its mathematical approach to campaign strategy. It was 'rococo absurdity', for example, to argue that the angle made by the point of an army's operations and its base line should always be more than 90 degrees – regardless of the movements of the enemy army.[11] Nonetheless, Bülow, impressed by Napoleon's victory at Marengo in 1800, picked up important themes in the new form of warfare. He pointed out that Napoleon's ability to control large forces allowed strategic movement to envelop and crush smaller formations. He noted how Napoleon maximised use of his armies – like money in commerce, they needed to be kept active rather than simply held for possible future use.[12] He favoured conscription and opening careers to talent, and observed that war shaded into foreign policy and domestic politics. Clausewitz, despite his tirade, recognised merit in some of Bülow's ideas.[13] Bülow's thinking, however, lacked theoretical awareness, and his good ideas remained largely undeveloped.[14]

The only English military theorist of note in this period was Major General Henry Lloyd (c.1718–1783) whose multi-volume *The History of the Late War in Germany* began appearing in London in 1766 and was soon translated into French and German. The book distinguished two aspects of war, a mechanical side that lends itself to analysis and can be learned; and a 'sublime' side that consists of applying fixed and immutable principles of war but is difficult to grasp. A theoretical work in 1781 (*Principles*) took up the idea of a line of operations – the link between an army and its base for purposes of advance and retreat, supply and communications. From this Lloyd deduced principles such as the importance of short lines of communication, contributing to the idea that a set of principles of strategy could be identified.[15] Napoleon dismissed his theorising as a pathetic joke.[16] But Lloyd also emphasised the importance of psychology in matters of leadership, morale and human weakness[17], and his attempt to incorporate both material and psychological factors inspired followers of both schools.[18]

Georg Heinrich von Berenhorst (1733–1814) was the first major figure of the Counter-Enlightenment to challenge the Enlightenment hegemony. His book, *Reflections on the Art of War* (1796–99), proved popular at a time when the German School was exploring nationalism and romanticism. For Berenhorst who fought under Frederick the Great war was anarchic rather than scientific. He emphasised chance and accident which defied calculation and challenged human beings to heroic effort. Immense obstacles could be overcome and the conventional principles of war overturned by energy, genius and luck.[19] Will-power and fighting spirit, Berenhorst claimed, produced victories for Frederick despite supposedly objective factors such as the numbers and weapons of the opposing army.[20] Frederick was at fault, however, in failing to understand the importance of morale and patriotism among his troops, which Berenhorst believed more valuable than immaculate drill and brutal discipline or the science and learning of their officers.[21] Some strategic theories, Berenhorst conceded, might have limited use but only as long as rivals failed to follow suit. Once others adopted them, courage, energy, skill, together with chance and luck, returned to centre stage.

Antoine Jomini (1779–1869) was a Swiss-born soldier who, though never in command of troops, saw service in both French and Russian armies – including the battle of Jena, the occupation of Berlin, the war in Spain and, with sensible timing, as military adviser to Tsar Alexander from 1813.[22] Prolific and disputatious as a military theorist, Jomini readily proclaimed his own merits and criticised the work of others including Clausewitz. His first major study published in 1804, *Traité de grand tactique*, was regularly succeeded by revised versions and additional volumes, culminating in his *Précis de l'Art de la Guerre* in 1838. Setting down principles and maxims in a clear and straightforward fashion, Jomini sought to be accessible to his readers and offer practical advice. Unlike Clausewitz, he avoided complexity and remained 'learnable'.[23] The result was, in terms of popularity, 'the greatest military text-book of the nineteenth century'.[24]

Though his ideas shifted over time, Jomini took from Lloyd the notion that universal and timeless principles of strategy could be identified. Analysing the campaigns of Frederick and Napoleon, however different in character, could identify common ingredients of success.[25] Focusing on 'lines of operation', Jomini emphasised the importance of manoeuvre, maintaining 'interior' lines and striking with great mass and speed at the 'decisive point'. Jomini did not ignore the human element, especially the need for a military spirit among the people and high morale in the army. But his focus was on the heroic, aggressive and inspired military leader as supreme expounder of timeless principles of strategy.[26] Like Clausewitz, Jomini saw the clash of arms as the single decisive means in war. Unlike Clausewitz, he saw little value in examining psychological, institutional and political factors to explain the course and character of war.[27] Suspicious of mass armies as a threat to political and social order, he preferred wars conducted by professionals.[28]

Gerhard Johann David Scharnhorst (1755–1813) was a major influence on Clausewitz both intellectually and personally. Educated in the progressive military academy founded by Count Schaumburg-Lippe-Bückeburg, Scharnhorst valued education and the dissemination of ideas, and to this end founded three military periodicals. While a strong believer in the utility of military theory, he recognised its limits and the need for a critical approach as well as a careful study of history. Scharnhorst's principal theoretical contribution was to stress the importance of determining the 'correct concepts' that permit analysis of the important elements of war.[29] These are derived from experience and from the 'nature of things' (a concept drawn from Montesquieu), and allow the theorist to grasp the connections between the parts and the whole and between theory and reality. While principles of war can be deduced from historical and analytical study, Scharnhorst recognised that human judgement was required to apply those principles and he strongly opposed any attempt to present them as formulae. His essentially undoctrinaire approach shaped much of Clausewitz's early thinking.

Individual theorists did not fall neatly into one school. Differences between Enlightenment and Counter-Enlightenment were often a matter of emphasis and some common ground existed. All theorists accepted the distinction between material and psychological factors and all agreed the latter had an impact on war. All believed that chance could never be eliminated. In dispute was the relative importance of these factors. At the heart of the debate was the question whether rules or principles could be identified with sufficient precision to guide the conduct of war by the commander.

Debate about tactics – line versus column, the role of skirmishers and so on – could be tested in exercises and on the battlefield and reasonably hard and fast rules deduced. But campaign strategy was a tougher nut to crack. Could timeless principles be developed of practical use to the commander? Were they to be gleaned from history and experience or from abstract reflection? How could their validity be tested? Related to this was the question of military genius. Do brilliant generals follow the principles of strategy, break them or create new ones? Can their ideas and methods be emulated or taught to others? Underlying different views was a profound disagreement over the relationship between theory and practice in war. How much could or should theory influence the actual conduct of strategy? What is the relationship between theory and success in the campaign? Some like Bülow offered rules of mathematical precision. Others like Berenhorst dismissed the usefulness of rules altogether: 'What is the use of rules when one is covered up to one's ears with exceptions?'[30]

Many military theorists in the eighteenth and into the nineteenth century also recognised the importance of the political and social context in which war was fought. Lloyd, Jomini and Bülow amongst others understood that war could be viewed as a means by which states promote policy. The relevance of social and political change to a nation's military potential was widely recognised. That the collapse of the *ancien régime* in France led to a dramatic increase in military strength through the rise of patriotism and popular enthusiasm was irrefutable. But was autocracy capable of achieving such results without revolution? How should governments and armies be related? Theories of war, it was clear, needed to address social and political questions as well as military.

Enter Clausewitz

Clausewitz drew on theorists of war in his own time but like them owed debts to earlier writers on war, politics and philosophy. The greatest influence was undoubtedly Machiavelli (1469–1527) whose *Discourses on Livy*, *The Art of War* and *The Prince* Clausewitz read as a student in Berlin. He did not share Machiavelli's belief in timeless principles of war or his interest in ancient warfare, but accepted his view of the unchanging character of human nature and of political struggle, both within and between states. Clausewitz's interest was further stimulated by Fichte whose essay on Machiavelli he read in early 1809.[31] Many Germans turned to Machiavelli at this time, seeing a parallel with Italy after 1494 when French armies had routed the mercenary forces of the Italian states. Machiavelli had denounced their weak policies and ineffectual methods of war, calling for unity and energetic action to restore independence and advocating a peacetime militia and conscript army for Florence.[32] In such tasks a prince was duty bound to put national interest before personal morality or ethical ideals. Clausewitz found himself in full accord with such views. If Machiavelli attracted criticism his principal fault was simply that 'with a certain lack of decency, he had called things by their proper names'.[33]

The influence of Montesquieu (1689–1755) whom Clausewitz read eagerly is more difficult to pin down. Scharnhorst, also familiar with Montesquieu, helped transmit his ideas to Clausewitz. The single reference in *On War* is Clausewitz's aspiration in revising chapter 1 of Book I to emulate Montesquieu's concise, aphoristic approach. [63] More generally, Clausewitz's analysis of war borrowed the concept of necessary relationships between component parts from *De l'esprit des lois* (1748) which examined the distinct functions performed by legislature, executive and judiciary, and the relationships between them that seemed inherent in their very nature. Clausewitz also developed Montesquieu's idea that war can be differentiated according to types of society.[34] As society changes, so too does war. Montesquieu's notion of the spirit of the people also pointed to intangible elements in politics interacting with more concrete factors such as population, climate and terrain. It was precisely this blending of diverse and complex factors, of abstract and concrete, that Clausewitz sought in regard to war.

The direct influence on Clausewitz of Immanuel Kant (1724–1804) and G.W.F. Hegel (1770–1831) is much debated. While Clausewitz probably did not read Kant's major works on philosophy and ethics at first hand, they were the subject of popularising lectures in Berlin given by Johann Kiesewetter, an instructor at the War College.[35] Clausewitz attended some of these and his methodology is certainly indebted to Kant whose ideas he adapted in rough and ready fashion. The hierarchy of laws, principles, rules, prescriptions and methods in *Critique of Practical Reason* of 1788 thus finds a clear echo in Clausewitz's approach to strategy and tactics.[36] The concept of Absolute War also owes a debt to Kant whose concept of 'pure reason' identified reason in the abstract in contrast to 'practical reason' that applies in the real world. Clausewitz found this distinction useful in 1827 when he was puzzling whether two very different types of war – limited and unlimited – and the manifold variations of war over history could all be subsumed under a single concept. Absolute War, uncontaminated by particular historical or political contexts, could be contrasted with the great variety of wars in reality.

Hegel lectured on the philosophy of history in the 1820s at the University of Berlin of which he was rector. Clausewitz did not attend the lectures, but was probably personally acquainted with him and certainly shared many views: a reverence for the state and its civilising role in human history; a perception of the state as impartial arbiter of the struggle between different interests in society; and a belief that war serves to purify and energise the life of the state.[37] Both also found inspiration in Machiavelli and dismissed international law as of little significance.[38] Clausewitz found interesting Hegel's dialectic that proposed the ultimate unity of diverse and contending elements of reality – thesis and antithesis interacting to form a synthesis that in turn becomes a new thesis. But he was no Hegelian and perhaps never fully understood his philosophy. Like many thinkers at the time, he thought in terms of opposites, polarities, contradictions, positive and negative, active and passive, all of which applied easily to war.[39] Clausewitz's approach was dualistic rather than genuinely dialectic.[40] A military man can discuss offence and defence, means and ends, moral and physical factors without being Hegelian.

A work of its time

Clausewitz reflected the philosophical ideas swirling around him without being a philosopher. Typical of the educated person of his age, he 'drew scraps of ideas at second and third hand from his cultural environment'.[41] Of particular interest were questions of methodology: the distinction between means and purpose (where Clausewitz borrowed from late Enlightenment theories of art, a topic on which he wrote a number of pieces[42]), the problem of change versus continuity, the construction of pure concepts, the play of contradictory forces, the idea of positive and negative poles, the relationship between knowledge and action, and so on. In relation to war, he picked up ideas about the significance of moral as well as physical factors, the role of chance and uncertainty, the value of training and instruction, the problem of rules and principles for the conduct of war, and the view that war serves as a political instrument.

All this was done in eclectic rather than systematic fashion. Rejecting the Enlightenment's faith in reason as a means of subordinating war to human control, he welcomed its emphasis on analysis and education. In the Counter-Enlightenment he found emphasis on the psychology of the individual and the pervasiveness of chance liberating and challenging. Yet he did not surrender to emotion, religion or mysticism.[43] The intellectual climate of the time established the important questions, stimulated his desire to analyse war and suggested some of the means by which to do so. Clausewitz, a pragmatic military man with a remarkable analytical ability, considerable breadth of mind and an unusual openness to ideas, made his own mark in the history of ideas about war.

6
On War

'It was my ambition to write a work that would not be forgotten after two or three years, and that possibly might be picked up more than once by those who are interested in the subject'. [1]

Writing *On War*

Contemplating a major study of war, Clausewitz was aware of the burden he assumed. A note from 1816–18 sought to disillusion those who expected 'a complete system and a comprehensive doctrine'.[2] Rather than 'a complete theory it offers only material for one', and a 'greater mind' would be needed to replace his 'small nuggets of pure metal' with 'a single whole, cast of solid metal, free from all impurity'. [61–2] Cautious and modest, these remarks probably referred to a set of essays that Clausewitz planned to write on strategy rather than what became *On War*.[3] Nonetheless, by 1818 Clausewitz had decided to write a work that did not simply reproduce 'every commonplace, everything obvious that has been stated a hundred times'. A 'spirit of analysis' and a 'systematic approach' to war would yield 'a book that would not be forgotten after two or three years, and that possibly might be picked up more than once by those who are interested in the subject'. [Author's Comment, 63] Clausewitz's intellectual aspirations were now more ambitious, if still modestly stated.

By 1827 the first six Books were drafted, a mix of new material and passages from essays, lectures and memoranda written since the early 1800s.[4] A Note by Clausewitz, undated but probably written at this time, detailed his dissatisfaction with Book VI which he called 'only a sketch'.[5] 'It is a very difficult task to construct a scientific theory for the art of war, and so many attempts have failed that most people say it is impossible, since it deals with matters that no permanent law can provide for'. But, he concluded, sufficient propositions about the conduct of strategy had already been demonstrated 'without difficulty' to show the quest for such a theory is not an idle undertaking. [71] Only the first chapter of Book I could be regarded as finished. [70]

A different 'Note' by Clausewitz dated 10 July 1827 described the draft as 'a rather formless mass of ideas that must be thoroughly reworked once more'. But he was hopeful that, for all their imperfections, the reader would 'find they contain the basic ideas that might bring about a revolution in the theory of war'. Much work remained to be done. Two further books were to be written and major revision undertaken of the first six books in the light of two complementary ideas about the nature of war and its relationship to politics. One focused on the distinction between two kinds of war which Clausewitz saw as 'a matter of actual fact' and which could be deduced from historical observation; the other focused on how states choose to employ war to achieve their objectives. [69–70]

Where he had earlier assumed that every war required maximum effort and always sought victory whatever the object, Clausewitz now accepted that two types of war were equally valid: one to overthrow the enemy, the other to secure limited objectives. Book VI, entitled simply 'Defence', helped bring Clausewitz to the realisation that defensive operations often sought to delay, to avoid confrontation, to wear the enemy down; for the defender preservation of the status quo was a legitimate objective of war.[6] The last chapter of Book VI – chapter 30, the second longest in the entire book – included in its title the qualifying clause 'Where a Decision Is Not the Objective' and began to address the second type of war in some detail. Books VII and VIII incorporated this distinction more fully.

The second key idea was Clausewitz's perception that war needed to be understood not as an independent variable but as a function of policy: 'this point must be made absolutely clear, namely that *war is nothing but the continuation of policy with other means*'. [69] The reader, Clausewitz advised, should keep this proposition firmly in mind throughout since 'it will greatly facilitate the study of the subject and the whole will be easier to analyze'. [69] In the event only Book VIII deals at all fully with war in its political context. Clausewitz, who had gone back to writing military histories, made little progress with the planned revisions. The first chapter of *On War* – out of a total of 125 – remained the only one revised to his satisfaction, though even here obscurities remain.[7]

After his death Clausewitz's papers were organised into volumes by Marie and publication began in 1832. In her preface to the first edition of *On War* Marie stated that, while no word had been added or deleted, 'a good deal of work' had been required in arranging material, including the insertion of intended revisions. [67] Unlike most classic texts which represent a writer's considered views at the time of publication, the book we know as *On War* contains chapters ranging from unrevised, early drafts to more or less final versions written over a period of 12 years or more. It also incorporates sections of essays, lectures and memoranda dating back to the reform era. An apt description of *On War* might be 'Clausewitz's workshop'.[8]

Reading *On War*

There are many problems in reading *On War*. As well as the eclectic philosophy and the jury-rigged methodology already noted, there is the ambiguity resulting from Clausewitz's failure to fully incorporate the new ideas mentioned in the Note of 10 July 1827. The book consequently embraces both his earlier emphasis on battle and victory, and his later concern with moderation and limited objectives. This mixture of earlier and later ideas helps explain diverse and often contradictory interpretations of Clausewitz: the glorifier of battle and all-out war and the sober advocate of restraint and political control. *On War*, it might be said, contains both a militant 'Old Testament' and a more measured 'New Testament' – but they are interwoven rather than conveniently divided.

On War is also at times inconsistent, obscure and opaque. For example, Clausewitz fails to apply his distinction between two types of war to the defence as well as the offence, and does not provide a promised chapter on political-military relations. Nor is he always rigorous in his use of terms and definitions. *On War* also employs numerous passive constructions and abstractions, often in convoluted fashion.[9] The French military historian, Hubert Camon, in his book on Clausewitz of 1911, expressed a common view, calling Clausewitz the 'most German of Germans ... In reading him one constantly has the feeling of being in a metaphysical fog'.[10] This is too harsh a judgement but even admirers concede that *On War* is 'densely packed' with ideas and needs frequent pause for reflection.[11]

Yet *On War* has many strengths – including its prose. Though often dense and abstract, Clausewitz's words can also illuminate by simplifying complex issues and dramatising the human element of war. Vivid metaphors drawn from everyday life, including games, nature and commerce, remain in the memory: effort in war is like walking under water, moving armies is like transplanting trees, battle resembles payment in cash. He can make what is complex seem simple, a quality which may cause the casual reader to think 'he is reading mere commonplaces'.[12] When in 1858 Engels commended *On War* and pointed out the analogy between war and commerce, Karl Marx replied that '[t]he fellow possesses a common sense bordering on wit'.[13]

Above all, however, *On War* is marked by Clausewitz's passionate involvement in his subject – personally, politically and intellectually. His work derived from '[y]ears of thinking about war, much association with able men who knew about war, and a good deal of personal experience'. [Author's Preface, 62] Unlike many theorists, he saw at first hand everything from the suffering of the common soldier to the highest levels of strategic planning. As a citizen of Prussia, too, Clausewitz felt driven to analyse and understand war which had inflicted the deepest humiliation on his country and constantly threatened its independence. To grasp what makes successful armies was a matter of urgency. As a scholar and a practitioner, Clausewitz was *engagé* in every sense of the word.

Yet for all his involvement in war and loyalty to Prussia *On War* is detached and objective. Not intending to publish it in his lifetime, he wrote primarily for his own satisfaction and for a few friends prepared to read him carefully.[14] Nor did he desire celebrity of the kind Jomini and others had achieved. He thus felt few constraints in his military writing – in contrast to his political essays that sought to influence opinion. He could freely criticise Frederick the Great or praise Napoleon.[15] He attacked writers on strategy whom he thought in error and denounced 'the tyranny of fashion' in strategic thinking. [162] He could not resist jibes at Jomini, Bülow and others, and used irony and sarcasm to effect. The distinctly 'combative posture' in *On War* has its attraction.[16] But typically he also feared misunderstanding by lesser minds, expressing concern that his ideas would be 'liable to endless misinterpretation ... the target of much half-baked criticism'. [70]

Another strength of *On War* derives from Clausewitz's profound knowledge of and objective approach to military history in which he read and wrote widely. Though his contributions to military history were never recognised (partly because most of his work was not published until well after his death) and have long since been overtaken, his work displayed considerable originality and constitutes an important transitional stage in historiography.[17] Less concerned with battles and tactics than with strategy, historical discipline led him to take a critical approach to evidence, recognise the importance of the circumstances under which decisions are made, and perceive the changing social and political context of war. For Clausewitz, history was not a search for lessons, but a concrete manifestation of the inter-action of individual actions – by great leaders and humble followers – and of complex forces such as social change, nationalism and the spirit of armies.

Clausewitz drew not only from history but from a wide range of dis-ciplines, including philosophy, epistemology, social science methodo-logy, political theory, international relations, politics, psychology, sociology, public administration, military strategy and tactics. He could not be expert in all of them and perhaps was master of none. Specialists in these areas have found fault.[18] Yet without his insistence on its heterogeneity, Clausewitz's understanding of war would lose much of its value. He was also writing at a time when social science was in its infancy, and his analysis of the social and psychological factors in shaping decisions in war and influencing the performance of armies was itself part of the development of modern social science.[19]

Above all, *On War* is a battleground between the Enlightenment and Counter-Enlightenment. Clausewitz had a foot in both camps. In the Enlightenment tradition he believed in the application of reason to human affairs. Enduring elements and principles can be identified in war. Sufficient regularities exist from one campaign to the next so that commanders need not throw up their hands altogether. But no math-ematical or mechanical principles – such as geometry of movement, spatial relationships of armies or the calculus of numbers and supply – exist or could exist. War itself, however, should be subject as far as pos-sible to rational control in order to serve the aims of governments.

Yet there are inescapable limits to the role of reason in human affairs, and to what reason can explain. Clausewitz's emphasis on the role of passion and chance, friction and human intuition meant that war was never a simple exercise of reason. Judgement, creativity and boldness were essential, qualities Clausewitz found in the Counter-Enlightenment. He stressed the emotional and intuitive nature of human action and the importance of moral forces in war – from the fighting spirit and patriotism of the soldier to the inspiration of the general.[20] With the romantics he was attracted to the idea of the heroic leader struggling against the odds and the great battle on which the fate of nations turned. With the historicists he believed that each event had some unique qualities, that each war reflected its own era and that war in general remained in a process of continuous change. With the nationalists he praised the vitality of the nation and the readiness of citizens to make great sacrifices. And with the idealists he believed in the importance of the state and its central role in human affairs – while he accorded Prussia no anointed destiny. Familiar with all these schools of thought, he was an adherent of none.

Clausewitz's achievement

On War seeks to reconcile the theoretical rigour demanded by the Enlightenment with the intractability of war claimed by the Counter-Enlightenment. If Clausewitz must be placed in one camp, his faith in reason makes him a follower of the Enlightenment. But the Counter-Enlightenment keeps him alive to the limits of scientific analysis. This constant tension is one reason why Clausewitz explores at length the relationship between theory and practice which is one of the principal achievements of *On War*. Though Clausewitz's methodological struggles by no means produce complete answers, and though theories of war in his time were by no means as lifeless and mechanical as many have suggested, including Clausewitz himself, *On War* represented a major advance in its comprehensiveness and its intellectual rigour.

Clausewitz's achievement was to identify the important parts of the complex activity that is war and to propose a framework for linking them in their 'necessary relations'. In the terms used in the first paragraph of *On War*, he identified the '*elements* of the subject', its '*various parts*' and finally '*the whole* in its internal structure'. For 'in war more than in any other subject we must begin by looking at the nature of the whole'. [75] For Clausewitz war consists of four principal elements:

(i)   war is fighting, a human activity with unique characteristics – the perspective of the soldier;

(ii) war is a contest between armies, a struggle that has its own dynamics and raises the question of how each side best pursues its aims – the perspective of strategy and the general;

(iii) war is – or, at least, should be – an instrument of national policy – the perspective of the statesman; and

(iv) war is social behaviour, a form of activity between states that originates in and takes its shape from the totality of politics and society, including institutions and movements – the perspective of the observer rather than the participant.

These four levels of interpretation form the subject of this book and are outlined briefly here.

War, first and foremost, is fighting. It may resemble other forms of human behaviour, but it has its own special and enduring characteristics. The eternal element in war is the clash of arms – the physical and mental struggle between groups of people seeking to kill and injure one another in battle. Clausewitz never forgot the human face of war, the emotions and actions of men on the battlefield. He brought these 'moral forces' – among them courage, fear, and the spirit of armies – into the centre of war, the first theorist to do so with a degree of analytic rigour. And with the human element came friction, an elusive factor that escapes measurement and ensures fighting is never the same in reality as it is in theory.

Second, war is a clash between two armies each led by a commander. This contest is shaped by forces outside war itself – the interests of states and the political, social and cultural context of warfare – and is replete with contingencies and accidents, unknowns and variables. But the interaction between armies has specific characteristics, notably the relationship between offence and defence and the possibility that reciprocal efforts might cause a 'rise to extremes'. How best to conduct such a dynamic activity? Can there be rules or principles to guide those responsible for waging war? How can they be derived and tested? How, if at all, does theory influence the actions of commanders? These were questions relevant to all wars though answers might vary from war to war and age to age.

Clausewitz is torn between asserting that strategic principles can be easily demonstrated and arguing that they are difficult to establish and of limited usefulness. This is one reason why military people are frequently disappointed with him.[21] In reality *On War* is less valuable for its propositions on strategy than for its analysis of the nature of strategy as an activity. It offers an understanding of the creative quality of strategy, and explores the relationship between knowledge and action. Clausewitz is the first military theorist to discuss in any depth how strategic propositions might be derived from history and analysis, and how those propositions can influence the conduct of war. He does not resolve all of the epistemological problems and his attempt to develop a distinct approach to the evaluation of commanders (*Kritik*) is open to question. But he remains a pioneer of the methodology and epistemology of military strategy.

Third, Clausewitz offers a doctrine on the relationship between war and politics. War exists because the interests of states inevitably clash and war is thus a necessary part of their relations. The state employs war to promote its aims, whether national survival or conquest, over-turning or restoring the balance of power, resolving greater or lesser disputes. The use of force is therefore to be understood as an instrument of policy – and one that should be subject to political control. This is the heart of Clausewitzian doctrine: war ought to serve purposes determined by the state. The normative element is clear even though, as was common in his time, he made no great distinction between 'is' and 'ought'.[22] Clausewitz was the first to analyse war as a means to an end in systematic fashion.

Finally, Clausewitz offers an interpretation of war as social activity. War is simultaneously fighting, a contest, a form of political activity and, most broadly, social interaction. Though a distinct activity, war is tied closely to the social, political and economic structures of states, their traditions and values, and their perceptions of the world. As well, like any significant social interaction, war evokes human passion and emotion, demands the application of human reason and skills, and remains ever subject to chance and fortune. This 'remarkable trinity' of passion, reason and chance is the key to Clausewitz's understanding of war as a social phenomenon.

Clausewitz's approach to war thus operates on several levels though it is not always clear which he is addressing. Similarly, by going deeper than mere battles and campaigns, while retaining his sense of the reality of war, he can appear 'too philosophical for the practitioners of war and too practical for the philosophers'.[23] But for those interested in a subtle and intelligent mind coming to grips with a complex subject, Clausewitz offers a profound analysis of war as a human and social phenomenon at different levels. In doing so, he established a firm place for the study of war among other intellectual inquiries.[24]

Clausewitz also expounded a paradigm of war that has dominated Western thinking for some 200 years. What can be called 'modern war' is to be conducted primarily by armies (against one another) and employed by states as a rational instrument of policy. This doctrine has not gone unchallenged. The enormous growth in the destructiveness of weapons, the spread of hostilities far beyond the battlefield and the entry onto the scene of many other types of warrior – revolutionaries, terrorists, freedom fighters and the like – all challenge Clausewitz's relevance. Yet debate about war and conflict almost always starts from his paradigm even if it does not always return to it.

Part IV
The Levels of War

7
War as Fighting

'War is no pastime ... no mere joy in daring and winning, no place for irresponsible enthusiasts'. [86]

Clausewitz's first perspective is that of the soldier. At the centre of war is the clash of arms – soldiers killing and being killed, injuring and being injured. This is the unique and defining characteristic of war that makes it different from every other human activity. 'What remains peculiar to war is simply the peculiar nature of its means'. [87] Any definition of war must recognise its true character, avoiding the pedantic or legalistic definitions advocated by some eighteenth century writers. Clausewitz goes 'straight to the heart of the matter': war is violence, 'an act of force'. [75] Clausewitz adds 'to compel our enemy to do our will' but the question of purpose will be considered later. Quite simply, 'war is fighting'. [127]

Though war bears some resemblance to other activities such as commerce or litigation, its unique methods define its nature. 'There is only one means in war: combat' [*das Gefecht*]. [96] Everything in war therefore must be subordinate to combat:

> The end for which a soldier is recruited, clothed, armed, and trained, the whole object of his sleeping, eating, drinking, and marching *is simply that he should fight at the right place and the right time*. [95]

Combat is the 'strand that runs through the entire web of military activity and really holds its together'. [96] War can thus never be made less bloody as some theorists proposed for 'it is always true that the character of battle, like its name, is slaughter, and its price is blood'. [259] The German word for battle – *Schlacht* – also means slaughter.

To focus on combat Clausewitz drew a line between 'war proper' and activities which are 'merely preparations for war'. [131] War itself includes only fighting and activity directly related to it, extending to marches, camps, billets and requisitions which, though in a sense administrative, involve troops in the field and hence the possibility of combat. [129] Supply, maintenance and administration are in constant interaction with fighting and with strategy, but they remain activities 'essentially separate' from the use of soldiers. [131] Clausewitz therefore dismissed the notion that supply could be seen 'as a final arbiter for the conduct of war'. [135] Further removed from fighting are matters such as fortifications and the creation and training of armed forces. War takes these as given even though they ultimately influence combat.

While war is about killing it is not simply 'mutual murder'. [259] No military leader is totally indifferent to the spilling of blood: '[a]s a human being a commander will recoil from it'. [259] But those engaged in war must never forget its true character: '[i]t would be futile – even wrong – to try and shut one's eyes to what war really is from sheer distress at its brutality'. [76] Misplaced humanitarianism can lead to greater carnage than war seriously pursued.

> The fact that slaughter is a horrifying spectacle must make us take war more seriously, but not provide an excuse for blunting our swords in the name of humanity. Sooner or later someone will come along with a sharp sword and hack off our arms. [260]

For 'war is such a dangerous business that the mistakes which come from kindness are the very worst'. [75] War has no place for the kind-hearted or 'irresponsible enthusiasts'. [86]

Clausewitz nonetheless recognised some limits to the brutality of war. First, he takes as given that fighting is a matter for soldiers, not civilians. The immunity of non-combatants reflected the chivalrous tradition in military conduct and was a concept towards which eighteenth century international lawyers were groping.[1] Sieges of cities which refused to surrender in good time and the repression of rebels were notable exceptions. Reprisals against civilians, as in Spain, also claimed legitimacy. But like most professional soldiers, Clausewitz had an instinctive revulsion against barbarities such as slaughtering civilians and killing prisoners committed by ill-disciplined guerrillas in Spain or the Cossacks in Russia.

Second, rules for the conduct of war do exist among soldiers. [187] Honour, chivalry and custom demand observance of conventions surrounding such matters as acceptance of a surrender, negotiation of a truce, sparing the wounded, taking prisoners and their subsequent exchange or ransom. An attempt by the French government after mid-1793 to 'exterminate' the nation's opponents by granting no quarter and killing all prisoners was resisted by those in uniform and the decree was repealed at end of 1794.[2] Shared values among the aristocratic classes in the officer corps naturally helped, and the generous treatment of August and Clausewitz as prisoners of war was no surprise.

Third, Clausewitz argued, civilised nations bring a degree of intelligence to the conduct of war. Reason teaches that crude methods may be ineffective and even counter-productive:

If, then, civilized nations do not put their prisoners to death or devastate cities and countries, it is because intelligence plays a larger part in their methods of warfare and has taught them more effective ways of using force than the crude expression of instinct. [76]

By the seventeenth century, for example, laying waste to the cities and countryside of defeated enemies was

rightly held to be unnecessarily barbarous, an invitation to reprisals, and a practice that hurt the enemy's subjects rather than their government – one therefore that was ineffective and only served permanently to impede the advance of civilization. [590–1]

Self-interest, economy of effort and civilised standards thus coincide to reduce the superfluous barbarities of war.

But force, 'equipped with the inventions of art and science', remains at the heart of war and can only be moderated in small degree. As Clausewitz observed, '[a]ttached to force are certain, self-imposed imperceptible limitations hardly worth mentioning, known as international law and custom, but they scarcely weaken it'. [75] He thus hardly touches on laws and customs in warfare and minimises their important sociological functions – for example, allowing the soldier to distinguish between war and murder, and strengthening discipline and cohesion in conditions of danger.[3] Law brings a degree of order to an otherwise chaotic activity but for Clausewitz order in war comes primarily from political direction and military control.

The psychology of war

War is 'a special activity, different and separate from any other pursued by man'. [187] Soldiers set themselves apart from the rest of society and 'think of themselves as members of a kind of guild, in whose regulations, laws, and customs the spirit of war is given pride of place'. [187]

> No matter how clearly we see the citizen and the soldier in the same man, how strongly we conceive of war as the business of the entire nation ... the business of war will always remain individual and distinct. [187]

Special qualities are demanded of those who take part in this activity marked by 'danger, exertion, uncertainty, and chance'. [104]

Clausewitz was not the first to emphasise the psychological element in war.[4] Berenhorst, for example, considered the psychology of soldiers a 'major factor in the conduct of war', especially when 'motivated by patriotic enthusiasm'. He criticised Frederick the Great – who could barely speak German – for his lack of national consciousness and for treating his army as a machine.[5] Napoleon's dictum – *à la guerre, les trois quarts sont des affaires morales* – and his simple but effective means of maintaining morale also lent salience to psychology.[6] But from his earliest writings Clausewitz emphasised the key role of what he called the 'moral' element. Any understanding of war, he argued, is deficient if it does not 'reckon with and give full value to moral qualities' – for they 'constitute the spirit that permeates war as a whole'. [184]

The moral element adds a whole dimension of uncertainty to fighting. As Clausewitz observes, the physical effect of a cannonball moving at a speed of 1,000 feet per second on any living creature in its path is self-evident and measurable; but the psychological effect of cannon fire among troops is far less obvious and predictable yet just as important, if not more so.[7] Similarly, the advent of crude firearms in the Middle Ages was significant more for its psychological than its physical impact on soldiers. [170] Moral factors, indeed, often have an 'incredible effect'. 'One might say that the physical seem little more than the wooden hilt, while the moral factors are the precious metal, the real weapon, the finely-honed blade'. [185]

Contemporary psychology was poorly equipped to understand the moral factor, being largely descriptive, static and focused on personality types. Clausewitz complained of the backwardness of this 'obscure

field' of which he had 'slight scientific knowledge'. [106] He contrasted
the task of the physician who deals only with the body with that of the
psychiatrist [*Seelenartzt*] who must deal with the mind, suggesting that
the latter is far more highly valued because of the complexities of his
subject. [136–7] But it would lead only to platitudes to 'list the most
important moral phenomena in war and, like a diligent professor, try
to evaluate them one by one'. [185] It was preferable to 'treat the
subject in an incomplete and impressionistic manner', while making
clear its 'general importance'. [185] By modern standards Clausewitz's
analysis is primitive, relying on simple taxonomies and dichotomies,
but he was the first military theorist to place the psychological element
at the centre of the study of war.[8]

The friction of war

The imponderables of human psychology also contribute to a critical
phenomenon present in all fighting – friction. Clausewitz found this
concept in mechanics, a source of ideas for describing and analysing
human behaviour that won favour in the eighteenth century as the
wheels of the Industrial Revolution began to turn. In mechanics friction refers to all those factors that cause machines to work less
efficiently than is theoretically possible. The same applies to fighting.
'The conduct of war', Clausewitz wrote in *Principles of War*, 'resembles
the workings of an intricate machine with enormous friction, so that
combinations which are easily planned on paper can be executed only
with great effort'.[9]

Friction originates in the character and environment of war, and in
how the human mind reacts to these. Physical danger causes fear and
anxiety which lead to failure to perform at the optimum. Adverse
weather, poor terrain and equipment breakdown produce exhaustion
and loss of morale among soldiers and delay or disaster in the plans of
commanders. Friction is also cumulative as one problem exacerbates
another. 'Countless minor incidents – the kind you can never really
foresee – combine to lower the general level of performance, so that
one always falls far short of the intended goal'. Clausewitz gives
the example of a traveller making what should be an easy journey
who does not find fresh horses at the expected stage. [119] In war,
more than anywhere, human action invariably achieves less than the
theoretical maximum.

Friction affects all levels of war. An army might appear easily
managed as orders are issued and discipline ensures they are carried

out – just as a 'great beam turns on its iron pivot with a minimum of friction'. [119] But an army is far more complex and open to friction at every point from common soldier to general. For 'none of its components is of one piece: each part is composed of individuals, every one of whom retains his potential of friction'. [119] The soldier cannot avoid his constant battle with friction:

> Action in war is like movement in a resistant element. Just as the simplest and most natural of movements, walking, cannot easily be performed in water, so in war it is difficult for normal efforts to achieve even moderate results. [120]

Every war, therefore, even the most hard-fought, 'is chained by human weaknesses'. [216]

Clausewitz identifies four principal sources of friction, all of which depend upon the human reaction to the environment of war:

- the danger posed by the enemy;
- the efforts required of one's own forces;
- the difficulties presented by the physical environment; and
- the problem of knowing accurately what is occurring.[10]

The physical danger of war soon makes the novice realise that the battlefield is governed by forces totally outside his experience. [113–4] Clausewitz imagines accompanying a newcomer to the battlefield:

> As we approach the rumble of guns grows louder and alternates with the whir of cannonballs, which begin to attract his attention. Shots begin to strike close around us. … cannonballs and bursting shells are frequent, and life begins to seem more serious than the young man had imagined. Suddenly someone you know is wounded; then a shell falls among the staff. You notice that some of the officers act a little oddly; you yourself are not as steady and collected as you were … [113]

The shock of seeing 'men being killed and mutilated moves our pounding hearts to awe and pity'. The danger of war bears down on every soldier, leading to fear, mistakes, loss of effort, even panic. On the battlefield ideas and reason are thus 'refracted in a manner quite different from that which is normal in academic speculation'. [113]

Fighting also demands exertion by every soldier but it is hard to know what their limits are and what they can be made to achieve. Subordinate officers and soldiers, for example, 'frequently encounter difficulties which they declare insurmountable'.[11] Can a unit fighting a losing battle be encouraged to fight on despite fearful losses? Can soldiers be made to march great distances at speed? As Clausewitz observes, 'just as it takes a powerful archer to bend the bow beyond the average, so it takes a powerful mind to drive his army to the limit'. [115] All the more so, because that limit is elastic and cannot be known in advance. 'The inexperienced observer now comes to recognize one of the elements that seem to chain the spirit and secretly wear away men's energies'. [115]

The physical environment compounds the challenges to both soldier and general:

> Fog can prevent the enemy from being seen in time, a gun from firing when it should, a report from reaching the commanding officer. Rain can prevent a battalion from arriving, make another late by keeping it not three but eight hours on the march ... [120]

Similarly, adverse terrain such as mountains, marshes, rivers and woodland slows down movement or delays messengers, throwing plans out of kilter or making impossible the combining of forces in good time. For the soldier and the general fighting means close, constant and often unpredictable interaction with the physical environment.

Friction, finally, derives from the fact that commanders at all levels inevitably have unreliable knowledge not only about enemy forces but also about their own. It is natural to exaggerate the strength of the enemy and to believe bad news rather than good. In the heat of war the 'senses make a more vivid impression on the mind than systematic thought'. [117] As plans go wrong, caution and timidity arise. Fear, anxiety, indecision, and a reluctance to act until more information is available all contribute generously to friction. For such reasons '[e]verything in war is very simple, but the simplest thing is difficult'. [119] Clausewitz pays much attention to the qualities commanders need to deal with friction.

Friction also exists at the political level. In a letter to Marie in September 1806 Clausewitz had employed the term to criticise the complex arrangements for military advice that surrounded the king.[12] He also used the word freely in describing decision-making in the campaigns of 1812–15.[13] *On War* touches on this subject in discussing the nature of political-military relations. Nowadays, friction of this kind is taken for granted, but it was by no means obvious in the armies of Clausewitz's time which were 'the first truly large, modern organizations'.[14]

Of all human activities war is the most exposed to friction for '[i]n war more than anywhere else things do not turn out as we expect'. [193] Friction sums up this discrepancy, 'the only concept that more or less corresponds to the factors that distinguish real war from war on paper'. [119] It must therefore be incorporated in any understanding of war otherwise theory will not correspond to reality. Those who seek to eliminate it by sophisticated theories or simply ignore it are deluded. Though other writers mention the phenomenon, Clausewitz was the first to accord friction a central place in fighting. It is ever present even in the most experienced armies and commanders, and will challenge the ethos and spirit of an army as a whole.

The military virtues of an army

How can armies deal with friction? Given that friction 'is inconceivable unless one has experienced war', the best preparation is war itself. [119] The battle-hardened soldier grows accustomed to war as the eye becomes accustomed to the dark whereas 'the novice is plunged into the deepest night'. [122] Combat is really the only 'lubricant' that will reduce friction but even veterans of many campaigns do not escape its effects. [122] In fact most armies lack direct experience of war and must rely on exercises. But '[p]eacetime maneuvers are a feeble substitute for the real thing', albeit more valuable than routine, mechanical drill. [122] A useful, though limited, means of gaining familiarity with war in peacetime is 'to attract foreign officers who have seen active service'. Officers can also be sent to observe wars. [122]

The chief means of countering friction, however, lies in an army's military spirit – the sum of the military virtues displayed by its soldiers. This was what Prussia had lacked in 1806. It was far more important than

> the self-esteem and vanity of regular armies which are patched together only by service-regulations and drill. Grim severity and iron discipline may be able to preserve the military virtues of a unit, but it cannot create them. [189]

An army trained in this fashion may display discipline, skill, pride and high morale but still lack inherent strength. 'One crack, and the whole thing goes, like a glass too quickly cooled'. 'We should take care', he warns, 'never to confuse the real spirit of an army with its mood'. [189]

For Clausewitz an army is not a machine but a social organisation which should be animated by the 'true spirit of war' which, as he set out in a letter to Fichte in 1809, entails

> mobilising the energies of every soldier to the greatest possible extent and in infusing him with warlike feelings, so that the fire of war spreads to every component of the army instead of leaving numerous dead coals in the mass.[15]

Reforming the army was thus not simply a matter of setting up one kind of organisation or another but of restoring 'the single powerful idea of the honor of its arms' and hence 'the true military spirit'. [188]

Such moral and spiritual values, Clausewitz argued, 'permeate war like a leaven', affecting the capabilities of an army at every point before, during and after battle. [366] Moral factors are often decisive in the engagement while breaking the enemy's moral strength becomes 'the means of achieving the margin of profit'. [231] Military virtues are indispensable if defeat threatens. Without spirit an army loses heart as the danger slowly dawns on officers and spreads through the ranks. 'Worse still is the growing loss of confidence in the high command'. [254] But '[a]n army with spirit will never panic in the face of defeat'. [255]

> An army that maintains its cohesion under the most murderous fire; that cannot be shaken by imaginary fears and resists well-founded ones with all its might; that, proud of its victories, will not lose the strength to obey orders and its respect and trust for its officers even in defeat ... that is mindful of all these duties and qualities by virtue of the single powerful idea of the honor of its arms – such an army is imbued with the true military spirit. [187–88]

In war the spirit of an army makes a real difference, 'a definite moral factor that can be mentally subtracted, whose influence may therefore be estimated'. [188]

This military spirit is built on qualities found in individual soldiers. Foremost is courage in the face of danger. Since war is the realm of danger, '*courage* is the soldier's first requirement'. [101, 85] It will permeate all decisions: 'courage, the sense of one's own strength, is the principal factor that influences judgment. It is the lens, so to speak, through which impressions pass to the brain'. [137] The soldier finds courage for one of two reasons: a natural indifference to danger which is a permanent condition; or a temporary feeling such as ambition, patriotism or enthusiasm which overcomes fear of danger. [101] Courage of both kinds and the self-confidence it generates are the 'finest and least dispensable of military virtues'. [86]

Boldness is another vital quality, more at home in war than any other activity. 'A soldier, whether drummer boy or general, can possess no nobler quality; it is the very metal that gives edge and luster to the sword'. [190] Boldness is the greater, the less it is forced by necessity. [191] For the rank and file acting under orders boldness is 'like a coiled spring, ready at any time to be released'. [190] In more senior ranks it must be disciplined by reflection, though rashness is a 'laudable error'. Frequent, ill-timed boldness is in fact no bad thing; 'it is a luxuriant weed, but indicates the richness of the soil'. [190] Only boldness amounting to disobedience of an express order is to be condemned. [191]

Ambition is also praiseworthy. The soldier's longing for glory is the most powerful and constant passion inspiring men to fight. [105] Clausewitz criticises those who sneer at 'greed for honor' or 'hankering after glory'. These 'noble ambitions' may be abused but

> [i]n war they act as the essential breath of life that animates the inert mass. Other emotions may be more common and more vener-ated – patriotism, idealism, vengeance, enthusiasm of every kind – but they are no substitute for a thirst for fame and honor. [105]

Clausewitz himself could not be said to lack ambition.

Courage, boldness and ambition are necessary but more is required to make a strong and successful army. In the first place discipline and training are indispensable. High standards, however, do not always offer an advantage since 'the armies of practically all European states have reached a common level of discipline and training'. [186] Yet they cannot be ignored and Clausewitz warns that a long period of peace during which military spirit and combat experience decline makes training and discipline all the more important.

High morale is a second requirement and a responsibility of leaders. The commander who inspires trust and devotion among his troops can ask more of them than one 'ruled by delicate emotions'. [339] He will also reward his troops – 'whether prompted by sympathy or prudence'. [339] Nor should food supplies be based on the 'niggardly abstract calculation of the smallest ration that will keep a man alive'. [331] Clausewitz disputed the view that 'wretched food makes no difference to an army', suggesting that even Frederick the Great might have achieved more if he had fed his soldiers as well as Napoleon. [331] Yet in the final analysis such matters are secondary. Clausewitz cites with approval Napoleon's dismissal of the matter of provisions: *qu'on ne me parle pas des vivres*. [339] The health of troops is likewise a lesser matter and mentioned only occasionally.

Soldiers possessing genuine military spirit, discipline and high morale will bear enormous hardship and privation:

> What can be more moving than the thought of thousands of soldiers, poorly clad, their shoulders bent under thirty or forty pounds of equipment, plodding along for days on end in every kind of weather and on every kind of road, continuously endangering their health and their lives, without even a crust of bread to nourish them? [339]

This sort of episode occurs so frequently, Clausewitz observes, that it is surprising that 'heart and strength' do not give out more often. [339] As well as military spirit and morale, two other factors help explain such endurance: the cause for which the troops are fighting and the thought that 'hardship and privations, no matter how extreme, must always be treated as a temporary condition, which has to lead to a state of plenty – even at times luxury'. [339]

Regular armies, in particular, can be bouyed by professional pride. While they may possess military virtues, their spirit is sustained above all by two interrelated experiences, namely 'a series of victorious wars' and, less obviously, 'frequent exertions of the army to the utmost limits of its strength'. [189] Soldiers need to be shown what they can achieve.

> The more a general is accustomed to place heavy demands on his soldiers, the more he can depend on their response. A soldier is just as proud of the hardships he has overcome as of the dangers he has faced. [189]

A regular army imbued with professionalism alone can be effective, especially against other regular armies. But without true military spirit it is best kept in large formations and cannot easily be split up into smaller units, as is necessary when fighting a people in arms. [188] By contrast, the great conquering armies of history – from the Macedonians under Alexander to the French under Bonaparte – relied on their military spirit. [189] Such an army survives 'the wildest storms of misfortune and defeat, and even the indolent inertia of peace, at least for a while'. [189]

The heart of war

Though taking many different forms according to time and place, war 'must contain some more general – indeed, a universal – element with which every theorist ought above all to be concerned'. [593] This element is fighting – the spilling of human blood. Other elements of war such as supply and logistics, administration and equipment are secondary. Fighting, moreover, has both material and 'moral' dimensions which are inextricably interwoven. War as fighting also reveals the inevitability of friction, a phenomenon with physical and psychological origins that influences all combat and permeates war at all levels. It is greater in war than in any other human activity. Though Clausewitz never used the phrase 'fog of war' often attributed to him, it captures the idea.

An army is a human and social organisation, not a machine. To fight well it needs to be motivated by a military spirit that will allow it to overcome the friction, dangers and uncertainty of war. A blend of individual and collective qualities is required, including courage and boldness, discipline and high morale. This will allow an army to endure many hardships and enhance its prospects of victory. Much can be done to create the required virtues in peacetime but only fighting itself will create and can truly test an army's military spirit.

In contrast to many writers before and since Clausewitz takes a human-centred view of war. Fighting lies at its heart and is conducted by men with all their strengths and weaknesses. Once the human element is acknowledged there is room for wide disagreement about its nature and importance. For Clausewitz the psychological element of war is complex and critical but not so elusive and unfathomable as to defy analysis altogether.

8
War as Contest

> *'The effect that any measure will have on the enemy is the most singular factor among all the particulars of action'.* [139]

War is fighting but it is also fighting for a purpose against an opponent who resists by force. Fighting in war – unlike fighting among animals or fighting for the sake of ritual – entails forming intentions and pursuing objectives. It is designed – or should be designed according to Clausewitz – to achieve those ends. The purpose is fulfilled when the opponent accedes to our wishes. In its second dimension, therefore, war is 'an act of force to compel our enemy to do our will'. [75]

Contests other than war

Clausewitz begins his analysis by describing war as 'nothing but a duel on a larger scale'.[1] To expand this idea he employs various analogies, the first being in Book I, chapter 1 where he likens war to a wrestling match. Each wrestler uses physical efforts with the aim of throwing his opponent and compelling him to concede defeat. There are obvious differences between wrestling and war. The former employs bare hands and bodily strength, the latter operates with armies of thousands and vast arrays of weapons, often for extended periods of time and across great distances. In wrestling each contestant has a single mind; in war each belligerent consists of a collectivity of people and a complex organisation. Objectives in war are infinitely variable and liable to differ for each belligerent and to change in the course of the contest. Despite these differences, the parallels are compelling.

First, both physical and mental processes are at work. As well as making physical efforts, each wrestler thinks – much or little, competently or incompetently – about what he is doing and what he is trying to achieve. Each wrestler is seeking 'through physical force to compel the other to do his will'. [75] But while the means are physical, it is the psychology of each wrestler – the readiness to fight, the desire to win – that animates and pervades the whole contest. War is similarly a combination of mental and physical effort, 'a trial of moral and physical forces through the medium of the latter'. [127]

Second, Clausewitz's wrestlers demonstrate the importance of interaction. A move – or the threat of a move – by one contestant can be met by any number of counter-moves so that the course which the match can take is infinitely variable. War is similarly a reciprocal activity, characterised by 'the use of force under conditions of danger, subject to constant interaction with an adversary'. [133] War is never 'the action of a living force upon a lifeless mass (total nonresistance would be no war at all) but always the collision of two living forces'. [77] Important consequences flow from this. The best strategy for each belligerent, as for each wrestler, will depend on the opponent's actual and likely moves. As well, this interaction can create a dynamic that spurs contestants to greater effort.

Third, there is a distinction between means and ends. Wrestlers seek an immediate goal, namely throwing the opponent to the floor. In turn, this physical result is a means to produce the desired end, namely the opponent's defeat. In wrestling the rules stipulate that pinning the opponent to the ground for a certain period of time constitutes victory. Once this occurs the winner is decided and the match is at an end. The manner of determining winner and loser is also clear in the analogy of a duel which Clausewitz uses on occasion. In a duel inflicting a wound with a sword may by convention and tradition constitute victory. War similarly distinguishes between the intermediate physical result which Clausewitz calls the goal [*Ziel*] and the ultimate political object of the war [*Zweck*]. The latter is essential to understanding war but is not in principle part of the idea of war as a contest. Within war the goal 'takes the place of the object, discarding it as something not actually part of war itself'. [75]

As we shall see, the relationship between goal and object in war is far more complicated than in wrestling or duelling, not least because there are no clear rules to govern it. War is also different in that any means can be employed. If a wrestler takes a gun into the ring, the match is immediately at an end; if a duellist uses a firearm against an opponent equipped with a sword, it is murder. War, however, knows no such bounds. Opponents offer all kinds of violence to one another, even indiscriminate slaughter of civilians and prisoners, without bringing the contest to an end.[2] There are levels of violence below which war fizzles out, but there are in principle no upper limits. In this regard war resembles more a bar–room brawl in which rules, participants and bystanders alike may be thrown out of the window.

Another analogy occasionally employed by Clausewitz is with the law. Forcing an opponent to battle, for example, is like appealing to a higher court in which one may win or lose. [99] Early victories are not the end of the campaign since it is possible to 'win the first decision in a case but lose it on appeal and end by having to pay costs as well'. [597] Clausewitz also likens war to commerce 'which is also a conflict of human interests and activities'. (And 'it is *still* closer to politics, which in turn can be considered as a kind of commerce on a larger scale'.) [149] In commerce buyer and seller compete over the price to be paid; once agreed, payment follows according to accepted procedures. Trade, moreover, is often conducted on the basis of credit, a system that works so long as the trader settles up when required. So it is with war.

> The decision by arms is for all major and minor operations in war what cash payment is in commerce. Regardless how complex the relationship between two parties, regardless how rarely settlements actually occur, they can never be entirely absent. [97]

The analogy is not with a modern banking system that relies indefinitely on credit and book transfers. In Clausewitz's time banks regularly settled in cash.[3]

In the final analysis, of course, neither commerce nor wrestling are about life and death. Duelling may sometimes take a life but it remains small-scale and private in character. For Clausewitz war is uniquely 'a clash between major interests, which is resolved by bloodshed'. [149] It may resemble other contests in important respects but it alone entails the spilling of blood on a large scale for political ends.

The rise to extremes

The interaction [*Wechselwirkung*] between two sides each seeking to impose its will on the other by force of arms, Clausewitz believed, is in principle liable to lead to greater levels of violence. Three factors push it towards the extreme:

- once force has been introduced there is no logical limit to its employment;

- each belligerent fears that the other will seek to overthrow him; and
- each belligerent feels compelled to match or outdo the enemy's exertions.

Taken together these interactions make for a rise to 'extremes'. [77]

The first form of interaction is simply the condition of two sides contending by violence who can choose to employ any means:

> war is an act of force, and there is no logical limit to the application of that force. Each side, therefore, compels its opponent to follow suit: a reciprocal action is started which must lead, in theory, to extremes. [77]

This interaction is by no means certain to be restrained by reason or by moral qualms:

> The maximum use of force is in no way incompatible with the simultaneous use of the intellect. If one side uses force without compunction, undeterred by the bloodshed it involves, while the other side refrains, the first will gain the upper hand. That side will force the other to follow suit; each will drive its opponent toward extremes. [75–6]

Neither side can assume that it is safe to hold back in war since it will lose out against unrestrained violence by the other.

The second form of interaction arises because each side seeks to put the other in a position where demands will be accepted:

> if you are to force the enemy, by making war on him, to do your bidding, you must either make him literally defenseless or at least put him in a position that makes this danger probable. [77]

While war continues each side fears that the other will be able to put it in this position by disarming or defeating it:

> So long as I have not overthrown my opponent I am bound to fear he may overthrow me. Thus I am not in control: he dictates to me as much as I dictate to him. [77]

Each side seeks to put the other in a position where he will do one's bidding. Each side, Clausewitz assumes, thus has a breaking point at which it will give up the struggle and yield to the other's demands.[4]

A third pressure towards the extreme arises because each side is conscious of the level of effort both are putting in. Each assesses the other's strength in terms of 'two inseparable factors, viz. *the total means at his disposal* and *the strength of his will'*. [77] Once a reasonably accurate estimation is obtained:

> you can adjust your own efforts accordingly; that is, you can either increase them until they surpass the enemy's or, if this is beyond your means, you can make your efforts as great as possible. But the enemy will do the same; competition will again result and, in pure theory, it must again force you both to extremes. [77]

In Book VIII Clausewitz explores this calculation further:

> Since in war too small an effort can result not just in failure but in positive harm, each side is driven to outdo the other, which sets up an interaction.
> Such an interaction could lead to a maximum of effort if such a maximum could be defined. [585]

Each belligerent thus has an incentive at least to match the vigour with which its opponent is pursuing the war. The general must therefore 'decide from the start whether his opponent is both willing and able to outdo him by using stronger, more decisive measures'. [517] And he must never forget that his counterpart can at any time choose to appeal to 'that supreme tribunal – force' by seeking a major battle. The enemy's choice can thereby 'force us against our will to do likewise'. [98–9]

Two types of war

War is thus a kind of auction in violence with unlimited bidding as the German *Steigerung bis zum Äußersten* suggests. In theory this 'rise to extremes' occurs instantaneously and inevitably. It is war's 'natural tendency', but only in a 'philosophical, strictly logical sense'. [88] In reality many factors, including friction and politics, constrain war and most fall short of the extremes of violence. At certain periods in history even the idea of a rise to extremes appeared totally absent. In the eighteenth century each state could 'gauge the other side's potential in terms both of numbers and of time' so that war became predictable and hence

> deprived of its most dangerous feature – its tendency toward the extreme, and of the whole chain of unknown possibilities which would follow.... Safe from the threat of extremes, it was no longer necessary to go to extremes. [589–90]

This posed a further question for Clausewitz. Could wars so lacking in intensity and potential for escalation be counted in the same category as great wars fought for the control of Europe? Were there perhaps two fundamentally different types of violent contest?

In an early essay on strategy, written in 1804, Clausewitz identified two kinds of political objective in war – either to destroy the opponent totally or to weaken him sufficiently so that he accepts whatever conditions are demanded of him. In each case the immediate aim is to reduce his capacity to resist so that he cannot fight on at all or can continue only with the greatest risk. In both cases all-out military effort is required.[5] To Clausewitz at this time wars lacking such energy and urgency for decision hardly seemed to count as wars as all.

In unrevised sections of *On War* Clausewitz calls them 'mongrel affairs' or half-things [*Halbdinge*]. With no vital issues at stake war is reduced 'to something tame and half-hearted' and troops spend nine-tenths of their time 'occupied by idleness'. Military action is 'reduced to insignificant, time-killing flourishes, to skirmishes that are half in earnest and half in jest'. [218] With 'the hostile spirit of true war' held in check', what should be '[g]ambling for high stakes seems to have turned into haggling for small change'. [218]

The idea that war could embrace a wide range of goals, not all of which require maximum effort, is first evident about half-way through Book VI on defensive operations.[6] Discussing defence in mountainous country, Clausewitz asks whether resistance 'is intended to be relative or absolute. Is it meant to last only a certain time, or to end in definite victory?' Mountains, he concludes, 'are eminently suited to defense of the first type', allowing a defender to delay an attacker, harass his movements and ultimately to wear him down. [419] Such negative objectives, Clausewitz recognises, will rightly influence the intensity with which war is fought.

This limited type of war could also apply to the offence. An attacking state might aim merely at gaining 'a province, a strip of territory, a fortress, and so forth. Any one of these may be of political value in negotiations, whether they are retained or exchanged'. [526] Such a war does not seek a clear decision, the aim being to strengthen one's bargaining position or secure an advantage. The contest may be more 'a state of observation than a struggle of life and death'. [488] For a time Clausewitz remained somewhat dismissive of this kind of war. An attacker not bent on a decision is likened to 'an idler who strolls through a campaign and takes advantage of the occasional bargain that comes his way'. [501]

By 1827, however, Clausewitz had accepted the idea that political factors account for the existence of two genuine forms of war. The distinction could be made as 'a matter of actual fact'. Both kinds deserve the name 'war' but 'the fact that the aims of the two types are quite different must be clear at all times, and their points of irreconcilability brought out'. [Note of 10 July 1827, 69] The critical difference between the two types is whether they are fought to defeat an opponent totally or simply to gain an advantage over him. One is 'completely governed and saturated by the urge for a decision', an urge felt by at least one side if not both, while the other seeks to defend a position or secure marginal gains. [488–9]

Unlike wrestlers and duellists, states determine for themselves what the nature of the contest shall be. Political aims thus enter the picture and the implications must be accepted:

> Once this influence of the political objective on war is admitted, as it must be, there is no stopping it; consequently we must also be willing to wage such minimal wars, which consist in *merely threatening the enemy*, with *negotiations held in reserve*. [604]

The key conclusion is reached: 'Only if war is looked at in this way does its unity reappear; only then can we see that all wars are things of the *same* nature'. [606] In the revised Book I, chapter 1 Clausewitz can therefore accept

> without any inconsistency [that] wars can have all degrees of importance and intensity, ranging from a war of extermination down to simple armed observation. [81]

There is certainly a 'gulf that separates a war of annihilation, a struggle for political existence, from a war reluctantly declared in consequence of political pressure or of an alliance that no longer seems to reflect the state's true interests'. [94] But both types of war remain war and both are equally 'political':

> Only if politics is regarded not as resulting from a just appreciation of affairs, but – as it conventionally is – as cautious, devious, even dishonest, shying away from force, could the second type of war appear to be more 'political' than the first. [88][7]

Of course, actual wars do not fall neatly into one category or the other. While theory sees a sharp distinction between two types of war – 'perfect contrasts, the extremes of the spectrum' – Clausewitz observes that for those involved in war 'matters are not so sharply delineated' and 'as an actual occurrence, war generally falls somewhere in between ... these extremes'. [517]

Nonetheless, certain factors help push a given war towards one type or another. Where stakes are high, interaction naturally pushes violence to higher levels. A tense political relationship between two states may mean that 'the slightest quarrel can produce a wholly disproportionate effect – a real explosion'. [81] Similarly, ambitious policies will stir up powerful emotions so that war will tend towards its 'abstract concept'. [88] Where great goals are absent and the stakes are minor, all the friction and difficulties inherent in war conspire to reduce levels of effort. Governments are also constrained by strategic calculation: 'why should we make the enormous exertions inherent in war if our only object is to produce a similar effort on the part of the enemy?' [217] In fact, governments may find themselves seeking to stimulate emotions rather than hold them back. [88] Enthusiasm wanes, resources dwindle and governments procrastinate in the hope that something will turn up. 'Meanwhile, the war drags slowly on, like a faint and starving man'. [604]

Clausewitz suggests that wars with limited aims are more numerous – perhaps 49 out of every 50 wars.[8] Once war as contest takes into account political objectives, the constraints of friction, strategic considerations and limited resources, the rise to extremes no longer seems natural and inevitable. On the contrary, the burden of explanation for Clausewitz is to understand the few contests that overcome the natural shackles of warfare.

Deciding the outcome of contests

The idea of war as a contest prompts the question: how are winners and losers determined? What is it that leads one side to be recognised as victor, the other as loser? In some violent contests between individuals – brawls, street-fights, robberies with assault – the outcome is simply determined. If a thief knocks down a man in the street, he can remove the money he wants from the victim's wallet.[9] The object is achieved as an immediate consequence of the physical outcome: the thief takes the wallet from the unconscious victim. This is enforcement of one's will, pure and simple. Similarly, as Clausewitz observes, an invader prefers to take possession of a country with no resistance.

A different means of resolving a contest can be seen in the action of a criminal who starts to hurt his victim in order to coerce him into handing over money. This requires a measure of cooperation on the victim's part, albeit under duress, so that a psychological element enters the picture. A protection racket takes this relationship between criminal and victim to a higher level of sophistication. In such cases of coercion the victim decides to cooperate under pressure. Failure to concede, it is feared, will lead to more pain or even destruction. It is this kind of coercive relationship – the reluctant acceptance of one's demands by the opponent – that war normally seeks.

A third kind of resolution of a contest comes to the fore in sports such as wrestling or the duel – both analogies used by Clausewitz. Here winner and loser are determined by 'rules of the game' whether explicit as in wrestling or, more relevant to war, unwritten as in the duel. In duelling, for example, a minor wound may be accepted by convention as sufficient to end the duel, the honour of both participants being satisfied. Similarly in war, the spilling of blood, especially on a large scale, carries special significance and helps establish certain understandings whereby losses in battle are taken to signify that political concessions are appropriate.

These three processes for achieving a result – enforcement, coercion and convention – can be identified in Clausewitz's thinking. Interwoven in practice, they can be analytically separated. The focus is on how military results translate into political consequences, how the military aim [*Ziel*] produces its political purpose [*Zweck*].

(a) War as enforcement

The idea that physical destruction of enemy forces gives the winner a free hand to impose on the loser whatever outcome he wishes is a powerful one. It is found most clearly in the idea of war as '*an act of force to compel our enemy to do our will*'. [75] 'To secure that object we must render the enemy powerless [*wehrlos* or defence-less]; and that, in theory, is the true aim of warfare'. [75] In particular, the enemy's 'fighting forces must be *destroyed*: that is, they must be *put in such a condition that they can no longer carry on the fight*' and the country occupied so that fresh forces cannot be raised. [90]

Complete victory of this kind appears to carry 'the power of its own enforcement'.[10] Like the wrestler 'incapable of further resistance' [75], the enemy has no choice but to accept our will. Thus in theory everything is 'governed by a supreme law, the *decision by force of arms*'. [99] But as Clausewitz realised, pure enforcement is an ideal rarely achievable in practice. It is difficult to totally destroy an enemy (and quite possibly unwise in the longer term). And while an enemy is not totally destroyed, his will to fight may persist:

> Even after a defeat, there is always the possibility that a turn of fortune can be brought about by developing new sources of internal strength or through the natural decimation all offensives suffer in the long run or by means of help from abroad ... it is the natural law of the moral world that a nation that finds itself on the brink of an abyss will try to save itself by any means. [483]

In most wars, therefore, simple physical conquest will not be achieved and an element of compliance becomes necessary.

(b) War as coercion

If war entails some measure of compliance, this makes it a bargaining process that works on the mind of the opponent as much as on his physical capacity. War becomes a matter of coercion by threats (and in some cases promises) rather than simple disarming or destruction. Inflicting losses and threatening further losses are powerful inducements to concession:

> If the enemy is to be coerced you must put him in a situation that is even more unpleasant than the sacrifice you call on him to make. [77]

Harm is done or threatened not simply to destroy an opponent's capabilities but to coerce his thinking. Most wars are in fact concluded before the point of simple physical enforcement is reached:

> the aim of *disarming the enemy* (the object of *war in the abstract*, the ultimate means of accomplishing the war's political purpose ...) is in fact not always encountered in reality, and need not be fully

achieved as a condition of peace. On no account should theory raise it to the level of a law. Many treaties have been concluded before one of the antagonists could be called powerless. [91]

Yet the possibility is always present that an opponent will refuse to be coerced and the attacker must decide whether to pursue the contest to the point of enforcement.

(c) War as convention

Convention provides a third link between military action and political outcome. One of the 'rules of the game' in war is that victory on the battlefield carries certain prerogatives accepted by both winner and loser.[11] Ancient Greece developed the idea that victory in battle – defined as holding the field at the end of a clash of arms – should carry political consequences.[12] City-states could thereby settle differences in a matter of hours through a fierce and bloody encounter. Similarly, medieval custom granted victory and its prerogatives to the side that occupied the battlefield for three consecutive days.[13]

The clash of arms as a symbolic means of settling conflicts, Clausewitz argues, was most apparent towards the end of the seventeenth century when the conduct of war was reduced to 'a somewhat stronger form of diplomacy, a more forceful method of negotiation, in which battles and sieges were the principal notes exchanged'. [590] As in a sporting contest, winners and losers were decided according to accepted rules. Convention thus 'unnecessarily restricted many aspects of operations', especially exploitation of success on the battlefield. [265] Only exceptional generals such as Marlborough and Frederick the Great drove home their victories by vigorous pursuit. [266] To most commanders

> *[t]he very idea, the honor* of victory appeared to be the whole point ... Once a decision had been reached, one stopped fighting as a matter of course: further bloodshed was considered unnecessarily brutal. [265]

War limited in this way could not serve indefinitely as a means of resolving conflicts. As France demonstrated after 1789 '[t]his spurious philosophy was not the complete basis for a decision'. [265]

Nevertheless, an element of convention will be present in many wars, especially those with limited objectives. In some wars the military aim is identical to the political – Clausewitz gives the example of a war for the control of a province. But in most wars political objectives are complex and are not easily equated with a simple military goal or a single clash of arms. States must then agree, implicitly if not explicitly, that a military encounter or series of encounters is to 'serve the political purpose and symbolize it in the peace negotiations'. Agreement on a 'substitute' [*Äquivalent*] is easier when public passions are not aroused and the stakes are smaller. [81] The key idea is that 'abandonment of the battlefield' should equate with 'abandonment of intentions'. [234]

Why should states accept conventions about the outcome of a contest? The reasons seem to lie deeper than politics. In human society the organised injuring of human bodies invariably carries symbolic and ritual significance.[14] Many cultures follow rituals that require the shedding of blood – from human sacrifice to initiation ceremonies – and virtually all endow loss of life in war with special meaning. This symbolic element helps explain the readiness of communities both to sacrifice young men in war and to accept the result of battle. From this perspective war is a contest in which two sides seek to 'out-injure' each other in killing and wounding.[15] Clausewitz does not explore this aspect of war but it accords with his emphasis on the centrality of bloodshed and his interpretation of war as a social relationship.

The concept of contest

War as contest focuses on competitive interaction as two sides contend for advantage or for total superiority over the other. The analogy with a wrestling match captures this essence and reflects Clausewitz's emphasis on the role of the opposing commanders in the campaign – as if 'the whole monstrosity called war came down, in fact, to a contest between individuals, a sort of duel'. [577] The analogy draws attention to the reciprocity at the heart of war and the dynamics that ensue as each belligerent reacts to the other. What Clausewitz saw in the wars of his age was not simply expansion of resources committed to war but the more intense interaction of belligerents and reciprocal pressures to increase the level of effort. He was the first writer to begin to analyse the idea of a rise to extremes in war seen as a contest. Though not exploring the idea as fully as subsequent strategists, he provides the essential skeleton for a general theory of escalation.[16]

War embraces both conflicts aiming for total success and those seeking marginal advantage. But there is a natural divide, like a watershed, between wars embodying great ambitions and energy and wars that find states struggling to overcome friction and maintain

momentum. In practice, most wars are of the latter kind, a consequence of two sets of 'counterweights' to the rise to extremes: (i) those
within war itself such as the friction inherent in fighting and the
dynamics of the contest which can hold back as well as spur on belligerents; and (ii) those outside war relating to its political purpose and
the social and political conditions of the age. [388]

'The aim of war should be what its very concept implies – to defeat
the enemy. ... But what exactly does "defeat" signify?' [595] Clausewitz
recognises this is a complex process that can be pursued by various
routes. Enforcement appears to be the trump card but total subjugation
of an opponent is rarely achieved. Success in war usually requires a
measure of psychological coercion of the opponent, turning war into a
bargaining process in which one side makes concessions under threat.
The element of convention may also be present as contending sides
recognise the clash of arms as the symbolic equivalent of their political
struggle. War, in short, is a contest embodying complex physical, psychological and sociological relationships between two states.

9
War as an Instrument of Policy

> *'[War] cannot follow its own laws, but has to be treated as part of some other whole; the name of which is policy'.* [606]

The idea of war as a contest focuses on how belligerents interact and how outcomes are achieved. But Clausewitz also needs an external perspective to explain why belligerents engage in a contest at all. War, he proposes, should be seen as a means to achieve the political goals which states set themselves. Their goal is thus not victory in the contest but what victory brings. Were victory alone the objective, war would be an activity in itself and lack wider meaning:

> war cannot be divorced from political life [*Verkehr*], and whenever this occurs in our thinking about war, the many links that connect the two elements are destroyed and we are left with something pointless and devoid of sense. [605]

War might have its own dynamics but its *raison d'être* lies outside: 'Its grammar, indeed, may be its own, but not its logic'. [605] War in itself is 'incomplete'; it must be 'treated as part of some other whole; the name of which is policy'. [606].

Policy and politics

It is necessary to separate two senses of the German word *Politik*, a distinction not always clear in Clausewitz's writing. It may refer to 'policy', the conscious articulation of goals by states and their pursuit by whatever means are chosen. In this light war is a servant of policy which 'converts the overwhelmingly destructive element of war into a mere instrument'. [606] The second meaning of *Politik* refers to 'politics', the sum of political interactions within and between states. In this context, *'war is only a branch of political activity ... it is in no sense autonomous'*. [605] Clausewitz's idea of politics embraces not only political activity as such but also social change, economic relationships and the spirit of the age (technology came later), and he sometimes uses the term 'society' in this context. While his distinction between politics and society is vague, Clausewitz's point is clear: social and political processes and institutions shape both war in general and the particulars of policy.

War is thus not only an instrument of policy but an activity intrinsically bound up with politics: 'war is not a mere act of policy but a true political instrument, a continuation of political activity by other means'. [87] Both perspectives are important and each performs a different function. Policy reflects a state's particular interests and character, and contains an element of choice or subjectivity, however constrained by circumstances. Politics is more a matter of objective factors – political and social conditions such as the balance of power, the resources available, the character of governments and so on – which set limits on policy choices and push them in certain directions.

> [T]he aims a belligerent adopts, and the resources he employs, must be governed by the particular characteristics of his own position; but they will also conform to the spirit of the age and to its general character. [594]

Politics in this sense helps explain why war in the past was fundamentally limited and why in Clausewitz's time it became possible on a monumentally destructive scale.

There has been much debate as to whether Clausewitz gave priority to the subjective or objective perspective.[1] But it would be contrary to his usual approach to say that one always dominates the other. All elements must be comprehended. War for Clausewitz is 'a very peculiar form of duel' since its basis lies not simply in a

> mutual desire or willingness to fight, but in the purposes involved; and those always belong to a larger whole – the more so because war itself, considered as a single conflict, is governed by political aims and conditions that themselves belong to a larger whole. [245]

This chapter looks at Clausewitz's ideas about war as an instrument of policy. War as a product of political and social circumstances is considered in the following chapter.

Development of the idea

The idea of war as an instrument of policy is most closely associated with Clausewitz but was already familiar in the eighteenth century.[2] Many writers on strategy perceived some link between war and politics. The Prussian General Friedrich von Lossau expressed the concept as follows: 'Wars are therefore the exterior means of states to achieve by violence what they cannot achieve by peaceful means'.[3] Bülow's formulation of the idea – 'Political strategy relates to military strategy as military strategy to tactics' – was overly simple but may have impelled Clausewitz towards his classic definition.[4] Some doubted the usefulness of the concept. The editor of Scharnhorst's revised *Handbook for Officers* (1817–8) stated that 'war … always has an *ultimate political purpose*' but did not pursue the idea.[5]

From the time Clausewitz first started writing about war he was convinced that war and policy were related though the nature of the linkages had to be determined. His earliest thinking – such as the essay *On Strategy* in 1804 – focused on the importance of military effort, the decisiveness of battle and the role of the commander. Policy took its cue from the military imperative to destroy the enemy's forces and his will to resist. Limited aims did not mean limited effort. Over time, however, Clausewitz steadily placed more weight on policy.[6] A first modification was to require the commander to reconcile as best he could military and political imperatives neither of which was accorded superiority. Next he gave priority to policy, putting it before but not above war.

By 1827 Clausewitz could grant full primacy to the political purpose of war. Not only did policy determine the objective of war, it also explained the course which a war takes and the intensity with which it is fought. 'The political object – the original motive for the war – will thus determine both the military objective to be reached and the amount of effort it requires'. [81] Policy, moreover, reaches deep into war and beyond the end of hostilities: 'The main lines along which military events progress, and to which they are restricted, are political lines that continue throughout the war into the subsequent peace. How could it be otherwise?' [605] War is led by a hand – and 'this hand is policy'.[7]

The idea of war as an instrument or continuation of policy receives several other expressions in *On War*:

- 'war is nothing but the continuation of policy with other means'. [Note of 10 July 1827, 69]
- 'War, therefore, is an act of policy'. [87]
- 'The political object is the goal, war is the means of reaching it'. [87]
- 'war should never be thought of as *something autonomous* but always as an *instrument of policy*'. [88]
- 'war is simply a continuation of political intercourse, with the addition of other means'. [605]
- 'Once again: war is an instrument of policy. It must necessarily bear the character of policy and measure by its standards'. [610]

This 'formula', as it is sometimes called, contains several important features.

The resort to war, first of all, is an additional means for policy to employ; it does not replace policy or relegate it to a lesser position. Clausewitz is clear in the original German (if not always in translation) that the use of force supplements policy, never replaces it. It is always a continuation 'with' [*mit*] not a substitution 'by' [*durch*] other means.[8] War may certainly replace diplomacy – in the sense of formal dealings between states – but both remain subordinate to policy.

> The conduct of war, in its great outlines, is therefore policy itself, which takes up the sword in place of the pen, but does not on that account cease to think according to its own laws. [610]

Resort to war is simply to opt for 'a policy conducted by fighting battles rather than by sending diplomatic notes'. [607] For states, war is merely 'another expression of their thoughts, another form of speech or writing'. [605]

Second, whether or not diplomacy continues during hostilities, a political relationship still exists. Clausewitz spells this out unequivocally:

> it is apt to be assumed that war suspends that intercourse and replaces it by a wholly different condition, ruled by no law but its own.
>
> We maintain, on the contrary, that war is simply a continuation of political intercourse, with the addition of other means.

We deliberately use the phrase 'with the addition of other means' because we also want to make it clear that war in itself does not suspend political intercourse or change it into something entirely different. In essentials that intercourse continues, irrespective of the means it employs. [605]

Politics between belligerents does not cease. It is simply that war becomes part of their political relationship.

Third, the formula does not distinguish between saying that war is in practice a continuation of policy and saying that war ought in principle to be a continuation of policy. While war is by definition a continuation of *politics*, an outgrowth of political conditions, war in practice may or may not be a continuation of *policy*. Clausewitz knew that war might originate with no particular purpose, escape the control of governments or be mismanaged. His message is clearly that states *should* treat war as an instrument of policy. This fusion of analysis and doctrine accorded with much contemporary thinking which did not make the sharp distinction between 'is' and 'ought' demanded by modern philosophy. Clausewitz assumed that development of the centralised state and the idea of national interest made it natural for governments to approach war as means to an end. In Aristotelian fashion he focuses on the natural potential or *telos* of things. The state by its nature can and should make war into its instrument.

Initiating war

The immediate origins of war are matters of policy:

When whole communities go to war – whole peoples, and especially *civilized* peoples – the reason always lies in some political situation, and the occasion is always due to some political object. War, therefore, is an act of policy. [86–7]

War actually begins, however, only when one state resists the actions of another. The attacker naturally prefers to walk in without resistance:

The aggressor is always peace-loving (as Bonaparte always claimed to be); he would prefer to take over our country unopposed. To prevent his doing so one must be willing to make war and be prepared for it. [370]

It is thus the defender who in fact starts a war, 'who first commits an act that really fits the concept of war'. [377]

> Essentially, the concept of war does not originate with the attack, because the ultimate object of attack is not fighting: rather, it is possession. The idea of war originates with the defense, which does have fighting as its immediate object. [377]

In political terms war requires one state to seek change, another to defend the status quo. 'Politically, only one [side] can be the aggressor; there can be no war if both parties seek to defend themselves'. [216] Consequently, 'it is the weak, those likely to need defense, who should always be armed in order not to be overwhelmed'. [370] 'War', in short, 'serves the purpose of the defense more than that of the aggressor.' [370] The word 'aggressor', it should be noted, lacked legal or moral connotations in Clausewitz's time.

As an instrument of policy war embraces everything from maximum violence to the merest hint of force:

> The terrible two-handed sword that should be used with total strength to strike once and no more, becomes the lightest rapier – sometimes even a harmless foil fit only for thrusts and feints and parries. [606]

A major objective such as 'a war of extermination' naturally requires great efforts but where stakes are small 'simple armed observation' may suffice. [81] Whatever the stakes, however, war should always be seen as a political instrument. What matters in the first instance is the ability of a state to determine accurately the type of war which it initiates or is forced into by another state. It is not uncommon for national leaders to misjudge the situation, in particular by underestimating the effort that is required. This may have disastrous consequences but is not uncommon.

Contemporary statesmen, for example, had clearly failed to recognise the nature of the war against France:

> Woe to the government, which, relying on half-hearted politics and a shackled military policy, meets a foe who, like the untamed elements, knows no law other than his own power. [219]

Yet some explanation can be suggested. It was natural to assume that war would follow past patterns and remain limited since the great bulk of wars are of the lesser kind. [501] Against France, Prussia and Austria simply assumed 'the diplomatic type of war' was required. [591] Statesmen were caught in the old paradigm of limited war for limited aims.

> Such a transformation of war might have led to new ways of think-ing about it. In 1805, 1806, and 1809, men might have recognized that total ruin was a possibility – instead it stared them in the face … They did not, however, change their attitude sufficiently … They failed because the transformations of war had not yet been sufficiently revealed by history. [583–4]

Indications of a new potential for war were missed and 'cus-tomary means' of response were chosen – a clear failure of political judgement. [609]

Clausewitz poses the question: 'Would a purely military view of war have enabled anyone to detect these faults and cure them?' The answer is emphatically negative. A 'thoughtful strategist' might have been able to understand events and even foresee the con-sequences but 'it would have been quite impossible to act on his speculations'. [609] Policy requires political choices, not simply military analysis.

> Not until statesmen had at last perceived the nature of the forces that had emerged in France, and had grasped that new political conditions now obtained in Europe, could they foresee the broad effect all this would have on war; and only in that way could they appreciate the scale of the means that would have to be employed, and how best to apply them. [609]

Political misjudgements also account for the fact wars may be started by states with inadequate military capability. Reason suggests this should not occur but reality is different. [91]

Controlling the instrument

As an instrument of policy war must not only be suited to the objective but also remain under the control of the policy-maker. Ideally, it responds fully and immediately to whatever policy demands and as a passive tool never influences the choice of objectives. But the dynamics of violent interaction make this purely theoretical. In practice, controlling war for any period requires constant vigilance and effort since violence is never an inert element.

> Policy, then, will permeate all military operations, and, in so far as their violent nature will admit, it will have a continuous influence on them. [87]

War is thus not only a blunt but also an unsteady instrument and any resort to war must take this into account.

First, Clausewitz suggests that a state cannot be confident in advance of the course and outcome of war due to its complexity:

> Its violence is not the kind that explodes in a single discharge, but is the effect of forces that do not always develop in exactly the same manner or to the same degree. [87]

Accurate appraisal of how a war will develop cannot be done by 'sheer methodical examination' but requires 'the intuition of a genius'. It depends on complex factors such as relative strengths, available resources, the character of the nations concerned, the spirit of their armed forces and the 'political sympathies of other states and the effect the war may have on them'. [586] 'Bonaparte was quite right when he said that Newton himself would quail before the algebraic problems it could pose'. [586]

Second, governments must reckon with the fact that war has its own dynamics that influence and may even transform the goals with which they began. War is not a single decision but entails a series of decisions each of which is shaped by what has gone before. While the original purpose of the war must be kept in mind,

> That, however, does not imply that the political aim is a tyrant. It must adapt itself to its chosen means, a process which can radically change it. [87]

Again,

> the original political objects can greatly alter during the war and may finally change entirely *since they are influenced by events and their probable consequences*. [92]

The interdependence of means and ends in war are described even more clearly in a work on the campaigns of 1799:

> in war more than elsewhere, purpose and means exist in permanent *reciprocal relationship*. However valid it is for political intentions to give events their initial direction, the means – that is, fighting – can never be regarded as an inanimate instrument. Out of the rich vitality of war grow a thousand new motives, which may become more significant and dominant than the original political considerations.[9]

Though Clausewitz does not use the term, he has identified the phenomenon of feedback.

Third, there is the possibility that costs will increase to the point where they outweigh gains. To avoid this a belligerent must adopt

> the principle of using no greater force, and setting himself no greater military aim, than would be sufficient for the achievement of his political purpose. [585]

The risk is that 'all proportion between action and political demands would be lost'. [585] In such a case policy ought to be reversed since

> means would cease to be commensurate with ends, and in most cases a policy of maximum exertion would fail on account of the domestic problems it would raise. [585]

It is quite possible that 'the exhaustion of the belligerents increases to such an extent that, instead of making the war more expensive, they are driven to make peace'. [338] Yet states are reluctant to acknowledge their strength is running out: 'That sort of thing is long kept confidential, possibly forever'. [388] Other, plausible explanations for abandoning a war must be offered to the world.

Finally, war taken up as an instrument of policy may simply escape the control of governments. The emotions of combatants, for example, can be 'so aroused that the political factor would be hard put to control them'. [88] To the extent that governments find it difficult to contain hostilities or bring them to a halt, war ceases to be an instrument of policy. This is not an idea Clausewitz explores at length since paying it too much attention might undermine his central argument that war can and should remain an instrument of policy.

Criticism

Several criticisms have been directed against Clausewitz's notion of war as an instrument of policy. Three relate to the distinction between war and peace. First, some claim that he is morally indifferent to the horrors of war. Walzer, for example, argues that he ignores or radically underestimates the significance of taking up an instrument that entails violence and killing.[10] It is true that Clausewitz says next to nothing about legal and moral restraints on the resort to war or on its conduct, that he advocates all-out violence with equanimity where necessary and that he claims humanitarian scruples in war can be positively dangerous. While he places violence and killing at the centre of war, however, he insists they should not follow their own law but remain subordinate to the political purpose.

Second, the formula is said to blur the line between war and diplomacy by putting them side by side in the armoury of the policy-maker without adequate differentiation. Scarry, for example, sees a certain sleight of hand in the way that the formula elides war with the relatively benign and peaceable activity of diplomacy.[11] On this view the formula makes the difference with diplomacy appear almost a technical matter, a simple choice of one means rather than another. Clausewitz's response would be that in the nature of foreign policy war and diplomacy must exist side by side and that any effective diplomacy needs ultimately to be backed by a capacity to use force. Diplomacy without armaments, Frederick the Great had said, is like music without instruments. This is not to say that war is a preferred means, only that the capacity for it is essential.

Third, some commentators have seen in Clausewitz too great a readiness to resort to war, even a preference for war. Rapoport, for instance, suggests that a 'clear distinction among readiness, willingness, and eagerness can hardly be made on objective grounds', and that in some measure politics will adapt itself psychologically to war.[12] Certainly, Clausewitz emphasises preparation for war and nowhere talks of war being a last and reluctant resort of states. Yet his whole position suggests that war is a dangerous and costly business that brings great uncertainty in its wake. Though a necessary and useable instrument, war is not to be taken up without careful weighing of the consequences.

A fourth and more fundamental criticism of Clausewitz's formula is its assumption of rationality. The means-end approach to war, it is argued, assumes a degree of rationality unlikely in practice – a typically liberal or utopian belief that reason can control politics.[13] Clausewitz certainly takes as given that reason will play a significant part in decisions about war:

> War moves on its goals with varying speeds; but it always lasts long enough for influence to be exerted on the goal and for its own course to be changed in one way or another – long enough, in other words, to remain subject to the action of a superior intelligence. [87]

War is thus a rational undertaking in which belligerents weigh losses, past and future, against the benefits to be secured:

> Since war is not an act of senseless passion but is controlled by its political object, the value of this object must determine the sacrifices to be made for it in *magnitude* and also in *duration*. Once the expenditure of effort exceeds the value of the political object, the object must be renounced and peace must follow. [92]

In the light of the uncertainties Clausewitz himself describes this is a rather sanguine assumption about the ability of states to break off war when it is no longer worth the candle. In a war for low stakes 'the very faintest prospect of defeat might be enough to cause one side to yield' even though it has the capacity to continue. [91] But in a war where stakes are high and passions aroused the assumption is indeed tenuous. Clausewitz, however, cannot admit that war aims may be overridden by the war itself since this would 'destroy his basic contention that war is the instrument of policy and not the reverse'.[14]

A final criticism is that war may be of such overwhelming importance to a state engaged in a struggle for survival – as when a small state is attacked by a major power – that it is misleading to describe war as simply an 'instrument' serving the 'policy' of the community.[15] Means and ends merge as war itself takes over and becomes policy for the time being. Whether war for survival falls within the concept of policy or even politics is a matter of debate. Certainly, Clausewitz finds it hard to imagine wars driven by pure feeling and containing no element of policy:

> That the political view should wholly cease to count on the outbreak of war is hardly conceivable unless pure hatred made all wars a struggle for life and death. [607]

Even a people engaged in such a struggle, Clausewitz implies, will normally have some end in sight – survival, or even victory, however remote – and some kind of organised leadership to sustain the objective of the war. Though patriots in arms may think only of fighting, their leaders will give some thought to appropriate means and eventual ends.

Clausewitz's realism

Clausewitz's view of the resort to war appears somewhat detached, a pragmatic calculation that has little time for some of the more subtle restraints on foreign policy such as international and domestic law, public opinion, and the popular appeal of peace. Though he recognises the risks and costs in war, he seems ready to face them. What lies between Clausewitz and many of his critics is ultimately the doctrine of realism: war is a common and necessary means of pursuing state policy, states must be ready to undertake war in pursuit of their interests and war, once begun, needs to be pursued in businesslike fashion. Clausewitz foreshadows the positivist doctrine of the nineteenth century that treats decisions on war and peace as the prerogative of a sovereign under no higher authority. If he has anything to offer just war thinking, it is not in the matter of justification but in the duty of prudence, the obligation on states to apply reason to their decisions.

For war is not a purely passive instrument like a surgeon's scalpel, but complex and uncertain with many inherent problems: the difficulty of assessing costs and benefits, the potential for unforeseeable consequences, the influence that the dynamics of hostilities have on the political purpose, the possibility that objectives will not be achieved despite heavy costs, and so on. Careful thought must therefore be given to all the implications of a resort to war:

> No one starts a war – or rather, no one in his senses ought to do so – without first being clear in his mind what he intends to achieve by that war and how he intends to conduct it. The former is its political purpose; the latter its operational objective. [579]

The greater the war in prospect, moreover, the greater the need for caution and 'the more imperative the need not to take the first step without considering the last'. [584]

War, says Clausewitz, *should* be a continuation of policy – that is, as a matter of prudence and national interest statesmen *should* regard war as a means to an end and should act rationally as far as they can. (On statesmanship see chapter 17.) The idea of war as an instrument of policy is thus an ideal to be sought by keeping war subordinate to political guidance and rational control. The doctrine is needed precisely because war is a dangerous and difficult instrument to wield. Whether those involved in war in fact treat war as an instrument of policy and whether they succeed in doing so always remain open questions. The fact that war is sometimes not approached in rational fashion or slips out of control in the course of hostilities is, in Clausewitz's view, to be regretted. But these real possibilities underscore the need for the doctrine rather than undermine it.

10
Pure War and Real War

'But move from the abstract to the real world, and the whole thing looks quite different'. [78]

Clausewitz's three perspectives on war as fighting, contest and policy focus on human behaviour that influences the course of events: how men fight, how generals conduct strategy and how statesmen pursue policy. But war is also shaped by the wider context: the nature of politics within and between states, forms of government, the structure of societies, the economy of nations, the level of civilisation, military institutions and the development of technology. This is Clausewitz's most comprehensive view of war – as a social activity.

To illustrate the influence of external factors on war, he adopted a method common in contemporary German thought, namely defining an activity in its 'ideal' or pure form, uncontaminated by non-essential elements. Once the pure concept is established, the effect of factors that influence and shape the activity in the real world can be gauged. Kant examined aspects of human behaviour – including reason – in this fashion. There are also clear parallels with Newton's mathematical model of planetary movement and Adam Smith's notion of a perfect market.[1] For Clausewitz the concept of 'pure war' promised to identify the many and varied factors shaping war in reality. This concept he called Absolute War [*absoluter Krieg*].

Absolute War

To see war in its purest form, it must be deprived of all incidental characteristics – soldiers and commanders, armies, campaigns, generals, statesmen, the political and social context. It must be stripped of its usual dynamics – friction, strategic interaction and political objectives. In such a war human weakness is absent, action proceeds without resistance, and plans are carried out successfully. All strategic calculations are completed beforehand and all necessary resources are available at the start of the war. The use of force is concentrated in a single action with no pause in activity, no waiting for a better time to act. [79]

Three characteristics in Clausewitz's formulation of Absolute War refer to its origins, its course and its outcome:

- 'a wholly isolated act, occurring suddenly and not produced by previous events in the political world';
- 'a single decisive act, or a set of simultaneous ones';
- 'the decision achieved [is] complete and perfect in itself, uninfluenced by any previous estimate of the political situation it would bring about'. [78]

Absolute War thus lacks political and social context, as if fought between abstract entities without ambitions, interests, histories or concerns over the future. No considerations of policy, no thought for budgets, allies, opinion at home or future risks modify or shape such a war. War is not an instrument of policy since there is no policy. It remains a thing in itself, a violent collision pure and simple.

The usual translation of *absoluter Krieg* is Absolute War, a term easily and often misunderstood as a recommendation that every war should be fought with utmost energy and ferocity. But Clausewitz developed the concept for the theorist, not the statesman or general. A better translation is 'pure war', a term that suggests war unadulterated by considerations extraneous to fighting and avoids the implications of 'total war'. On occasions Clausewitz uses a similar term, namely 'pure concept of war' [*reiner Begriff des Krieges*]. [90] He also employs *bloßer Begriff* translated as 'pure concept' [78] and 'pure definition' [580] of war.

A further source of confusion is *On War* itself since Clausewitz took some time to clarify the concept. His first reference is tentative – in Book VI, chapter 28 (written before the revised Book I, chapter 1) he writes of 'true war, or absolute war, if we may call it that'. [488–9] Observing the wars of Napoleon, Clausewitz found it hard to imagine anything more decisive and devastating. More than once he cannot resist describing war in his time as a realisation of the absolute. Thus war 'assumed its absolute state [*absolute Gestalt*] under Bonaparte'; and 'with our own eyes we have seen warfare achieve this state of absolute perfection. [580]

But this left him in a quandary. If Napoleon's wars achieved perfection, 'what are we to say about all the wars that have been fought since the days of Alexander – excepting certain Roman campaigns – down to Bonaparte?' [580] Are they to be dismissed as inferior? Might not future wars reach higher levels of violence? Clausewitz realised that the actual level of violence and energy does not provide the standard by which to define pure war. Not even wars fought with maximum effort and violence, he concludes, match the abstract concept of war which belongs to the realm of theory. He can now assert without qualification that 'absolute war has never in fact been achieved'. [582] In his era war only 'closely approached its true character, its absolute perfection'. [593] In Clausewitz's final thinking Absolute War is a 'logical fantasy' to which the human mind us unlikely to submit itself. [78] Pure war is pure theory.

What, then, is the value of the concept? The most obvious reason for it is simply the methodological imperative. To understand war it must be imagined in its purest form, without the restraints of reality:

in the field of abstract thought the inquiring mind can never rest until it reaches the extreme: a clash of forces freely operating and obedient to no law but their own. [78]

It follows that '[t]o introduce the principle of moderation into the theory of war itself would always lead to logical absurdity'. [76] Absolute War is like Absolute Zero on the temperature scale. Major wars might approach the pure form but a gap between idea and reality is always present.

Another benefit of the concept is to assist in developing a theory of war (see chapter 14). The closer real wars approach the pure form, the more evident are the principles of war.

A war in which great decisions are involved is not only simpler but also less inconsistent, more in concert with its own nature, more objective, and more obedient to the law of inherent necessity. [516]

This is so because human weaknesses are more likely to be overcome, strategic interaction is less likely to stall, and political complexities and compromises carry less weight. Thus Napoleon's campaigns, while not strictly pure war, 'make it easier for us to grasp the concept of modern, absolute war in all its devastating power'. [584] In lesser wars, by contrast, the inner logic is concealed by all manner of twists and turns and by 'peculiar features that are often incomprehensible, and sometimes astonishingly odd'. [517]

Above all, the concept illuminates the factors that shape war in reality: 'move from the abstract to the real world, and the whole thing looks quite different'. [78] Clausewitz identifies four factors that modify Absolute War, each broadly corresponding to his four perspectives on war. First, those actually waging war are not abstract persons but human beings and organisations which

> are always something short of perfect and will never quite achieve the absolute best. Such shortcomings affect both sides alike and therefore constitute a moderating force. [78]

Real war is thus shackled by human limitations at every level. It is simply 'contrary to human nature to make an extreme effort'. [80]

Second, in real war time and human calculation enter the picture. Mobilising forces takes time and preparations for war are never complete. Strategic interaction itself is never simultaneous or a single decisive act since 'war consists of several successive acts [and] each of them, seen in context, will provide a gauge for those that follow'; indeed, 'the very nature of those resources and of their employment means that they cannot all be deployed at the same moment'. [79] Decisions are delayed and actions always less than optimal. War, in short, is an uphill struggle in which there is usually not enough 'energy' to 'overcome the vast inertia of the mass'. This explains why actual 'war turns into something quite different from what it should be according to theory – turns into something incoherent and incomplete'. [580]

Nor, thirdly, is war the last word in policy:

> even the ultimate outcome of a war is not always to be regarded as final. The defeated state often considers the outcome merely as a transitory evil, for which a remedy may still be found in political conditions at some later date. [80]

As a consequence tension often slackens and belligerents reduce their efforts. This leads Clausewitz to what he sees as the most important modifier of Absolute War – the political object.

> The political object – the original motive for the war – will thus determine both the military objective to be reached and the amount of effort it requires. [81]

Of all the 'counterweights that weaken the elemental force of war' and cause it to fall short of the absolute, the political is the most important. [388] It is also the one that can occasionally push states close to the absolute. Only the huge ambitions of Napoleon, underpinned by radical political and social change, allowed him to conduct war close to its limit.

Real war

Clausewitz also wanted to capture the nature of actual war as a social and political phenomenon. For him war in its broadest conception 'is part of man's social existence'. [149] Like all human activity it contains elements that are irrational and cannot be controlled, elements that are subject to human reason, and elements that are simply unknowable. These three 'dominant tendencies' make war into 'a remarkable trinity' [*wunderliche Dreifaltigkeit*] that consists of:

- passion – hatred and enmity, which give rise to primordial violence and can be seen as 'a blind natural force'[2];
- reason – war's 'element of subordination, as an instrument of policy, which makes it subject to reason alone'; and
- chance – 'the play of chance and probability within which the creative spirit is free to roam'. [89]

In varying combination these elements exist in all wars: the passion on which war ultimately depends for its energy, the reason that states apply – well or badly – to the pursuit of objectives in war, and the wayward impact of chance or fortune. They are precisely the elements lacking in Absolute War.

These three variable elements give war a chameleon-like character, but the variations go deeper than mere surface change: 'War is more than a true chameleon that slightly adapts its characteristics to the given case'. Passion, reason and chance are 'like three different codes of law, deep-rooted in their subject and variable in their relationship with one another'. To understand war a theory is needed that 'maintains a balance between these three tendencies, like an object suspended between three magnets'. It is not possible to ignore any one of the trinity or to establish a fixed relationship between them. Any such theory would 'conflict with reality to such an extent that for this reason alone it would be totally useless'. [89]

The elements of reason, passion and chance can be found in all social activities of significance – from affairs of the heart to the creation of wealth and the conduct of politics. This trinity was not original to Clausewitz, dating back at least to Ancient Greece and finding fashion among contemporaries, including his friend, the Prussian politician and diplomat Wilhelm von Humboldt (1767–1835).[3] But Clausewitz applied this perception most thoroughly to war, and though *On War* nowhere discusses passion, reason and chance at length, these elemental forces permeate his entire work.

(a)   Passion

Clausewitz saw a fundamental connection between war and passion:

> If war is an act of force, the emotions cannot fail to be involved. War may not spring from them, but they will still affect it to some degree, and the extent to which they do so will depend not on the level of civilization but on how important the conflicting interests are and on how long their conflict lasts. [76]

In major wars passionate feelings are likely to be the wellspring of enmity between states, influencing relations before and after the war and underpinning hostilities from start to finish. In some cases peacetime hostility is so great that a minor dispute can precipitate a major war:

> Between two peoples and two states there can be such tensions, such a mass of inflammable material, that the slightest quarrel can produce a wholly disproportionate effect – a real explosion. [81]

Antagonism can also be easily aroused and stimulated in the course of a conflict.

> Even where there is no national hatred and no animosity to start with, the fighting itself will stir up hostile feelings: violence committed on superior orders will stir up the desire for revenge and retaliation against the perpetrator .... [138]

Passion, in short, is unpredictable. Policy must therefore understand that the emotional reactions of others are highly variable: 'The same political object can elicit *differing* reactions from different peoples, and even from the same people at different times'. [81] Emotions, once aroused, make war difficult to control as an instrument of policy.

Nor is it a question of civilization. While savage people, Clausewitz believes, 'are ruled by passion, civilised peoples by the mind',

> [e]ven the most civilised of peoples can be fired with a passionate hatred for each other. ... Consequently, it would be an obvious fallacy to imagine war between civilized peoples as resulting merely from a rational act on the part of their governments and to conceive of war as gradually ridding itself of passion. [76]

Wars in his time, Clausewitz observes, 'are seldom fought without hatred between nations'. [138] Passion is a dynamic, ever-present factor, feeding into war and feeding off it.

(b) Reason

While passion is essential in war, hatred alone does not suffice. War requires a hostile intention directed against another party that channels the emotions involved.

> Two different motives make men fight one another: *hostile feelings* and *hostile intentions*. Our definition is based on the latter, since it is the universal element. Even the most savage, almost instinctive, passion of hatred cannot be conceived as existing without hostile intent. [76]

In other wars hostile intentions may predominate though feelings are never totally extinguished. In either case it is the element of intention – the desire to achieve a result – that provides a foothold for reason, albeit sometimes a precarious one.

For Clausewitz reason is, firstly, a condition in people whereby they act in accord with healthy common sense [*gesunder Menschenverstand*]. This is practical reasoning which is found in leaders who display judgement and understanding, and is a quality Clausewitz finds ennobling and often commends. Discussing military talent, for example, he describes 'the urge *to act rationally at all times*' as part of 'the sense of human dignity, the noblest pride and deepest need of all'. [106]

Clausewitz, secondly, refers to reason in the abstract or intelligence [*Intelligenz*]. In this sense reason is what links ends and means. Like Max Weber subsequently, Clausewitz saw rationality in the selection of appropriate means to achieve specified ends and for this reason can be ranked 'among the founders of a sociology of action'.[4] Goal-oriented rationality means calculation of how best to achieve given objectives with the means available, while taking into account the effect of one's own actions and anticipating those of an opponent. Strategy and foreign policy cannot exist without some element of reason in this sense.

Civilised states, Clausewitz thought, even though they could be driven by great passions, are better able to bring reason of both kinds to bear on war. Common sense creates order in a potentially chaotic activity, and helps dignify an essentially brutal form of behaviour. Reason as intelligence imposes a purpose on an otherwise meaningless activity. In limited wars reason tends to play a larger role since policy-makers and generals can retain greater control over the course of events:

> The less involved the population and the less serious the strains within states and between them, the more political requirements ... will dominate and tend to be decisive. [81]

In major conflicts reason must deal with and on occasion retreat before more intense passions. In both types of war goal-oriented rationality seeks to subordinate violence to human objectives.

This contrasts with the theoretical case of Absolute War where there is no policy to tame and direct the violence of war towards a purpose:

> Were it a complete, untrammeled, absolute manifestation of violence (as the pure concept would require), war would of its own independent will usurp the place of policy the moment policy had brought it into being; it would then drive policy out of office and rule by the laws of its own nature. [87]

True to the Enlightenment, Clausewitz believes that humans can exercise some control over events, that reason can and should be applied to ensure war remains simply a means to an end – despite many pressures to the contrary and the heroic efforts sometimes required. Yet reason alone does not provide the motivating force of war and can never fully control it.

(c)   Chance

While Clausewitz does not elaborate on passion and reason in war, he frequently comments on chance and probability, emphasising that the accidental and the unknowable give war a special character:

> Only one more element is needed to make war a gamble – chance: the very last thing that war lacks. No other human activity is so

continuously or universally bound up with chance. And through the element of chance, guesswork and luck come to play a great part in war. [85]

War is the realm of chance: No other human activity gives it greater scope: no other has such incessant and varied dealings with this intruder. Chance makes everything more uncertain and interferes with the whole course of events. [101]

Why do chance and uncertainty feature so strongly in war? Clausewitz points to both objective and subjective factors. As a complex and dynamic set of interactions, war is simply unpredictable. There cannot be sufficient information and reliable enough theories to foresee its course. Moreover, the unknown and the unknowable – which decision-makers can only guess or estimate – are often critical in shaping a war, even its outcome.

Chance is also important in subjective terms. Soldiers and generals know that they take decisions of great consequence on inadequate information in rapidly changing and unpredictable situations. These decisions require not only careful analysis but moral qualities. While reason and calculation help tackle the uncertainties of war, courage is needed to deal with the attendant fears:

The element in which war exists is danger. The highest of all moral qualities in time of danger is certainly *courage*. Now courage is perfectly compatible with prudent calculation but the two differ nonetheless, and pertain to psychological forces. Daring, on the other hand, boldness, rashness, trusting in luck are only variants of courage, and all these traits of character seek their proper element – chance. [85–6]

Clausewitz therefore pays considerable attention to the qualities of mind and temperament necessary in war. (See chapter 13.)

Chance presents some problems to Clausewitz. He cannot grant it too great a place for that will undermine the importance of both material factors such as the size of armies and of psychological factors such as the morale of an army or the genius of commanders. To ascribe victory or defeat in battle purely to chance, for example, means that 'a commander's personal merits, and thus also his responsibility, become irrelevant'. [167] In reality, chance is reduced by the skilful and challenged by the daring. If we find that success or failure are repeated by the same man, we must conclude that 'luck in war is of higher quality than luck in gambling'. [167]

Chance is neither malevolent nor benign. It may be confronted, but it will never be eliminated from war:

> From the very start there is an interplay of possibilities, probabilities, good luck and bad that weaves its way throughout the length and breadth of the tapestry. In the whole range of human activities, war most closely resembles a game of cards. [86]

While a card game has no element of danger, the analogy emphasises the importance of the unknowable. Without uncertainty in the minds of those engaged in it war would still require reason and passion but the outcome would be determined and known in advance. Like Machiavelli's *fortuna* chance for Clausewitz pervades every facet of war. Whatever certainties reason or passion might promise, chance ensures that nothing can be taken as given.

The trinity

The idea of a trinity of reason, passion and chance appears explicitly only in chapter 1 of Book I but its elements are found throughout *On War*. Reason is central to the concept of war as an instrument of policy, necessary to distinguish means and ends. Passion gives war its original motivation and ultimate objective. Chance is all-pervasive at all levels – fighting, contest and policy. Clausewitz always preferred to give such abstract speculation more concrete form. He thus linked each element of the trinity with the three institutions he identified in European society: people, army and government or the three 'estates' of commoners, warriors and rulers. The links, however, are not direct. As Clausewitz puts it, passion 'mainly concerns' the people, reason the government, and chance the commander and his army. [89]

The blind, natural force of passion is thus associated primarily – but not solely – with the people, with popular feelings and national animosities that create hostility between peoples and move them to fight: 'the passions that are to be kindled in war must already be inherent in the people'. [89] Reason pertains primarily to government which sets the aims of war and determines the necessary means. Clausewitz does not say that reason is found only in the political leadership, nor that political leaders will always be rational. He explicitly criticised monarchs who put personal honour before the needs of the state, and implicitly criticised Napoleon for allowing personal ambition to lead him into desperate folly. Rather, Clausewitz is pointing to what he sees as a necessary relationship between government and reason if war is to serve as an instrument of policy: 'the political aims are the business of government alone'. [89]

Chance and probability are the natural province of the army and its commanders. Soldiers deal constantly with uncertainty and friction in war while commanders continually assess probabilities and attempt to exploit chance. In this environment the art of war requires a creative spirit as well as courage and endurance: 'the scope which the play of courage and talent will enjoy in the realm of probability and chance depends on the particular character of the commander and the army'. [89] Chance is not the exclusive preserve of the military man but he is the one most familiar with it.

As Clausewitz recognises in his tentative formulation, the links between the elements of the trinity and elements of the state are not exclusive. Governments can be irrational, armies can flee from uncertainty, the people can be indifferent. Simple correlations are rarely Clausewitz's mode of thinking. A more satisfactory pattern of relationships can be proposed by introducing three further concepts which correspond to Clausewitz's three perspectives on war: fighting, strategy and policy. It is now possible to suggest a set of relationships between the elements of war, its activities and the institutions of the state in a trinity of trinities. (See Figure 10.1)

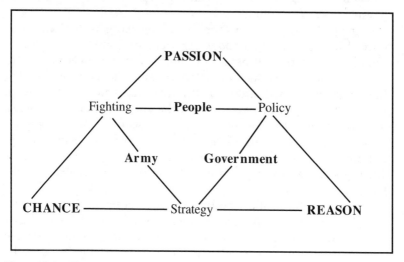

Figure 10.1   The Trinity of Trinities

In this schematic representation the three central activities of war – fighting, strategy and policy – can be depicted as the interaction of two of the three fundamental elements of war – passion, reason and chance. In turn each of these central activities has a primary link with two of the three institutions of the state.

Fighting is the interplay between passion and chance. While wars can be fought with little emotion, some hostile feeling towards an opponent is necessary. At the same time chance pervades the violence of war and influences the course hostilities take. In institutional terms the people engage in fighting while the army seeks to conduct it in an organised and skilful fashion. Both people and army are moved by passion – to a greater or lesser extent, according to circumstances – and both must reckon with chance. In itself, fighting is distant from reason but governments through strategy and policy seek to control and impose a purpose on the violence of war.

Policy represents a combination of reason and passion – like Friedrich Meinecke's concept of *Staatsräson* or *raison d'état* that exists in the 'obscure twilight zone between impulse and reason'.[5] Passion motivates the pursuit of objectives but must ally with reason to achieve those objectives. In institutional terms, policy derives from the interaction between government and people. Even autocracies must take popular feelings into account, democracies more so. In principle, policy is remote from chance since it seeks only logical relationships and aims to bring war under its control; in practice, the uncertainties of war constantly intrude.

Strategy can be seen as reason coming to terms with chance and uncertainty, seeking to impose a pattern on fighting in order to achieve its objectives. It pertains to both army and government. For the former strategy is the art of effective leadership and command in the campaign; for the latter it is the art of the statesman or foreign policy. The people, by contrast, lack the knowledge and experience necessary to engage directly in either strategy or policy-making. In principle, strategy is furthest removed from passion, being the application of reason to secure given ends. In reality, strategy cannot safely ignore the passions of the people – or their indifference – for too long.

From an institutional perspective, army, government and people are linked to their distinctive activities. For the army, deployment of violence and exercise of strategic skills in an uncertain environment are characteristic skills. For the government, strategy and policy must be combined in order to make war an instrument of policy, though achieving this is often elusive in practice. And for the people, war means engaging in violence – fighting and dying for the state. Depending on the political system, the mass of citizens may have greater or lesser influence over national leaders and their policies.

Clausewitz makes no explicit reference to such a schematic relationship but his whole analysis accords with this approach. The suggested relationships also meet the criticisms of those who rightly question the simple attribution of reason to the state and passion to the people.[6] The institutions of people, army and government play different but interlocking roles. Any war worthy of the name will manifest the complex relationships between Clausewitz's underlying trinity of passion, reason and chance and his principal institutions of government, army and people.

A human activity

Clausewitz draws an analogy with electrical discharges, suggesting that actual war is not the collision of 'two mutually destructive elements' as if in a vacuum but rather a case of

> tension between two elements, separate for the time being, which discharge energy in discontinuous minor shocks.
> But what exactly is this nonconducting medium, this barrier that prevents a full discharge? ... The barrier in question is the vast array of factors, forces and conditions in national affairs that are affected by war. [579]

Factors inherent in war and those pertaining to its political and social context ensure real war never achieves its pure form. Some wars come closer than others and provide a glimpse of the ideal but can never realise it.

The ghost of Absolute War, once raised, proved difficult to exorcise. Many readers have seen it as an exhortation to wage war at maximum intensity, sometimes praising this view, sometimes condemning it. Clausewitz's ideas began with a certain reverence for all-out war and at times he suggested Napoleon had achieved perfection. But in his final thinking the idea of war in its pure form is a theoretical device adopted to better understand the nature of war in reality. Intended for the theorist not the practitioner, the concept of pure war was designed to show that war is an activity that can only be understood in its wider context.

Like other significant human activities war is characterised by passion, reason and chance. These are the primary colours of war, capable of combining in infinitely variable ways. And all are essential. War with reason alone would be an intellectual game – 'a kind of war by algebra' [76]; with passion alone simply a fight among unthinking creatures; and with chance alone an accident of nature. Though war is a chameleon that can appear rationalist one moment, romantic the next and stochastic at another, no element can be omitted. Some contemporary theorists looked to reason in the hope it would eliminate war altogether; some gave primacy to passion and the romantic and heroic virtues of war; some sought to eliminate chance by reducing war to mathematical calculation. But Clausewitz embraced and even welcomed all three elements. Real war must be understood 'not on the basis of its pure definition, but by leaving room for every sort of extraneous matter'. Actual wars 'must allow for natural inertia, for all the friction of its parts, for all the inconsistency, imprecision, and timidity of man'. [580]

If there is one element, nevertheless, to which Clausewitz accords a certain priority, it is reason. A war of pure passion lacks all purpose and contains no element of chance; war is valued for its own sake. A war of pure chance denies all scope for the calculation of means and ends, for statesmanship or military virtues, turning it into a plaything of the gods. Only reason offers a way of understanding war and of enhancing the capacity of human beings to control their own destiny when passions motivate men to fight, and the complexities of war cause chance to intrude. In Clausewitz's concept of war reason is not dominant but it is the one element that offers mankind the prospect of controlling war in some measure and of making some sense out of its violence.

Part V
Strategy

11
The Nature of Strategy

'[T]he main lines of every major strategic plan are largely political in nature, and their political character increases the more the plan applies to the entire campaign and to the whole state'.[1]

On War devotes much attention to the campaign and the problems facing the commander (broadly corresponding to what is now called operational strategy). The issues are complex because strategy not only deals with factors on its own level but also constantly interacts with the fighting of soldiers and the policies of national leaders. This chapter looks first at the general characteristics of strategy and then at a number of key ideas that underpin it:

- the significance of battle
- the relationship between the three levels of activity in war – tactics, strategy and the war plan
- centres of gravity which seek to link military victory with political success, and
- characteristics of strategy in wars seeking outright defeat of an opponent and wars seeking marginal gains.

The following chapter addresses the dynamics of the campaign itself.

Characteristics of strategy

Strategy, of course, is shaped by the higher level of policy, by the purpose of the war. The main lines of every strategic plan reflect decisions by national leaders about the political aim of the war, the level of risk to be taken, the losses to be borne, the resources to be invested and so on. But strategy itself is concerned first and foremost with fighting: 'strategy is the use of force, the heart of which, in turn, is the engagement'. [227] Nothing can be achieved without success in the field: 'all strategic planning rests on tactical success alone ... this is in all cases the actual fundamental basis for the decision'. [386] Though battle may sometimes not take place, strategy always focuses on the engagement: 'even where the decision has been bloodless, it was determined in the last analysis by engagements that did not take place but had merely been offered'. [386]

Strategy, however, cannot rely on threats alone. Clausewitz rejects the eighteenth century idea of bloodless contests decided by manoeuvre and position. On this view, battle was merely the result of miscalculation. To Clausewitz this was 'a morbid manifestation' [259] and a delusion that leads many generals to failure. [98] Commanders who believe – whether out of misconception or kindness – that war can be conducted without loss of life are dismissed: 'We are not interested in generals who win victories without bloodshed'. [260] Military success without fighting is the exception, not – as writers like Sun Tzu have it – an ideal to be sought.[2]

While fighting is the currency of strategy, its defining characteristic is that decisions are taken in a process of interaction with an opponent. A campaign is rarely a single blow but a series of engagements such that each stage bears upon subsequent ones.[3] The most effective strategy depends on a general's assessment of his opponent's present and future actions. Strategy therefore entails the 'skillful ordering of priority of engagements ... indeed, that is what strategy is all about'. [228] In this process, chance and uncertainty characterise the campaign, more so than at lower or higher levels of war. In tactics chance can be managed through drill and routine. Thus battles are rarely decided by some unexpected factor that changes the whole outcome – these 'usually exist only in the stories told by people who want to explain away their defeats'. [249] At the national level, too, uncertainty may be less. The relative resources and capabilities of two states may be such that the outcome of a war can hardly be a matter of chance in the longer term.[4]

In the campaign the element of uncertainty is always high, the more so if forces are approximately equal. This means that in strategy

> success is not due simply to general causes. Particular factors can often be decisive – details only known to those who were on the spot ... issues can be decided by chances and incidents so minute as to figure in histories simply as anecdotes. [595]

Clausewitz gives several examples where a different strategic decision or a different outcome to a battle might have changed the outcome of a campaign. [595] Strategy is always a gamble and the greatest gambler of all was Napoleon. At Waterloo he

> staked his last remaining strength on an effort to retrieve a battle that was beyond retrieving; he spent every last penny, and then fled like a beggar from the battlefield and the Empire. [252]

Clausewitz suggests this last gamble was 'desperate folly'. [252] The Duke of Wellington was less confident: 'A damned nice thing – the nearest-run thing you ever saw in your life'.[5]

The battle in strategy

For the greater part of *On War* – Books II to V – Clausewitz worked on the assumption that the purpose of every campaign is to bring about a clear and decisive result and that this is best achieved by defeating enemy forces in battle. Thus in Book IV, chapter 11 entitled 'The Use of the Battle', he puts forward a set of 'unequivocal statements':

1. Destruction of the enemy forces is the overriding principle of war ...
2. Such destruction of forces can *usually* be accomplished only by fighting.
3. Only major engagements involving all forces lead to major success.
4. The greatest successes are obtained where all engagements coalesce into one great battle. [258]

In short, for both attacker and defender, '[b]attle is the bloodiest solution'. [259] This is the original Clausewitz, advocating battle and the 'dominance of the destructive principle' as the only true means of decision. [228]

A decisive battle [*Hauptschlacht*], moreover, is 'not only the natural but also the best means' of securing a major goal in war. 'As a rule, shrinking from a major decision by evading such a battle carries its own punishment'. [259] Contemporary war, in fact, shows 'there is nothing to prevent a commander bent on a decisive battle from seeking out his enemy and attacking him'. The defender therefore must fight or abandon his position. [246, 545–6] A great battle can 'act – more or less according to circumstances, but always to some extent – as the provisional center of gravity of the entire campaign'. [260] Only with the campaigns of his era, Clausewitz acknowledged, had it become 'fairly common' for the campaign to be decided by a single battle; and it had always been exceptional for a battle to settle the result of the entire war. [260]

For Clausewitz in this vein 'destruction of the enemy's forces is part of the final purpose' and 'must always be the *dominant consideration*'. [228] Battle takes its importance both from the material losses sustained and from its differential psychological impact. 'Every engagement is a bloody and destructive test of physical and moral strength. Whoever has the greater sum left at the end is the victor'. [231] The dispiriting effect of defeat is particularly important, Clausewitz argues, having 'a greater psychological effect on the loser than on the winner'. [253] One gains in vigour and energy, the other loses moral strength; and this, in turn, is liable to cause further material losses. Battles where material losses are comparable can thus produce seemingly disproportionate effects for the loser. The effect is 'rather a killing of the enemy's spirit than of his men'. [259]

Battle thus lies at the heart of strategy: 'the *violent resolution of the crisis*, the wish to annihilate the enemy's forces, is the first-born son of war'. [99] But Clausewitz came to recognise that in many campaigns neither side seeks a decisive result. In some circumstances, therefore, battle is to be avoided:

> If the political aims are small, the motives slight and tensions low, a prudent general may look for any way to avoid major crises and decisive action, exploit any weaknesses in the opponent's military and political strategy, and finally reach a peace settlement. [99]

Such a general is not to be criticised if he has judged the situation aright. Yet he 'must never forget that he is moving on [slippery] paths where the god of war may catch him unawares' – for an opponent may always confront him with sudden and overwhelming force. [99]

On War never fully escapes the spirit of all-out war that values the great, decisive battle. Yet is it fair to conclude that in the end Clausewitz reduced the centrality of battle in his understanding of war.[6] Most popular and many academic accounts of war make a feature of battles and engagements. While the engagement is undoubtedly the foundation of war, for Clausewitz it is primarily a means employed by the commander to promote wider aims. Battles, in fact, are determined less by tactics and the feats of units and individuals than by factors external to it – the number and deployment of troops, their training, discipline and morale, the quality of the general and the strategy he pursues.[7] These factors, which relate to the commander and the political leadership, concern Clausewitz more than the fighting itself.

Three levels of war: tactics, strategy and war plans

If war is to serve a political purpose and remain subject to rational calculation, its diverse and complex activities must be held together conceptually. Without such a framework war disintegrates into disconnected armed clashes. Clausewitz offers a simple but vital distinction between three levels of war (or, more accurately, levels of command) – tactics, strategy and the war plan:

> tactics teaches *the use of armed forces in the engagement*; strategy, *the use of engagements for the object of the war.* [128, also 177]
>
> War plans cover every aspect of a war, and weave them all into a single operation that must have a single, ultimate objective in which all particular aims are reconciled. [579][8]

The three levels are linked by a hierarchy of purpose, an approach Clausewitz adopted as early as 1804.[9] Some theorists, by contrast, saw tactics embracing all military activity including the raising and training of armies.[10] Bülow defined tactics as action within the range of vision of the enemy, strategy as action out of sight of the enemy. To Clausewitz such distinctions were quite 'artificial'. [128] Mere proximity could not turn minor administrative matters into strategy.

Clausewitz's approach was not entirely original but introduced an intellectual coherence lacking in most other writers. In essence, three levels of war were identified in terms of time and space. Episodes of fighting or the engagement occupy the shortest time – usually a few days at most – and are focused on a limited area. The campaign occupies a longer period – perhaps months or years – and extends to a wider theatre of operations. The war refers to the entire period of conflict and may cover the whole country or several countries. Tactics, strategy and the war plan thus progressively extend in time and broaden in scope. Clausewitz also discusses two further dimensions: the type of unit at each level – a force, an army and the nation; and the particular objective each seeks – victory in battle, securing the goals of the campaign, and realising the nation's policy objectives. Again, each dimension takes on a successively broader scope. Though Clausewitz did not set out an explicit schema, the full relationship en tactics, strategy and the war plan can be seen in the following

Activity	Unit	Space	Time	Aim
tactics	force	position	engagement	victory
strategy	army	theatre of operations	campaign	campaign goals
war plan	nation	country	war	policy

Tactics relate directly to the engagement – one military force fighting another in a given position. This may or may not take the form of a battle which is simply fighting on a larger scale, concentrated in time and position, and regarded by both sides as potentially decisive. Tactics, uniquely, aim at victory which consists of three elements:

1. The enemy's greater loss of material strength
2. His loss of morale
3. His open admission of the above by giving up his intentions. [234]

Engagements are usually bounded geographically by 'the range of *personal command*' and limited in terms of time by the idea of a turning-point at which the outcome becomes clear. [128] Tactics, in short, are about fighting, the domain of the soldier.

Strategy operates in a theatre of war, 'a sector of the total war area which has protected boundaries and so a certain degree of independence' – due, for example, to fortifications, natural barriers or distance. In a theatre there is normally – and desirably – a single commander exercising authority over an 'army' though two or more allied armies constitute a common exception. [280–1] The commander shapes the campaign and 'decides the time when, the place where, and the forces with which the engagement is to be fought'. [194] He must assess the significance of tactical victories for the campaign since these may have 'a noticeable influence on its planning and conduct' [142] and be alert to new tactics since 'a change in the nature of tactics will automatically react on strategy'. [226] Strategy thus seeks to exploit tactical victories for the purpose of the campaign.

The objective is not victory since 'in strategy there is no such thing as victory'. [363] Whereas in the engagement triumph or failure can readily be established, 'strategic success cannot be defined and delineated with the same precision'. [208] Strategy seeks intermediate objectives, often of different types, since the purpose of the war 'is usually remote, and only rarely lies very near at hand'. [194] Indeed, at the highest levels 'there is little or no difference between strategy, policy and statesmanship'. [178] The commander as strategist seeks to provide coherence to episodes of fighting and serve as the link between fighting and the war plan.

The war plan relates to the purpose of the war, the armed forces as a whole and the entire country. It closely shapes any campaigns designed to support it.

> A war plan is, after all, the source of all the lesser plans of attack and defense and determines their main lines ... in war, more than anywhere else, it is the whole that governs the parts, stamps them with its character, and alters them radically. [484]

This is the realm of national leadership where political factors come into full play in both major and minor wars.

The three levels, Clausewitz recognises, are not always easily distinguished. Strategy and the war plan may shade into one another. Thus operations in a particular theatre of war may be designed to have 'direct political repercussions' such as disrupting an enemy alliance or gaining new allies. [92] Strategy and tactics may coincide if a single 'great battle' comes to be regarded as a decisive clash in a theatre of war. [260] Clausewitz's distinctions also reflect limitations on warfare now much reduced by technological advances: physical barriers, problems of fighting at night or in winter, the general's span of command, speed of communications. Yet his broad, flexible distinctions have so far proved durable, based as they are on specific activities – fighting, strategy and policy – and on a clear hierarchy of purpose.

Centres of gravity

Strategy requires some link between military activity and the political objective. One popular contemporary notion was the 'key to the country', that geographic part of a nation which is difficult for the offence to seize and easy for the defence to support but which, once captured or occupied, inevitably leads to success.[11] Clausewitz dismisses this piece of conventional wisdom as 'one of those pseudoscientific terms with which critics hope to show their erudition', and a 'prize exhibit' in innumerable campaign histories which has never been clearly defined or proven its worth. [456] What he offers instead is nothing new but a concept that underlies 'the actions of every general in history'. [486]

To link the campaign to the political aim of a war, Clausewitz prefers a term borrowed from mechanics – the 'centre of gravity' [*Schwerpunkt*] – referring to the imagined point where all the forces of gravity bear on an object.[12] In war a centre of gravity is not in itself a point of weakness or strength but is the focus 'of all power and movement, on which everything depends'. [595–6] It concerns not the enemy's strength – nor the source of his strength – but his unity and cohesion. [485–6][13] The centre of gravity is important because it offers an opportunity to throw an enemy off balance (to maintain the mechanical analogy) and end his resistance. It is therefore 'the most effective target for a blow' [485] and 'the point against which all our energies should be directed'. [596]

Clausewitz's interest is primarily in wars designed to achieve a decisive result. If the aim is simply to gain an advantage, centres of gravity cease to be dominant and strategy has many more options. Operations may be conducted to disrupt an opposing alliance, win new allies or favourably alter the political scene. It may suffice, for example, to seize 'a lightly held or undefended province' which is of no intrinsic military value but causes anxiety to an opponent. [92] Where a decision is sought, however, determining the centre of gravity is 'a major act of strategic judgment' that influences the whole course of the war. [486] The particular centre in a given case varies according to the circumstances and the characteristics of each belligerent, and it may be that more than one must be identified. 'The first task, then, in planning for a war is to identify the enemy's centers of gravity, and if possible trace them back to a single one'. [619]

Clausewitz discusses four possible centres of gravity: territory, the capital of a country, its armed forces and its alliances. These relate to the three principal elements within a state – people, government and army – and to its external sources of support. Territory is of obvious importance since its loss means that some or all of a country's population and resources fall under enemy control. In a major war, however, loss of territory may not be decisive. Temporary occupation by an enemy means that the territory 'is merely lent to him'. [488] Even occupation of large tracts of a country may not suffice to defeat an opponent. The Russian army, for example, fought on and eventually triumphed over the French despite the loss of much territory and the occupation of Moscow. [595]

An enemy capital may be the centre of gravity since it is 'not only the center of administration but also that of social, professional, and political activity'. [596] In some wars it represents a government's will to resist. 'If Paris had been taken in 1792', Clausewitz suggests, 'the war against the Revolution would almost certainly for the time being have been brought to an end'. It was not even necessary to defeat the French armies first since they were not particularly strong. [595] As a general rule, too, the capital is the centre of gravity in countries divided by internal strife. [596] In some circumstances, however, capture of a nation's monarch rather than the capital may be decisive, this being one of the reasons why the Prussian king left the army after the defeats at Jena and Auerstädt.[14]

In some wars a nation's principal ally can be the best centre of gravity to attack. [596] The task then is to identify the centre of gravity of the ally and to strike accordingly. Fighting against an alliance as such raises somewhat different problems. Its cohesion in the field, based on precarious political agreement, 'will usually be very loose, and often completely fictitious'. [486] Here it is preferable to direct efforts against the ally whose defeat will cause the collapse of the alliance; this makes it 'all the easier to concentrate our principal enterprise into one great blow'. [596]

The preeminent centre of gravity, however, is the opponent's army:

> no matter what the central feature of the enemy's power may be –
> the point on which your efforts must converge – the defeat and
> destruction of his fighting force remains the best way to begin, and
> in every case will be a very significant feature of the campaign. [596]

To destroy the enemy army is to destroy a symbol of the country and expose its people and government to foreign control. This was the case with Alexander, Gustavus Adolphus, Charles XII and Frederick the Great who would have 'gone down in history as failures' if their army had been eliminated. [596] Napoleon, likewise, fell when his armies were defeated in 1814 and again in 1815. The army is in fact ultimately more important than territory.

> If the forces are destroyed – in other words overcome and incapable of
> further resistance – the country is automatically lost. On the other
> hand, loss of the country does not automatically entail destruction of
> the forces; they can evacuate the country of their own accord, in order
> to reconquer it the more easily later on. [484–5]

In wars fought to a decision there is a 'natural' but by no means inevitable progression from defeat of an enemy's armed forces to

occupation of its territory and possibly its capital, and then to diminu-
tion or destruction of its will to resist. [90–1] The symbolic element of
defeat on the battlefield together with the recognition that further
destruction may be inflicted and that fresh forces cannot be raised,
mean that the enemy will most likely cease to resist and can be
brought to 'the peace table'. [91]

Clausewitz's discussion of France's attempt to defeat Russia in 1812
is illustrative. Two possible routes to success were open to Napoleon.
The first was to defeat Russian forces in the field seeking to induce the
Tsar to negotiate a peace. But Russia's instinct was to avoid direct confrontation with Napoleon's army, pulling back its forces over 500 miles
while wearing down the French. 'The highest wisdom could never have
devised a better strategy than the one the Russians followed uninten-
tionally'. [615] Nor was occupation of Russian territory a practical alternative since the country was too vast to control and left the invader
unable to protect his rear.[15] Russia was not a country that could be
'formally conquered – that is to say occupied' even with the half
million men Bonaparte had mobilised. [627]

This left a second principal option, namely capture of Moscow –
Russia's principal city, albeit not the political capital – in the hope that
this would 'shake the government's nerve and the people's loyalty and
steadfastness'. Though not certain to succeed, this was Napoleon's
'only rational war aim'. [627] In the event Moscow was occupied – by
90,000 men – and Napoleon waited in vain for the Tsar to make peace.
The burning of the city did nothing to convince the Russians to capitulate. Nor did Napoleon's last hope eventuate, namely a revolt by the
Tsar's subjects. 'Only internal weakness', Clausewitz observes, 'only the
workings of disunity can bring a country of that kind to ruin'. [627]
Napoleon failed because the government 'kept its nerve and the people
remained loyal and steadfast'. [628] Destruction of the Russian army
was really the only sure way to succeed.

Clausewitz, in short, sees the armed forces as the principal centre of
gravity: 'The real key to the enemy's country is usually his army'. [458]
This is the reason why in some wars a single battle can be decisive –
when it represents a direct collision between two centres of gravity.
[489] Yet each war produces different centres of gravity and a strong
nation will often have more than one. In contemplating an attack on
France, for example, Clausewitz says its centre of gravity 'lies in the
armed forces and in Paris'. [633] Nor does defeating an enemy's armed
forces guarantee success. A nation may fight on through popular resistance, hoping to restore its army or receive support from allies.

Clausewitz's centre of gravity is focused on ends not means so that those responsible for strategy 'must keep the dominant characteristics of both belligerents in mind'. [595] In modern terminology it is 'effects-based' rather than 'capability-based.[16]

Strategy in major war

Some interpreters, notably the German historian, Hans Delbrück, have argued that Clausewitz distinguished two main types of strategy: that of overthrow or annihilation [*Niederwerfungsstrategie*] which focuses on the single 'pole' of destroying enemy forces in battle, and that of attrition [*Ermattungsstrategie*] which relies on the twin 'poles' of battle and manoeuvre.[17] All generals, Delbrück argued, tend to follow one strategy at the expense of the other, the choice depending on the nature of the armies involved and the political situation. Battle was the only thing Napoleon knew, while Frederick the Great, an exponent of attrition, mostly saw battle as the last resort. Strategy could also change in the course of a war, most likely from a strategy of overthrow to one of attrition as energies flag and resources dwindle. Presented in the 1870s, Delbrück's arguments caused much controversy as they contradicted the received wisdom of the General Staff that – in line with Clausewitz's supposed views – annihilation of enemy forces was the only correct strategy.[18]

In a war seeking a decisive outcome Clausewitz's main tenet was clear: only 'by constantly seeking out the center of his power, by daring all to win all, will one really defeat the enemy'. [596] An all-out campaign is more natural, being simpler and offering fewer risks than one taken slowly.

> no conquest can be carried out too quickly ... to spread it out over a *longer period* than the minimum needed to complete it *makes it not less difficult but more.* [598]

If one is strong enough to be certain of success, there is no point in proceeding by 'stages'. As Clausewitz puts it, '[a] short jump is certainly easier than a long one: but no one wanting to get across a wide ditch would begin by jumping half-way'. [598] It is wrong to assume that 'a slow, allegedly systematic occupation is safer and wiser than conquest by continuous advance'. [598] Yet even where decisive victory is sought a strategy of attrition can bring a state 'to the last extremity by degrees'. [626] The enemy is made to concede by 'using *the duration of the war to bring about a gradual exhaustion of his physical and moral resistance'.* [93]

Typically, in fact, Clausewitz sees no sharp dichotomy between these two forms of strategy since they are never distinct in practice. Annihilation resembles absolute war in which 'there is only one result that counts: *final victory*' but which is never achieved in reality. Actual wars therefore always contain some element of attrition by progression, consisting in the extreme case of

> separate successes each unrelated to the next, as in a match consisting of several games. The earlier games have no effect upon the latter. All that counts is the total score. [582]

In reality neither concept can be totally disregarded. For Clausewitz, moreover, it was the political effect that mattered. His strategy of attrition, in contrast to Delbrück, focused on the political intentions of the opponent. In this respect it may be better termed a war plan rather than a strategy in itself.[19] Similarly, Clausewitz's strategy of overthrow looked beyond destruction of the enemy's army to his political will.

Strategy in limited war

Where a decisive outcome is not the objective, matters look very different:

> When we attack the enemy, it is one thing if we mean our first operation to be followed by others until all resistance has been broken; it is quite another if our aim is only to obtain a single victory, in order to make the enemy insecure, to impress our greater strength upon him, and to give him doubts about his future. [92]

The 'destructive principle' and centres of gravity take second place. Simple control of territory can then be a legitimate aim:

> If one drops the idea of a decision, the centers of gravity are neutralized and ... possession of the country, the next most important component of the theatre of war, will become a direct objective. [488]

Pauses in military operations also become normal as neither side seeks out battle, risks are less readily taken, efforts diminished, and negotiations explored. Both sides may be so reluctant to press for a decision, indeed, that the distinction between offensive and defensive campaigns disappears and belligerents 'confront each other basically in a state of mutual observation'. [513]

The diversity of political objectives also means that the methods employed by strategy will vary immensely:

> We can now see that in war many roads lead to success, and that they do not all involve the enemy's outright defeat. They range from *the destruction of the enemy's forces, the conquest of his territory, to a temporary occupation or invasion, to projects with an immediate political purpose, and finally to passively awaiting the enemy's attacks*. [94]

As incentives to seek a decision diminish, military activity falls away:

> the art of war will shrivel into prudence, and its main concern will be to make sure the delicate balance is not suddenly upset in the enemy's favor and the half-hearted war does not become a real war after all. [604]

The structure of strategy

For Clausewitz the war plan underlies the whole nature of strategy which attempts to harness the violent business of war to the purposes of the state. War always entails fighting or the prospect of fighting and will, given the presence of passion and chance, resist subordination to policy. It must therefore be articulated in hierarchical fashion to permit whatever degree of control might be possible. The hierarchy of purpose also serves as a reminder that neither the dangers inherent in fighting nor the dynamics of the contest should distract attention from the ultimate objectives of war.

Within the political aims of war, the strategist has many critical judgements to make: the importance of battle; the centre(s) of gravity to serve as the focus of the campaign; whether military aims are best achieved by stages or by a single great effort. The strategist must also be aware of the diversity and variability of the political aims of a war and the possibility that a limited war may be transformed into an unlimited one – a danger that should be of constant concern to generals and national leaders. The strategist, finally, must take into account the dynamics of the campaign itself which, as the following chapter suggests, are far from simple.

12
The Conduct of the Campaign

'Strategic theory ... attempts to shed light on the components of war and their interrelationships, stressing those few principles or rules that can be demonstrated'. [177]

On War reflects campaign strategy in Clausewitz's time. Physical barriers such as fortresses, rivers and mountains were more influential than they later became. Lines of supply had assumed great importance in the eighteenth century and their relevance to Napoleonic warfare had to be assessed.[1] But there are enduring elements in the interaction of forces in a theatre of war which Clausewitz examined and which are still debated by strategists. This chapter first discusses the asymmetry of offence and defence and the factors making for success in each, then examines the principal dynamics of the campaign – the culminating point of the attack, surprise, and pauses in activity. It concludes by discussing Clausewitz's much-disputed claim that defence is the stronger form of war.

The asymmetry of offence and defence

All theorists distinguish between offence and defence, a distinction that reveals an important asymmetry. In tactics, it is about attacking a position or retaining it. In politics, it is about changing or preserving the status quo. In strategy, offensive and defensive operations share characteristics with the tactical and political levels but also reveal distinctive forms of interaction.

At all levels, the essential 'concept of defence' is 'the parrying of a blow' and its 'characteristic feature' is 'awaiting the blow'. [357] While defence seeks to preserve what it holds, the offence has an active or positive aim. [358] Defence and attack also differ in psychology: the 'true spirit' of defence is marked by prudence, the attack by courage and confidence. [545] But defence does not mean passivity. This would be 'completely contrary to the idea of war, since it would mean that only one side was waging it'.

> Even in a defensive position awaiting the assault, our bullets take the offensive. So the defensive form of war is not a simple shield, but a shield made up of well-directed blows. [357]

Similarly, 'a defensive campaign can be fought with offensive battles, and in a defensive battle, we can employ our divisions offensively'. [357]

Moreover, whereas the attack may be conceptually 'complete in itself', it is not possible to 'think of the defense without that necessary component of the concept, the counterattack'. [524] For Clausewitz defence incorporates the idea of retaliation and a shift to the offence. [380] He also notes the psychological importance of the switch: 'A sudden powerful transition to the offensive – the flashing sword of vengeance – is the greatest moment for the defence'. [370] But just as defence does not exist without offence, so in practice – if not in theory – attack inevitably entails defence. The realities of time and place mean that an offensive operation can never be conducted in a 'single steady movement', but has to defend its own forces and the ground it has gained. [524] Strategy thus entails constant interplay between offence and defence.

Factors favouring strategic defence

Clausewitz argued that certain factors in the campaign pertain primarily to defence. Properly exploited, they bolster the defence and trouble the attacker. Since the defence generally seeks to hold ground, the factors that assist it tend to be static and depend on the fact that the defence normally operates in its own territory. Five specific factors – terrain, fortresses, supply, the militia and morale – are of particular value to the defence and of limited, if any, benefit to the attacker.

For two principal reasons Clausewitz maintained that '[i]n strategy as well as in tactics, the defense enjoys the advantage of terrain'. [363] First, geographical features such as the location of roads, mountains and rivers often constrain the enemy's lines of attack. The direction of attack can normally be foreseen while defence remains 'virtually invisible' until the moment the attack is launched. [361] Second, features of the terrain such as rivers and mountains can provide protection and cover for the defence. If proper methods of defence are adopted, these advantages will 'always' accrue to the defender. [362]

The defence, however, can become complacent. Rivers and mountains, Clausewitz observes, are often assumed to be strong barriers but this makes them 'dangerous and alluring objects, which have often led to wrong decisions'. [433] Rivers need particular care, being 'like a tool made of a hard and brittle substance: they either stand the heaviest blow undented, or their defensive capacity falls to pieces'. [433] In fact successful defence of rivers is rare. [433]

Fortresses are of major value to the defence, providing secure depots, tactical points of support, staging posts for supplies and a refuge for weak or defeated units. Fortresses also protect large towns and camps in their vicinity, constituting a real barrier against an invader by delaying his operations and often compelling him to lay siege before advancing. [393–402] If the advance as a whole is halted to besiege a fortress, Clausewitz argues, the offence has 'as a rule' reached its culminating point. [625] Fortification alone, however, will not protect a region as it once did. [393] Only those fortresses that attract enemy forces and are able to hold out against them will weigh heavily 'in the scales of war'. [372] The defender must also avoid the trap of splitting his army into small garrisons, thereby losing the benefits of concentration. [393] In the attack only fortresses close to the frontier will play a role and then only a minor one. [372]

Lines of supply are shorter and more secure for the defender. The local population will likely be a major asset in this regard through the loyalty of citizens or the tradition of civil obedience to the government. [373] In short, at home 'every kind of friction is reduced' [365] and 'everything works more smoothly – assuming the public is not wholly disaffected'. [373] An attacking army, by contrast, inevitably suffers from extended supply lines, and is weakened by the detachment of garrisons to protect rear areas. [365] At the same time, lack of cooperation from a country's inhabitants generally means that nothing is done for invading troops except under 'force majeure' which they 'must apply at the expense of their own strength and exertions'. [373]

Compared with a regular army, the militia offers the defence 'a reservoir of strength that is much more extensive, much more flexible, and whose spirit and loyalty are much easier to arouse'. [372] As Prussia's militia demonstrated in 1813–15, such forces can contribute significantly to defence on home territory while being far less suited to attack on enemy territory.

The resilience of a people fighting in defence of their homeland constitutes a final significant factor for the defence. Close relations and innumerable daily contacts between troops and populace ensure a valuable flow of information about friend and enemy alike. [373] In some cases the people take up arms directly as they did in Spain – providing not simply 'an intensification of popular support but ... a genuine new source of power'. [373] At the same time an attacker may benefit from 'disaffected enemy subjects', a region opposed to the government [563] or 'the workings of disunity' [627] The defence loses much of its advantage if its political house is not in order.

Factors favouring strategic offence

Several factors can favour the offence. These tend to be more dynamic than those favouring the defence since the attack is usually in motion while the defence is relatively static. [367] Knowledge that it is advancing, for example, may raise an army's spirit though this will not survive serious resistance. [545] The more substantial factors that may favour an attacker – numbers, disposition of forces, concentric attack and continuity of effort – are examined below. But they do not accrue inevitably and exclusively to the attacker who must work for his success. The following discussion assumes that a decision is being sought in the campaign.

Clausewitz begins by emphasising the value of numbers. Though not essential to success numerical superiority is the most important single factor in strategy, and can be 'great enough to counterbalance all other contributing circumstances'. [194–5] 'The first rule, therefore, should be: put the largest possible army into the field. This may sound a platitude, but in reality it is not'. [195] In the eighteenth century, Clausewitz points out, size of armies was not considered of great significance and military histories often failed to mention numbers or did so in a casual way. [195–6] There were also 'strange ideas that haunted some authors: that there is a certain optimum size for an army, an ideal norm, and that any troops in excess of it are more trouble than they are worth'. [196] [2]

In Clausewitz's time, however, the size of the force to be put in the field had become a key political decision that had to be seen as part of strategy: 'This decision marks the start of military activity – it is indeed a vital part of strategy'. [196] Of course, the spirit of the army and good generalship can make up for lack of numbers, although 'in modern Europe even the most talented general will find it very difficult to defeat an opponent twice his strength'. [195] Obviously, it is absurd to seek 'to reduce the whole secret of the art of war to the formula of numerical superiority'. [135] But while they are not the final determinant, numbers count.

The disposition and deployment of those numbers – 'the skillful concentration of superior strength at the decisive point' – is a vital part of the art of the general. [197] There is rarely any excuse for failing to concentrate forces:

> the best strategy is always *to be very strong*; first, in general, and then at the decisive point. ... There is no simpler law of strategy than that of *keeping one's forces concentrated*. No force should ever be detached from the main body unless the need is definite and *urgent*. [204]

Commanders sometimes divide their forces out of confusion [546] or a sense that 'this was the way things ought to be done'. [204] Clausewitz rebukes the Austrian Field Marshal Schwarzenberg for spreading out his forces on reaching French soil in 1814: 'The attack should be like a well-hammered wedge, not a bubble that expands till it bursts'. [635, 620]

The principle of concentrating forces also governs employment of strategic reserves. Reserves are necessary, amongst other things, 'to counter unforeseen threats' and allow for a degree of uncertainty. [210] But they exist to be used and it is absurd to maintain them for their own sake – supposedly 'the peak of wise and cautious planning'. [211] While tactical reserves have a rather different function – to prolong and renew an action – a strategic reserve must be intended 'to contribute to the overall decision'. [210–11] While too many soldiers in the field may represent wasted effort, it remains true that 'all available force must be used simultaneously'. [207] The penalty for inadequate force is far greater than the cost of excess force.

After numbers and disposition of forces, a third element in strategic success is concentric attack i.e. the envelopment of enemy forces by flanking movements. Clausewitz emphasises operations designed to outflank an enemy using 'exterior' lines of attack, associating 'interior' lines primarily with defence. [542] The key advantage of concentric attack is that forces are directed 'toward a *common destination*' and become increasingly concentrated – unlike an attack on divergent lines. The benefits are most apparent at the tactical level, notably the intensified effect of cross fire and the ability to cut off an enemy's retreat. In general, too, the smaller the force under attack – down to a single soldier – the harder it is to resist attack from different directions. [368]

At the strategic level these advantages lessen or disappear. Cross-fire becomes irrelevant 'since one cannot fire from one end of a theater of operations to the other'. The large areas involved also lengthen and expose the attacker's lines of communication. [364] As well, the attack finds it more difficult to cut off retreat by defence.. [368] Strategic envelopment, moreover, must be translated into tactical envelopment if it is to produce results that matter, namely destruction of enemy forces. [547] But in some cases defensive positions are so extensive that they provide a 'kind of absolute security ... where the line of defense may run from sea to sea or from one neutral country to another'. [367] Envelopment thus becomes impossible.

Strategic defence, by contrast, has difficulty exploiting concentric movement, being unable to deploy troops in the depth required or conceal its movements sufficiently. [364] 'The defender cannot, as he can in tactics, surround the surrounder'. [364] Yet Clausewitz does not rule out flanking operations by the defence which, though more difficult promise high rewards if carried through successfully. They can be particularly valuable to the defence when employed toward the end of a campaign, during a retreat into the interior, or in conjunction with armed insurrection. [465]

Again, qualifications are in order for both offence and defence. Flanking operations, which are 'more popular in books than in the field', should not be overrated. [347] Of no value in themselves, they depend on effective combination with other factors. [460] In a typical summation Clausewitz observes: 'The convergent form pays dazzling dividends, but the yield of the divergent form is more dependable'. [368] Neither is inherently superior in part because 'an attempt at one will naturally evoke the other as the obvious countermove, the proper antidote'. [542] What is certain is that 'no rules of any kind exist for maneuver, and no method or general principle can determine the value of the action'. [542] The furthest Clausewitz goes is to say that envelopment is 'the most natural form of attack, and should not be disregarded without good cause'. [547]

Finally, Clausewitz sees continuity of effort as essential to strategic success. The very idea of a halt in the attack is anathema: 'any kind of interruption, pause, or suspension of activity is inconsistent with the nature of offensive war'. [599] There is no excuse for delay other than the time inevitably required to mobilise and move forces [598] or if the risks are too great. [626] Pauses are 'necessary evils' which generally help the defence as much as, if not more than, the offence. A commander who calls a halt out of weakness will generally find that

> a second run at the objective normally becomes impossible; and if it does turn out to be possible it shows that there was no need for a halt at all. When an objective was beyond one's strength in the first place, it will always remain so. [600]

Exceptions may arise, Clausewitz concedes, but these result more from changes in the political situation than from strategy itself.

Continuity of effort extends to pursuit of a defeated enemy which can turn tactical gains into strategic success. Often both sides lose heavily in a battle but '[t]he really crippling losses, those the vanquished does not share with the victor, only start with his retreat'. [230–1] Successful pursuit explains 'why guns and prisoners have always counted as the real trophies of victory' – tangible evidence in terms of materiel and morale. [232] Clausewitz spoke from experience. In 33 days after Jena and Auerstädt Murat's cavalry took 140,000 Prussian prisoners.[3]

Two principal difficulties face the commander in initiating and sustaining a pursuit. First, troops must be regrouped and re-equipped after the battle for 'the winning side is in almost as much disorder and confusion as the losers'. [263] Leadership is severely tested as the desire of soldiers for rest, safety and enjoyment of triumph demands a halt. Second, the commander must maintain control over his troops during rapid and dispersed movement, possibly including operations at night. The difficulties of pursuit are demonstrated by the frequency with which defeated armies rally quite rapidly without reinforcements. [271]

The culminating point of the attack

In the struggle between offence and defence Clausewitz argues that there is a point in time and space by which the offence should have achieved success and beyond which the balance tips in favour of the defence. The idea goes back at least to Machiavelli.[4] It arises because the attacker assumes an increasing burden over time which, unless success is achieved, sooner or later becomes too heavy to bear. For Napoleon capture of Moscow was the intended culminating point, the moment when he could consider himself 'over the ridge'.[5] In other cases attacks 'lead up to the point where their remaining strength is just enough to maintain a defense and wait for peace'. [528] Just as the defence ends with the counter-attack, the attack ends at the culminating point.

Several factors diminish the force of the attack. First and most obviously, the defence is better able to draw on the elements that favour it – terrain, fortresses, local supply, militia forces and high morale. For its part, the attack simply lacks such assets or cannot draw on them to the same extent.

Second, the attacker loses momentum – from casualties in battle, sickness, the need to besiege fortresses, difficulties of supply, a natural reduction in energy and, at the political level, the possible defection of allies. [527, 567–9] Any omission by the attack – whether from poor judgement, fear or indolence – accrues to the defender's benefit. Needing more things to go right, the attack faces greater risk of breakdown and delay, and the longer the time taken by the attack the greater the friction. Hence 'time which is allowed to pass unused accumulates to the credit of the defender. He reaps where he did not sow'. [357] And time, unlike space, as Napoleon observed, can never be regained.

Third, the attacker is increasingly pushed into defensive positions – to defend against counter-attacks, to avoid losing what he has gained or to provide respite for his troops. Attack entails defence:

> the superiority of *strategic defense* arises partly from the fact that the attack itself cannot exist without some measure of defense – and defense of a much less effective kind. [524]

For the offence, therefore, defence is a 'necessary evil, an impeding burden created by the sheer weight of the mass. It is its original sin, its mortal disease'. [524] Defence conducted by the attacker, moreover, is 'weakened in all its key elements' and ceases to 'possess the superiority which basically belongs to it'. [572]

Clausewitz offers historical examples for his assertion that the offence must achieve success before the burden of attack grows too great. In his war against Austria Frederick the Great gradually went on to the defensive after 1758 since 'even victories cost too much'. [614–5] It was 'as if the whole Prussian war-engine had ventured into the enemy's territory in order to wage a defensive war for its own existence'.[6] Frederick himself warned against advancing too deeply into foreign territory, beyond what he called the 'point'.[7] Napoleon clearly

went too far in his campaign against Russia in 1812, having to withdraw from Moscow 'because he had fallen victim to the illness of
strategic consumption, and had to use the last strength of his sick body
to drag himself out of the country'.[8]

The commander must judge whether he can reach the culminating
point with sufficient strength remaining. He must assess his own capabilities and make an informed 'guess' whether the initial attack will
heighten an opponent's resolve or shatter it. [572–3] Critically, too, he
must be able to recognise when the culminating point has arrived, a
decision likely to be strongly influenced by the 'dangers and responsibilities' he faces. [573]

> It is even possible that the attacker, reinforced by the psychological
> forces peculiar to the attack, will in spite of his exhaustion find it
> less difficult to go on than to stop – like a horse pulling a load
> uphill. [572]

Unable to determine the right moment to halt, he may 'overshoot the
point at which, if he stopped and assumed the defensive, there would
still be a chance of success'. [572] It is fear of this very possibility that
explains

> why the great majority of generals will prefer to stop well short of
> their objective rather than risk approaching it too closely, and why
> those with high courage and an enterprising spirit will often over-
> shoot it and so fail to attain their purpose. [573]

It is a fault to which the attack is uniquely prone.

Gaining strategic advantages

During a campaign both offence and defence look for courses of action
to secure advantages that do not seem warranted by the overall balance
of forces. Such 'strategems' rely on deceiving the opponent as to one's
intentions. Clausewitz briefly discusses two minor strategems – diversions and deception – and examines at length one that has always
appealed to strategists – surprise.

Diversions are attacks designed to draw enemy forces away from the
main objective. The target threatened must be of sufficient value to
encourage the enemy to defend it with more men than are employed
in the attack. Clausewitz is cautious about their value. 'If small forces

are to draw off larger ones, there must obviously be special circumstances at the root of it' – such as targets where the enemy is particularly vulnerable or which will yield substantial war materiel. [562–3] These 'favourable opportunities do not arise very often'. [563] By way of caution, Clausewitz mentions landings by British troops in North Holland in 1799 and on Walcheren in 1809. Both failed to tie up French forces or win support from the local population, their only justification being that British forces could not be employed in any other way. [563] Intended as diversions, they became merely harassing operations.

Deceptions or feints are designed to induce 'the intended victim to make his own mistakes' by creating an illusion and concealing one's purpose. [202] The use of cunning is an age-old and almost irresistible human urge in war, Clausewitz acknowledges, since plans issued for appearance only or false reports designed to confuse the enemy seem easy and cheap. But strategy, '[u]nlike other areas of life ... is not concerned with actions that consist only of words'. [202] Time and effort are required to prepare 'a sham action' on a scale sufficient to make a significant difference. Using forces 'merely to create an illusion' risks leaving troops unavailable if the opponent sees through the stratagem. [203] Only when one's forces are exceedingly weak and prospects bleak does cunning offer 'a faint glimmer of hope', so that combined with boldness and daring it 'may yet kindle a flame'. [203] Strategy should never rely on deception but use it only when 'a ready-made opportunity presents itself'. [202–3] If Napoleon used diversions and deceptions to effect, this was because they were used in conjuction with his already superior forces.

Surprise is a more significant stratagem, referring to any move or disposition of forces the enemy does not expect, and is open to the defence as well as the attack. [200] The desire to achieve surprise 'is more or less basic to all operations, for without it superiority at the decisive point is hardly conceivable'. It delivers material superiority over and imposes important psychological disadvantages on an opponent. Surprise, though basically a tactical device, can be found at all levels. [198] The characteristics of surprise – 'secrecy and speed' – are most evident at the tactical level where it can more readily be achieved 'simply because ... time and space are limited in scale'. [198] Darkness can also be exploited. [274] But in itself surprise does not bring great results at the tactical level. It may cause 'panic and confusion in the enemy's ranks' but the decisive factor remains the overall strength of the attack. [366]

Only at 'the higher levels of policy' does surprise promise great rewards although it faces many difficulties. [198] Launching a surprise attack against another country requires a high degree of energy on the part of the government and commanders, as well as great efficiency on the part of the army. 'Preparations for war usually take months', involving troop movements and concentrations and the establishment of depots the purpose of which 'can be guessed soon enough'. [198] Referring to defence against a possible aggressor, Clausewitz observes:

> the direction from which he threatens our country will usually be announced in the press before a single shot is fired. The greater the scale of preparations, the smaller the chance of achieving a surprise. [210]

Genuine preconditions for surprise war are thus rarely met. [199] Nonetheless, if the attacker 'contrives to keep his preparations sufficiently secret, he may well take his victim unawares'. But surprise of this kind 'has nothing to do with war itself, and should not be possible'. [370] It reflects failure of political leaders to anticipate the threat and take necessary precautions.

Clausewitz readily acknowledges the benefits of surprise in the campaign. Achieved on a large scale, and especially with attacks on the enemy flank or rear, it 'confuses the enemy and lowers his morale'. [198, 242], and 'loosens the bonds of cohesion' among enemy forces. [201] When a commander has psychological superiority over his opponent surprise may yield him 'the fruits of victory where ordinarily he might expect to fail'. [201] In exceptional cases 'momentous surprises' occur [200] and even bring 'the whole war to an end at a stroke'. [363] Occasional results of this kind ensure that 'the wish to achieve surprise is common and, indeed, indispensable' among commanders. [198]

But the popular idea that surprise is the dominant factor in success did not appeal to Clausewitz. Not only are many other factors at work in a campaign, but surprise requires the commander to act with remarkable 'energy, forcefulness and resolution' to ensure that 'lax conditions and conduct' do not give the game away. [199, 198] Inevitably 'the friction of the whole machine' is the enemy of surprise. [198] Successful surprise also usually requires 'major, obvious and exceptional mistakes on the enemy's part'. [363–4] Poor reconnaissance by Prussian forces meant failure to discover how Napoleon was massing forces at Auerstädt in 1806. In his overall assessment

Clausewitz adopts his standard line: 'the greater the ease with which surprise is achieved, the smaller is its effectiveness, and vice versa'. [199] Hence 'surprise and initiative ... are infinitely more important and effective in strategy than in tactics' but are difficult to achieve and ought to be countered by proper defence. [363] The equation is intuitively appealing though not easily demonstrated in practice.

Explaining pauses in the campaign

Even in the most vigorous campaigns, Clausewitz observed, commanders often halt their activities in apparent defiance of the fundamental nature of war:

> suspension of action in war is a contradiction in terms. Like two incompatible elements, armies must continually destroy one another. Like fire and water they never find themselves in a state of equilibrium. [216]

If delay is likely to improve the position of one belligerent, surely the other has an incentive to attack immediately. Pause would occur only in situations of 'polarity' where incentives to attack are in perfect but temporary balance. [82–3] Yet the history of warfare shows that '*immobility* and *inactivity* are the normal *state* of armies in war, and *action is the exception*'. [217] Why is this the case?

Clausewitz rejects the view that pauses occur whenever the incentive to attack on each side is in balance – such a balance is unlikely to be stable for long. A more substantial reason is friction. '[I]mperfect knowledge of the situation' may lead commanders to suppose wrongly that the initiative lies with the opponent. [84] Commanders also tend to overestimate enemy strength – 'such is human nature'. [85] This 'imperfection of human perception and judgement [which] is more pronounced in war than anywhere else' more often induces belligerents to believe there will be a better moment for attack at some later time. As well, 'the fear and indecision native to the human mind' encourage anxiety and aversion to responsibility, slowing down action like a 'moral force of gravity'. [217]

A second explanation for pauses derives from a fundamental asymmetry in strategy, namely that defence is a stronger form of warfare than attack. Thus if one side postpones its attack to wait for a better moment, this does not mean the opponent is strong enough to launch an attack. Even if both commanders are seeking a clear-cut decision, the superiority of the defence undercuts continuous action. [84–5] After Borodino, for example, it was not in Russia's interest to seek another battle but it did not follow that battle would benefit Napoleon since he had to preserve sufficient forces to occupy Moscow. The greater strength of the defence, in short, acts 'like a ratchet-wheel, occasionally stopping the works completely'. [217]

Defence as the stronger form of warfare

Clausewitz's controversial proposition that attack and defence are unequal in strength ran counter to the prevailing wisdom of the age – and to much strategic thinking thereafter.[9] But Clausewitz was unequivocal:

- 'defense is a stronger form of fighting than attack'. [84]
- 'the superiority of the defensive (if rightly understood) is very great, far greater than appears at first sight'. [84]
- *'the defensive form of warfare is intrinsically stronger than the offensive'.* [358]
- 'defense is the stronger form of war, the one that makes the enemy's defeat more certain'. [380]

Put baldly, of course, the proposition means little. Clausewitz cannot claim that every campaign will see the defence victorious. His argument is rather that defence possesses inherent characteristics that make it in general stronger than offence.

Clausewitz first points to the different purposes of defence and attack, the former having negative goals which are intrinsically easier to achieve than positive goals which are easier to frustrate. In war as in law, *'beati sunt possidentes'* – blessed are those in possession. [357–8] Since the attack is the weaker form of war, the attacker needs some political reason to engage in it all. Conversely, if attack were the stronger form '[n]o one would want to do anything but attack: defence would be pointless'. [359] Seeking to maintain the status quo, the defender in practice has every reason to engage in the stronger form of war, though Clausewitz asserts one should use it 'only so long as weakness compels', abandoning it 'as soon as we are strong enough to pursue a positive object'. [358].

A second argument is that while some elements of strategy are in principle available to both sides – such as numbers, concentration and continuity of effort – others are available only or primarily to the defence. Terrain, fortresses, supply and national morale can be more fully exploited by an efficient defence, the more so over time. By contrast, few elements favour the attack alone. Critically, too, the attack faces ever greater burdens as it proceeds, eventually reaching a culminating point. Other factors normally favouring the defence are to be found in national and international politics (see chapter 18). Most of the advantages accruing to the defence, moreover, tend to be permanent or only marginally affected by historical changes.[10]

At the same time, when the defence shifts to the attack and moves into enemy territory, it loses its principal advantages. An army invading the territory of a state that launched the first attack not only loses the strength inherent in defence but transfers that strength to the side attacked. In a rare formula to emphasise the disparity Clausewitz points out that 'the difference between A + B and A – B equals 2B'. [218]

Both offence and defence naturally compete for supremacy, especially at the tactical level where a see-saw struggle centres on manoeuvrability. While the offence remained unable to move its forces rapidly, Clausewitz asserts, the defence benefited from freedom to adopt prepared positions. As armies became more mobile, defenders sought security behind rivers or on mountains. But this advantage lasted only until attacking forces increased their mobility in rough country and could turn the defender's flanks. This led to extended lines of defence which in turn allowed the offence to attack less well protected points in the line. [361–2] The tactical balance between offence and defence thus turned on position and movement. Clausewitz thought changes at this level that would shift matters decisively in favour of the offence were unlikely; in any case the defence would seek to nullify such initiatives. [362]

At the strategic level the relationship between offence and defence appeared more stable. Competition certainly exists as new methods of defence stimulate new methods of attack and vice versa but Clausewitz considered it fruitless to argue that 'for every method of defense there is an infallible method of attack'. It sufficed to show that while the defence might be overcome, the cost of doing so could be disproportionately high. [523] Political developments could create the kind of strategic advantage Napoleon enjoyed, at least temporarily, when his ambitious policies, aggressive campaigns and readiness to pay great costs left the defence flat-footed everywhere. Once Prussia and other powers began to conduct defence in vigorous and rational fashion, however, they were at an advantage.

Clausewitz's strategy

The popular view of Clausewitzian strategy – large numbers, concentration of forces, unrelenting effort, decisive battle, overthrow of the opponent – is not entirely unfounded. This was his early idea of strategy, reinforced by concepts of Absolute War and the rise to extremes. But once he accepted that war might have all kinds of purpose, including minor gains or preserving the status quo, strategy became a far more complex and subtle undertaking. Though he retained a preference for vigorous action and argued for counterattack by the defence whenever possible, these strategies were to be adopted only if they were clearly linked to the success of the campaign and the political objectives of the war.

Especially where objectives are limited strategy is more subject to political considerations and less governed by the dynamics of interaction. Pause, delay and indecision are commonplace. Surprise is less common because energy is lacking. Culminating points are not reached because there is no strength and ambition pushing attacks forward. The enemy is not driven to what might be called the 'breaking point' of the defence when the will of the attacker can be imposed on him (an important idea Clausewitz does not discuss at length[11]). Principles of strategy relating to numbers, concentration, envelopment and continuity of effort still apply to such a campaign but they are both less relevant and less evident.

Clausewitz also emphasised how any significant campaign will consist of a constantly changing compound of offence and defence. These are complex and demanding activities which cannot be separated and which involve both material and psychological factors. At some point the attack must put resources into defending what it has gained unless its opponent puts up no resistance. For its part the defence should not be totally passive but must throw something – even a few bullets – at an attacker. The attack seeks to reach a culminating point where the outcome is clear but the counter-attack by the defence is designed to prevent or delay this. It is a contest which may involve high or low levels of energy and violence but there is inevitably interaction between attacker and defender, each of whom exploits both offence and defence in some combination.

The factors which feed into the strength (or weakness) of the attack and the defence are varied and variable – principally terrain, fortresses, supply, the militia and morale. Clausewitz argues that these are in general more easily accessible to the defence than to the attack. Add to this the fact that the offence has a positive goal while the defence is seeking to prevent change, that offence normally faces a higher degree of friction than the defence, and that the passage of time usually adds to the burdens of the offence rather than the defence, and it is clear why Clausewitz reaches the view that offence faces the greater challenge. Nor does this take into account the international balance of power which sooner or later works against the state taking up arms.

Clausewitz pays greater attention to strategic defence than many other writers and Book VI on defence is the longest in *On War*. He was anxious to show that defence should

> no longer cut so sorry a figure when compared to attack, and the latter will no longer look so easy and infallible as it does in the gloomy imagination of those who see courage, determination, and movement in attack alone, and in defense only impotence and analysis. [371]

Indeed, he goes so far as to argue that, properly conducted, defence is the stronger form of war. In this he was broadly correct about the wars of his time. Even Napoleon, the brilliant exponent of offensive war, was eventually defeated as friction wore down his armies and as his opponents increased their military effort. How much of his analysis is relevant to other historical eras is more problematic. Clausewitz provides the factors in the equation; he does not necessarily offer a solution for all time.

13
Command

'...it is natural that military activity, whose plans, based on general circumstances, are so frequently disrupted by unexpected particular events, should remain largely a matter of talent'. [139–40]

Tactics deals in routines and regularities, politics in values and compromises. Strategy is about setting objectives in a campaign and carrying through a plan. This is the responsibility of the general or commander who faces heavy demands on his intellect and character. He confronts physical danger and bears heavy responsibilities in a 'relentless struggle with the unforeseen' from which his mind may not emerge 'unscathed'. [102] This chapter examines Clausewitz's understanding of the nature of military command, the environment in which strategic decisions are made, and the characteristics of military genius.

Armies and commanders

An army is a complex social organisation that performs best when imbued with military virtues and buoyed by victories in the field. But it also needs a strong sense of authority and command to overcome the friction and pressures for disintegration inherent in fighting. This is the first challenge for the commander. 'No army can be properly commanded in the absence of a dominant, authoritarian determination that permeates it down to the last man'. While an army is based on directives to subordinates, this is not a simple matter. Orders may prove 'inappropriate to the circumstances of the moment ... a completely unavoidable disadvantage'. A careful watch must be kept on all officers. Indeed, '[a]nyone who falls into the habit of thinking and expecting the best of his subordinates at all times is for that reason alone, unsuited to command an army'. [510]

The selection of subordinate commanders is critical and needs to take into account personal characteristics. Armies should recognise that 'even junior positions of command require outstanding intellectual qualities for outstanding achievement' and that 'the standard rises with every step'. [111] Fortunately, not every soldier needs a measure of genius – otherwise armies would be very weak. [100] But there are usually many officers with the necessary 'practical intelligence'. [111] Others need careful handling. Less imaginative generals copy their supreme commander's favourite device without regard to circumstances. [154] Most armies are also familiar with the 'officer grown gray in the service, his mind well-blinkered by long years of routine' but this 'brave but brainless fighter' will not achieve 'anything of outstanding significance'. Promoting such men contributes 'nothing to their efficiency, and little to their happiness'. [111]

How, then, can a nation produce good commanders? The emergence of truly great commanders, Clausewitz suggests, depends on factors beyond the control of armies, namely 'the *general intellectual development* of a given society'. A warrior spirit may be found among some peoples but they will never produce a truly great commander 'since this requires a degree of intellectual powers beyond anything that a primitive people can develop'. [100] Only societies marked by 'higher degrees of civilization' – such as France and Ancient Rome – produce genuinely outstanding commanders but even such peoples may lack 'the natural disposition' for war. [100–1]

For the rest armies must do what they can. They may, for example, encourage or stifle talent. As junior officers rise in rank and the responsibilities of command increase, the vital quality of boldness tends to be held in check and caution and timidity take over. 'Nearly every general known to us from history as mediocre, even vacillating, was noted for dash and determination as a junior officer'. [191] Boldness is thus all the more admirable when found at the highest levels. [191–2] Nor is successful performance at one level any guarantee of success at the next. An officer may make his reputation in one rank but on promotion have his incompetence exposed. [111] Clausewitz quotes with approval Voltaire's maxim : 'The same man who shines at the second level is eclipsed at the top'. [191]

Good education is vital. The important principle is that 'the simplicity of knowledge required in war' should not, as so often happens, be 'lumped together with the whole array of ancillary information and skills'. Armies should not listen to those 'ridiculous pedants' who believe it 'necessary or even useful to begin the education of a future general with a knowledge of all the details'. '[P]etty things will make a petty mind unless a man rejects them as completely alien'. [145] Far better to read history and learn the importance of moral factors: 'this is the noblest and most solid nourishment that the mind of a general may draw from a study of the past'. [185] However, study of the careers of military officers who reach the top is of little value since they rarely analyse their art: 'They read some history, and in the end do what they can according to their natural abilities'.[1]

The environment of decision

'Everything in strategy is very simple', Clausewitz observes, 'but that does not mean that everything is very easy'. [178] The commander exercises his talents in conditions of danger, uncertainty, friction and complexity. In no other area of human activity are decisions involving life and death so frequently and so peremptorily demanded in such difficult circumstances. All of these factors mean that a commander will require very special qualities of mind and temperament.

The physical dangers are self-evident, being inherent in the nature of fighting as each side seeks to harm the other.

Uncertainty means that decisions are made on inadequate and often unreliable information – both about a commander's own situation and about his opponent. [84] Hence in war

> all action takes place, so to speak, in a kind of twilight, which, like fog or moonlight, often tends to make things seem grotesque and larger than they really are. [140]

Uncertainty is the result not simply of lack of information but of psychological pressures.

> The difficulty of *accurate recognition* constitutes one of the most serious sources of friction in war, by making things appear entirely different from what one had expected. The senses make a more vivid impression on the mind than systematic thought. [117]

It is natural to see the worst in any situation: '[a]s a rule most men would rather believe bad news than good, and rather tend to exaggerate the bad news'. Fear and anxiety multiply 'lies and inaccuracies'. [117] And even additional information may not make decisions easier: '[w]e now know more, but this makes us more, not less uncertain'. [102]

As well as danger and uncertainty, the commander must deal with friction as his forces encounter the inevitable obstacles and burdens of war. Not least is the friction within those forces since they are a complex organisation with diverse skills and equipment. [144] Subordinates rarely respond simply and easily to directions. Even senior officers may resist proposed actions so that commanders find themselves seeking to persuade their colleagues. 'So few people have acquired the necessary skill at this that most discussions are a futile bandying of words'. The result is often agreement for the sake of agreement and 'a compromise with nothing to be said for it'. [Unfinished Note, 71]

The commander, moreover, faces the utmost complexity as he seeks to balance political direction, the realities of combat and strategic calculation. The options are countless. Of the campaign of 1814 Clausewitz wrote: 'Every campaign plan chooses one path among a thousand'.[2] It is like making a voyage at sea through dangerous and unknown waters:

> every war is rich in unique episodes. Each is an uncharted sea, full of reefs. The commander may suspect the reefs' existence without ever having seen them; now he has to steer past them in the dark. [120]

Nor will the commander be free of doubt that the course of action chosen is the right one. He 'must never ... expect to move on the narrow ground of illusory security as if it were *absolute*'. [517]

Strategy is thus never a routine activity: 'any method by which strategic plans are turned out ready-made, as if from some machine, must be totally rejected'. [154] It is in reality a creative activity, an exercise in imagination and intellect. It requires well-developed qualities of mind and character because of the serious dangers, constant uncertainties, inevitable friction and manifold options facing the commander. In tactics 'the pressures of the moment' mean decisions must be taken rapidly with little room for the doubt and indecision liable to beset strategy. [178] Important decisions in strategy are very different and demand particular qualities. What, then, are the qualities of the good commander? What are the characteristics of the commander of genius?

Qualities of the military commander

Clausewitz analyses the psychology of command at some length though acknowledging he is no expert in the discipline. Adopting his normal approach, he identifies opposing or contrasting elements and then suggests how they work in combination. We can begin with his discussion of four personality types which are based implicitly on two factors: the level of emotion which can be low or high, and the degree of stability which can also be low or high.

The first two types have low levels of emotion. The stable kind lack initiative and motivation but have the advantage of rarely making a serious mistake and being hard to throw off balance. The less stable kind can be stirred to act by trifles but may be overwhelmed by great issues and are unlikely to achieve much. [106] Generals of these two types have their place but are unlikely to secure great results.

The last two personality types have high levels of emotion. The more volatile of these can be valuable, being given to acts of bravery, but usually do not sustain their efforts and need close supervision. With courage and ambition such men will be suited to 'a modest level of command'. [106–7] It is the fourth type that Clausewitz believes has greatest potential for military genius:

> men who are difficult to move but have strong feelings ... who are best able to summon the titanic strength it takes to clear away the enormous burdens that obstruct activity in war. Their emotions move as great masses do – slowly but irresistibly. [107]

The allusion to Scharnhorst is unmistakable – a commander of powerful emotions but stable disposition who displayed the qualities of mind and temperament that Clausewitz believed essential in great military leaders.

Qualities of mind

Qualities of mind help overcome the 'feeble light' of war. [140] The most fundamental of all such qualities is undoubtedly intellect (which also contributes indirectly to qualities of temperament). Nothing will compensate for lack of intellect, and even the maximum use of force does not exclude 'the simultaneous use of the intellect'. [75] Quite simply, '[n]o great commander was ever a man of limited intellect'. [146] Such intellect is gained not by formal instruction but through experience and observation, reflection and study. [146] A good commander has 'an intellectual instinct which extracts the essence from the phenomena of life, as a bee sucks honey from a flower'. [146] Some leaders have a 'natural talent' for acquiring the necessary knowledge but the majority – Clausewitz no doubt had himself in mind – need to nurture and develop their talent through study and reflection. [147]

Among particular mental capacities, the first is *coup d'oeil*, a quality highly valued by most eighteenth century military writers because of the uncertain and changing circumstances of war.[3] Relying on the 'inward eye' as well as the physical eye, *coup d'oeil* is the capacity for 'quick recognition of a truth that the mind would ordinarily miss or would perceive only after long study and reflection'. [102] More than just rapid judgement on the basis of immediate impressions, it requires *'an intellect that, even in the darkest hour, retains some glimmerings of the inner light which leads to truth'*. [102]

A second quality is presence of mind or the capacity to assess and deal rapidly with the unexpected, to react speedily to events without being overwhelmed. Whether this is due to a particular cast of mind or to steady nerves depends on circumstances but both elements are present. [103–4]

The third quality reflects the fact that warfare is intimately associated with terrain. [109] A commander requires a well-developed sense of locality, 'a faculty of *quickly and accurately grasping the topography of any area* which enables a man to find his way about at any time'. [109] He needs to hold a vivid picture or map of a large or small area in his mind without fading or blurring. It is a faculty that owes much to '*the mental gift we call imagination*' – perhaps 'the only service that war can demand from this frivolous goddess, who in most military affairs is liable to do more harm than good'. [109–10]

Taken together these qualities of mind provide the sense of judgement essential to the commander:

> a sense of unity and a power of judgement raised to a marvelous pitch of vision, which easily grasps and dismisses a thousand remote possibilities which an ordinary mind would labor to identify and wear itself out in so doing. [112]

Yet even a 'superb display of divination', Clausewitz insists, will lack 'historical significance' if it is not based on the essential qualities of temperament. [112]

Qualities of temperament

If intellect is the most important of the qualities of mind, the most important quality of temperament is determination. [108] Already in the *Principles of War* written for the Crown Prince Clausewitz had identified the importance of this quality: 'Pursue one great aim with force and determination' – a maxim to which he granted 'first place among all causes of victory in the modern art of war'.[4] Determination or persistence is essential because once operations begin war is revealed as 'a flimsy structure that can easily collapse and bury us in its ruins'. [117] All the planning, directions and orders can come to nothing because of the unreliability of information and the effect of friction as well as losses inflicted by the enemy.

The commander also faces difficult inner challenges: doubt about the soundness of his plans, anxiety about dangers posed by enemy action, and 'the heart-rending spectacle of the dead and the wounded'. [104] He must therefore maintain confidence in his plans and decisions when everything is pressing in the opposite direction.

> In the dreadful presence of suffering and danger, emotion can easily overwhelm intellectual conviction, and in this psychological fog it is so hard to form clear and complete insights that changes of view become more understandable and excusable. Action can never be based on anything firmer than instinct, a sensing of the truth. Nowhere, in consequence, are differences of opinion so acute as in war, and fresh opinions never cease to batter at one's convictions. [108]

Reports of danger break like waves all around but he 'must trust his judgment and stand like a rock on which the waves break in vain'. [117] It is a test of the commander's psychological strength. [107]

Determination is also necessary to overcome friction among the commander's own troops who begin to resist his will – not from disobedience but the natural ebbing of moral strength as casualties mount, fears grow, the sense of purpose is lost and inertia takes over. Left unchecked, 'the mass will drag [the commander] down to the brutish world where danger is shirked and shame is unknown'. [105] The commander must combat friction but not expect an unrealistic standard of achievement. [120] And dealing with friction comes at a cost. 'Iron will-power can overcome this friction: it pulverizes every obstacle, but of course it wears down the machine as well'. [119]

Determination is particularly required at the point of victory when immediate pursuit of enemy forces pays great dividends – but it is also when troops want nothing more than rest, food and freedom from danger. This 'whole weight of human needs and weaknesses' constrains the general's freedom of action. [263]

> What does get accomplished is due to the supreme commander's *ambition, energy* and quite possibly his *callousness*. Only thus can we explain the timorous way in which so many generals exploit a victory that has given them the upper hand. [264]

For such reasons Clausewitz had criticised Wittgenstein for failing to inflict even more damage on the French in their retreat from Moscow.[5]

Perseverance acts as an 'essential counterweight' to uncertainty and danger. [193] Its proper role 'is to limit the agonies of doubt and the perils of hesitation'. [102–3] But a common pathology of generalship is that determination 'can degenerate into *obstinacy* ... a reluctance to admit that one is wrong'. [108–9] At Waterloo, for example, Napoleon went beyond the point at which 'persistence becomes desperate folly', staking 'his last remaining strength on an effort to retrieve a battle that was beyond retrieving'. [252] This kind of obstinacy is 'a fault of temperament', 'a special kind of *egotism*' that is more than mere vanity. [108] How can a commander know when to persist and when to alter or abandon plans? Clausewitz suggests the following advice: 'in all doubtful cases *to stick to one's first opinion and to refuse to change unless forced to do so by a clear conviction*'. [108]

Like all soldiers the commander also has need of courage. At this level Clausewitz identifies two kinds: 'courage in the face of personal danger, and courage to accept responsibility'. [101] The former may be a permanent indifference to danger or a less enduring emotion based on motives such as ambition or patriotism. [101] The latter kind is 'the courage to accept responsibility, courage in the face of a moral danger'. [102] The commander will be mindful of the lives of 'all those entrusted to him' – a 'sense of responsibility [that] lays a tenfold burden on [his] mind'. [138] And he knows he is accountable for his actions not just at the time but in future – 'either before the tribunal of some outside power or before the court of [his] own conscience'. [101] This moral courage is a quality created by the intellect – hence the term *courage d'esprit* – but becomes in reality 'an act of temperament'. In war 'the rush of events' means that men are 'governed by feelings rather than by thought'; the task of the intellect is 'to arouse the quality of courage'. [102]

A third indispensable quality in a great commander is boldness. Distinct from courage, it is a principle in itself, 'a genuinely creative force', that provides energy and support for the commander's analysis of the situation and the decisions he makes. More at home in war than any other activity, boldness can to an extent compensate for 'space, time and magnitude of forces'. [190] It 'does not consist in defying the natural order of things and in crudely offending the laws of probability', but is a force that 'can lend wings to intellect and insight'. [192] At lower levels boldness can be given free rein, but the commander's boldness must be tempered by a strong intellect:

> The higher up the chain of command, the greater is the need for boldness to be supported by a reflective mind, so that boldness does not degenerate into purposeless bursts of blind passion. [190]

Inevitably, boldness is less common at senior levels because the distance between 'necessity and action' increases and 'the more numerous the possibilities that have to be identified and analyzed before action is taken'. [191] A commander may have to convince himself of the need for boldness by employing 'fear of *wavering* and *hesitating* to suppress all other fears'. [103] The challenge for armies is to ensure that the general retains sufficient boldness to 'keep pace with his rise in rank'. [191]

Even when allied with intellect, boldness involves risk. The commander prepared to take risks is always preferable to the hesitant, cautious general and '[t]here are times when the utmost daring is the height of wisdom'. [167] In war, Clausewitz asserts, boldness usually succeeds over timidity since the latter – as opposed to deliberate caution – implies a loss of equilibrium. [190] 'Given the same amount of intelligence, timidity will do a thousand times more damage in war than audacity'. [191] Boldness is most evident when there is a choice between vigorous action and inaction. Clausewitz praises Frederick the Great's initiation of hostilities in 1756 when all indications pointed the other way. [191] Boldness undertaken from necessity is of a lesser order. For Clausewitz boldness is a response to uncertainty and a means of increasing the chances of success. In the eighteenth century luck had been much debated as an attribute of military commanders, many such as Frederick the Great seeing it as 'entirely capricious in its visitations'.[6] Clausewitz took a more positive approach. In modern terms the bold commander makes his own luck.

Military genius in practice

Clausewitz emphasises the challenge of high command. There is a 'major gulf' between the commander of an army or a theatre of operations and subordinate commanders who are subject to 'much closer control and supervision'. [111] Not only character is tested but also the mind, for the higher the rank 'the greater is the degree to which activity is governed by the mind, by the intellect, by insight'. [191] Only at the highest level can the term 'genius' be employed. [111]

Clausewitz is referring not to an abstract or general quality of mind but to 'a very highly developed mental aptitude for a particular occupation'. [100] Military genius in particular does not consist in 'a single appropriate gift' such as courage but a 'harmonious combination of elements, in which one or the other ability may predominate, but none may be in conflict with the rest'. [100] Mental capacities – *coup d'oeil*, presence of mind, a sense of locality, together with intellect – are combined with qualities of character such as courage, boldness and determination. An imbalance between mind and temperament is a recipe for failure. Highly intelligent people, for example, are often irresolute since 'their courage and intellect work in separate compartments'. [102–3]

Several qualities can be identified in the way in which great commanders go about their business. One is their 'strength of mind' – 'the ability to keep one's head at times of exceptional stress and violent emotion'. [105] This high degree of self-control is rooted in temperament rather than intellect and is thus distinct from presence of mind. The commander has powerful emotions but self-control ensures he is not overwhelmed by them. Self-control is an emotion 'which serves to balance the passionate feelings in strong characters without destroying them' and is based on 'the urge *to act rationally at all times*' – an urge Clausewitz refers to as 'the sense of human dignity, the noblest pride and deepest need of all'. [106] Strength of mind also means the capacity to make important decisions. Most generals, 'when they ought to act, are paralyzed by unnecessary doubts'. [179] For '[t]ruth in itself is rarely sufficient to make men act'. [112] Action results more from emotions than from intellect.

A second characteristic of great generals is their ability to simplify the complexities of strategy. They concentrate only on essential activities which, like streams combining into rivers, 'empty themselves into the great ocean of war'. [144] Strategy is thus made to appear simple:

A few uncomplicated thoughts seem to account for their decisions ... one is left with the impression that great commanders manage matters in an easy, confident and, one would almost think, off-hand sort of way. [577]

For such reasons 'the whole monstrosity called war' often seems to come down 'to a contest between individuals, a sort of duel'. [577]
The general also embodies the entire campaign in his person:

> When all is said and done, it is really the commander's *coup d'oeil*, his ability to see things simply, to identify the whole business of war completely with himself, that is the essence of good generalship. [578]

The desire to personify an army and its victories creates great energy and vitality. To some this looks like self-promotion but the 'thirst for fame and honor' is a noble ambition intrinsic to effective leadership. It gives the commander 'the ambition to strive higher than the rest' and 'a personal, almost proprietary interest in every aspect of fighting, so that he turns each opportunity to best advantage'. [105] No able commander-in-chief has lacked ambition and Clausewitz doubts such a figure is conceivable. [105] He fails to mention the crippling effects of petty rivalry, thwarted ambition and deep resentments that can also mark the careers of generals.

Finally, the great commander allows his intellect and temperament to express themselves to the full. As early as 1804 Clausewitz suggested that a commander's choice of strategy 'is a pure expression of [his] manner of thinking and feeling, and almost never a course chosen by free consideration'.[7] Generalship is a creative activity in which decisions are made as if by second nature. The Roman leader, Fabius Cunctator, for example, did not delay operations against the Carthaginian army because this was sound strategy but because he was a prevaricator by nature.[8]

The talents of great generals therefore largely innate.

> Most men merely act on instinct, and the amount of success they achieve depends on the amount of talent they were born with. All great commanders have acted on instinct, and the fact that their instinct was always sound is partly the measure of their innate greatness and genius. [Unfinished Note, 71]

The distinguished commander must be born with qualities of temperament, above all boldness. 'No man who is not born bold can play such a role, and therefore we consider this quality the first prerequisite of the great military leader'. [192] The significance of innate talent is further confirmed by the fact that 'in war men have so often successfully emerged in the higher ranks, and even as supreme commanders, whose former field of endeavour was entirely different'. [145] Whether the potential for leadership of genius can be identified before the event or actively developed, Clausewitz does not consider.

In sum, the great commander combines intellect and temperament, achieving the freedom needed 'to dominate events and not be overpowered by them'. [578] This emphasis on 'the creative personality' marks a clear point of difference from Scharnhorst who – typical of the Enlightenment – preferred to explain Frederick's victories in terms of Prussia's military deployments rather than personalities.[9] For Clausewitz it is essential to understand the personality of the leading figures in a war rather than simply the capabilities of each side.[10] The military genius imprints his own character on the campaign.

The psychology of strategy

Strategy is always a gamble, and the general always a gambler. Doubtful about his information, unsure of his own forces as well as of the enemy, uncertain of the future course of events, the general must wager with men's lives, with entire armies and ultimately with a nation's fate. Clausewitz's response to the play of chance and probability at the heart of war was to turn to the qualities of mind and temperament that allow commanders to deal with complex and dangerous situations: 'With uncertainty in one scale, courage and self-confidence must be thrown into the other to correct the balance'. [86] Given 'these finest and least dispensable of military virtues', 'the greater the margin that can be left for accidents'. [86] For the commander cannot eliminate uncertainty, only maximise his chances. This very uncertainty, indeed, provides the opportunity for the general to exercise his talent.[11]

Strategy is a product of the human mind – far more so than tactics. The general can dominate an opponent by his mental constructs as much as by his material resources. Thus boldness in the face of uncertainty is more valuable than timidity – just as a poker player improves his chances of winning by being prepared to lose. There is a distinctly romantic strain here. Though history is shaped by social forces, Clausewitz believed that individuals can play decisive roles. Especially in time of crisis, individual leaders can rise above circumstance.[12] This helps account for Clausewitz's frequent references to Napoleon (as well as his obvious admiration for Scharnhorst and Gneisenau).[13] His prescription for determination and boldness accorded with prevailing views of great military leaders, though he seems little troubled by the danger of relying on a heroic figure who may lead to disaster as much as to triumph.[14]

Clausewitz's approach to the psychology of command and leadership is not highly sophisticated or systematic. It identifies opposing factors and asserts the need for a balance. In the climate of war persistence must not be pushed so far as to become obstinacy, bold action needs to be tempered by reflection, confidence should combine with a degree of scepticism. Mind and temperament constantly interact. For Clausewitz the conduct of strategy is not only an intellectual exercise but draws on emotions and character. War, in short, engages the whole man – mind and temperament – revealing weaknesses more readily than any other activity.

Both Enlightenment and Counter-Enlightenment strands are found in Clausewitz's interpretation of command and commanders. Reason, intellect and knowledge must be brought to bear on the conduct of war in order to impose a degree of order and purpose on an activity inherently dangerous and chaotic. Yet war is also a matter of passion, emotion, inspiration and character which drive the general though he must not let himself be swept away by them. Whatever its limitations Clausewitz's analysis of strategic command was remarkably insightful and balanced for its time. Nor has it lost relevance altogether even if later analysts have added to and amended it.

Part VI
Theory and Practice

14
Theory

'Philosophy teaches us to recognize the relations that essential elements bear to one another'. [374]

The quest for strategic theory

Many have sought the holy grail of strategy – a set of rules or principles to deliver success to the general. The quest goes back to Ancient Greece and Rome and was revived in the Renaissance with the emergence of the Italian city-states. Machiavelli aspired to discover rational, universal principles such as the need for unified command and for a decisive battle. *The Art of War* thus offers a number of 'precautions' for the general as well as twenty seven 'general rules of military discipline' consisting of maxims and precepts dealing with strategy, tactics, administration and discipline.[1]

Interest in strategic theory revived in the eighteenth century. The establishment of military academies at this time raised the question of what, if anything, could be taught about strategy. Enlightenment thinkers sought systematic approaches while the Counter–Enlightenment looked to great generals and their genius for war. A 'maelstrom of opinions' engulfed the conduct of war, requiring 'some sort of resolution'. As war became 'more orderly and complex', Clausewitz believed, more sophisticated principles and rules were possible. [134] Above all, theory had to tackle the conduct of the campaign where the prize beckoned most alluringly.

In tactics, cause and effect are closely linked and the demands on soldiers much the same from engagement to engagement. Theory at this level will therefore 'present far fewer difficulties to the theorist than will *strategy*'. [141] In general, Clausewitz argued, '[t]he more physical the activity, the less the difficulties will be' in establishing precise rules. [140] Situations recur which are 'essentially alike' so that drill and routines can be developed on the basis of 'the *average probability* of analogous cases' and courses of action 'prescribed by method rather than general principles or individual regulation'. [151–2] Examples include not using cavalry against unbroken infantry or not opening fire until the enemy is within range (though even these precepts may be broken if the commander judges differently). What Clausewitz calls 'an average truth' produces better overall results. [152]

At the other extreme the war plan is primarily a matter of political judgement and the range of possible decisions and outcomes virtually unlimited. Clausewitz criticises in passing those who seek a theory of international politics by induction, examining individual cases on the basis of their 'most striking feature, the high point of the event' while failing to dig down to the underlying causes. Such theorists *'never rise above anecdote'* and their findings apply to no more than a single case. [374] Theory at this level promises little though Clausewitz does discuss important regularities such as pursuit of national interests and the balance of power.

The challenge of strategic theory

Clausewitz knew what was wrong with much contemporary strategic theory. In the first place, it sought fixed values, as theorists focused on what was measurable, on physical rather than psychological factors, and on unilateral action rather than interaction. [136] It also misused evidence in ways Clausewitz found reprehensible:

> three or four examples from distant times and places, dragged in and piled up from the widest range of circumstances, tend to distract and confuse one's judgment without proving anything. The light of day usually reveals them to be mere trash, with which the author intends to show off his learning. [169]

Many popular theories thus lacked any basis in reality.

A related problem of strategic theory was its susceptibility to fashion – a fault of military thinking as in society at large.[2] Words and phrases such as 'dominate', 'commanding position' and 'key positions', Clausewitz noted, had a 'charm' of their own that helped each become 'a sacred convention of military erudition'. [352] Some writers were also over-impressed by the revolutionary methods of the French: 'As usually happens, opinions outstripped fact, and faith in the old system was undermined even more than reality justified'.[3]

Ostentatiousness and 'vanity' also encouraged strategists to put forward grand systems that were patently narrow and one-sided. Strategists were too ready to adopt 'jargon, technicalities, and metaphors' which 'swarm everywhere – a lawless rabble of camp-followers'. [168] This often loses the reader and suggests the author does not understand what he is saying. Theory becomes a 'laughing-stock' among those with genuine military competence. [169]

Theory was also liable to promise too much – a handbook for success. But Clausewitz repeatedly states what strategic theory *cannot* do:

- 'construct a model for the art of war that can serve as a scaffolding on which the commander can rely for support at any time'. [140]
- 'be a positive doctrine, a sort of *manual* for action'. [141]
- 'serve as a guide which at the moment of action lays down precisely the path he must take'. [141]
- 'cover every abstract truth, so that all the critic had to do would be to classify the case studied under the appropriate heading'. [157]
- provide the commander 'with positive doctrines and systems to be used as intellectual tools'. [168]
- 'mark the narrow path on which the sole solution is supposed to lie by planting a hedge of principles on either side'. [578]

It is thus absurd to look for 'elaborate scientific guidelines as if they were a kind of truth machine'. [168] Theory which offers detailed instruction, in short, is 'absolutely useless'. [136]

A sound theory of war, by contrast, avoids 'arcane and obscure language', taking the form of 'plain speech, with a sequence of clear, lucid concepts'. [168] It will disappoint those who expect exotic theorems:

> The reader expects to hear of strategic theory, of lines and angles, and instead of these denizens of the scientific world he finds himself encountering only creatures of everyday life. But the author cannot bring himself to be in the slightest degree more scientific than he considers his subject to warrant – strange as this attitude may appear. [193]

Nor will theory be detailed enough to cover every possible case. This would make it absurdly cumbersome – 'one would drown in trivialities'.[4]

Yet theory must not be so broad, so platitudinous that it is of no relevance to actual war.[5] Useful in mathematics, abstraction is unhelpful in war:

> when abstractions must constantly discard the living phenomena in order to reflect the lifeless form ... the result is a dry skeleton of dull truths and commonplaces, squeezed into a doctrine.[6]

The danger is that commanders will 'be irresistibly dragged down into a state of dreary pedantry' where they must 'grub around in the under-world of ponderous concepts'. [578]

The problems of developing 'a scientific theory for the art of war' are clearly very great. As Clausewitz observed in a Note probably written in 1827:

> so many attempts have failed that most people say it is impossible, since it deals with matters that no permanent law can provide for. One would agree, and abandon the attempt, were it not for the obvious fact that a whole range of propositions can be demon-strated without difficulty. [Unfinished Note, 71]

By way of illustration he listed a number of propositions, among them:

- 'defense is the stronger form of fighting with the negative purpose, attack the weaker form with the positive purpose';
- 'major successes help bring about minor ones, so that strategic results can be traced back to certain turning-points';
- 'victory consists not only in the occupation of the battlefield, but in the destruction of the enemy's physical and psychic forces, which is usually not obtained until the enemy is pursued after a victorious battle';
- 'every attack loses impetus as it progresses'. [Unfinished Note, 71]

Several other 'laws' or 'principles' are mentioned in *On War* – for example, be very strong at the decisive point; keep forces con-centrated unless there is good reason for the contrary [204]; forces should be used simultaneously (hence strategic reserves exist not for their own sake but to contribute to the final decision). [211] General propositions of this kind, Clausewitz argued, may not apply to every single instance but encompass 'the general run of cases'. [374]

It is evident that these propositions do not amount to a comprehensive theory of strategy; certainly, some appear self-evident, trivial or of limited application. But Clausewitz's primary concern was not to propose a utilitarian strategic theory that would directly assist the commander. As he had written in 1808, this was one function of theory but there were two other functions – analytical and pedagogic.[7] In pursuit of the latter two purposes, Clausewitz set out to do two things: (i) examine the scientific basis for developing and testing strategic theory, identifying what is logically required for a theory that helps explain the real world; and (ii) demonstrate how theory works in practice – not directly by providing rules for the commander to follow but indirectly by educating his mind and assisting his judgement.

Developing strategic theory

In developing strategic theory a starting point can be found in the concept of Absolute War where cause and effect are tightly linked, subject to neither friction nor political pressure. Everything occurs for reasons related to war itself.

> In the absolute form of war, where everything results from necessary causes and one action rapidly affects another, there is, if we may use the phrase, no intervening neutral void. [582]

Absolute War is thus more likely to reveal clear and enduring principles of strategy by providing 'a general point of reference'. [581] The theorist might imagine that he is operating in 'the field of the exact sciences of logic and mathematics'. [585]

But since all wars fall short of the absolute, theory must take into account what happens in practice: 'Its purpose is to demonstrate what war is in practice, not what its ideal nature ought to be'. [593] Theory, indeed, has less scope the further war moves away from its pure form:

> The more [external] factors turn war into something half-hearted, the less solid are the bases that are available to theory: essentials become rarer, and accidents multiply. [218]

The actual conduct of war 'is bound to move from the strict law of inherent necessity towards probabilities'. [91] There is thus an inevitable gap between 'between principles and actual events that cannot always be bridged by a succession of logical deductions'. [108]

The gap between the ideal and the real can be filled in some measure by laws, principles, maxims and rules. Here Clausewitz follows Immanuel Kant's *Critique of Practical Reason*, in particular the first chapter of Book I entitled 'Principles of Pure Practical Reason'.[8] At the top of the hierarchy stands a law which represents directly 'the relationship between things and their effects' and which is objectively true and valid for everyone. Law has another parallel meaning as an imperative that determines human behaviour in the form of a 'decree' or 'prohibition'. [151]

A principle is 'a law for action' but not in the sense of a fixed relationship between cause and effect. Principles exist where 'the diversity of the real world cannot be contained within the rigid form of law' and their application requires and 'allows for a greater latitude of judgment'. [151] In so far as a principle rests on underlying truths, it is objective and 'equally valid for all'. By contrast, a principle based on 'subjective considerations' (generally called a 'maxim') is valid only for the person who adopts it on the basis of their judgement and experience. [151]

The term 'rule' is often used to mean the same as principle but in another sense it allows recognition of an underlying truth from a single, relevant instance. A short cut in mathematics is a rule of this kind. Likewise in war, the deliberate exposure of troops by the enemy indicates a feint 'as a rule'. 'This manner of inferring the truth may be called a rule because one deduces the enemy's intentions from a single visible fact connected with them'. [152]

Laws, principles and rules must match and explain reality, identifying important factors and indicating the relationships between them in consistent and logical fashion.[9] Clausewitz provides two formulations:

- 'Its [theory's] scientific character consists in an attempt to investigate the essence of the phenomena of war and to indicate the links between these phenomena and the nature of their component parts.' [Preface, 61]
- 'Theory will have fulfilled its main task when it is used to analyze the constituent elements of war, to distinguish precisely what at first sight seems fused, to explain in full the properties of the means employed and to show their probable effects'. [141]

At the same time theory will demolish ideas that are confused and false. 'Theory should cast a steady light on all phenomena so that we can more easily recognize and eliminate the weeds that spring from ignorance'. [578]

The difficulties in developing strategic theory are inherent in the nature of war. First is the problem of complexity. Cause and effect are frequently far removed:

> The greater the distance between the event and the cause that we are seeking, the larger the number of other causes that have to be considered at the same time. [159]

Any significant event in war, moreover, has complex and multiple causes operating simultaneously. Every action, every decision has an impact that will 'modify their final outcome to some degree, however, slight'. [158] Small events may have large effects and vice versa, and the effects may be intended or unintended. Outcomes are probabilistic rather than deterministic. A given action does not always produce a predictable effect, a phenomenon now called non-linearity.[10] Pursuit of the chain of cause and effect requires not only complex calculations but also hypotheses about the relative weight of different causes and about possible alternative outcomes. 'A great many assumptions have to be made about things that did not actually happen but seemed possible'. [159]

Second, interaction is of the essence in strategy, adding enormously to its complexity. Theorists who view actions from one side only fall into grave error. For there is 'a continuous interaction of opposites' in war as each action by one side prompts a reaction by the other. [136] Each action and reaction changes the situation, each new situation may require changes in strategy. The possible variations in a campaign are so immense that 'the very nature of interaction is bound to make it unpredictable'. [139] As Napoleon put it, one engages the enemy and sees what follows.

Third, the friction inevitable in war militates against development of theory. Whereas in mechanics friction can often be finely calculated, in war 'tremendous friction ... is everywhere in contact with chance, and brings about effects that cannot be measured'. [120] Nor is it possible to allow for friction in war:

> The military instrument resembles a machine with tremendous friction, which unlike in mechanics, cannot be reduced to a few points, but is everywhere in contact with chance.[11]

Hence friction in war 'is a force that theory can never quite define'; 'instinct and tact' will always be required. [120]

Fourth, strategic theory must embrace human psychology since '[m]ilitary activity is never directed against material force alone; it is always aimed simultaneously at the moral forces which give it life, and the two cannot be separated'. [137] War is thus an indissoluble union of moral and material forces, 'an organic whole which, unlike a metal alloy, is inseparable by chemical processes'. [184] The problem for theory is that 'moral values can only be perceived by the inner eye, which differs in each person, and is often different in the same person at different times'. [137] Two individuals will likely assess moral factors differently, just as architects or artists disagree on the aesthetics of a building or a painting. [136] 'Unfortunately' for theory, psychological factors in war 'will not yield to academic wisdom. They cannot be classified or counted. They have to be seen or felt'. [184]

In sum theorists must understand that 'in war everything is uncertain, and calculations have to be made with variable quantities'. [136] Nor can a campaign be explained purely in terms of visible actions on the part of armies. It requires some account of the intentions of the participants, and why they formed those intentions. Decisions of the commanders, moreover, are shaped in some degree by the theories of strategy they hold. For Clausewitz the campaign is a moving target which theory can only approximate.

Kritik

Against this background, Clausewitz's approach to strategic theory is through what he calls *Kritik*. Perhaps best translated as 'critical analysis', it is a three-stage process. The first establishes historical fact i.e. 'historical research proper' which has 'nothing in common with theory' but is the raw material with which theory must work. The second is 'critical analysis proper' i.e. 'the tracing of effects back to their causes'. The final step is the evaluation of strategy – 'criticism proper, involving praise and censure'. [156] This will be considered in the next chapter.

(i) Historical research

The initial task is 'the discovery and interpretation of equivocal facts' i.e. facts open to varying interpretations. But gaining accurate knowledge of the past is problematic. Lack of information about actions and the motives behind them, Clausewitz observes, is '[n]owhere in life … so common as in war'. Details may simply go unrecorded or may be 'intentionally concealed by those in command'. [156] Clashes of opinion among senior generals are rarely mentioned in history books or memoirs since they may 'touch political interests, or they are simply forgotten, being considered as scaffolding to be demolished when the building is complete'. [112] Mere passage of time means that 'military history, like any other kind, is bound ... to lose a mass of minor elements and details that were once clear'. The historical record 'loses some element of life and color, like a picture that gradually fades and darkens'. [173] Nor can memoirs be relied upon. Referring to Napoleon's account of the campaign of 1796, written 15–20 years after the event, Clausewitz concluded that it is 'a sad necessity for us not to accept fully the commander's evaluation of his own decisions'.[12]

It is one thing to say that the historical record is unreliable and incomplete. It is another matter to doubt its relevance. Military theorists of the eighteenth century were often more familiar with Caesar and Vegetius, Herodotus and Thucydides, than with contemporary commanders.[13] Clausewitz, however, argued that forms of war change significantly over time, thereby limiting the material on which 'practical lessons' can be based. Consequently, '[t]he further back one goes, the less useful military history becomes, growing poorer and barer at the same time'. Indeed, '[t]he history of antiquity is without doubt the most useless and the barest of all'. [173] The penchant of many writers to refer to ancient wars, Clausewitz suggests, reeks of 'vanity and quackery' and raises doubts about their 'honesty of purpose'. [174] Similarly, armies of the Middle Ages were so specialised in character and 'so completely divorced from the rest of political and civil life' that lessons drawn from that era are of limited use. [174, 586–7]

To be of value strategic theory must look to recent military history. Only those wars beginning with the War of the Austrian Succession (1740–48), Clausewitz argues, bear 'a considerable resemblance to those of the present day'. [173] Over 75 per cent of the references to military history in *On War* are to the wars of Frederick the Great.[14] But this raises an important problem. At what level of generality is a theory of strategy intended to operate? On the one hand, as a contest between two commanders a campaign is likely display types of interaction comparable with campaigns of any era – such as surprise, pursuit or decisive battle. Strategic theory may thus draw on any reliable history. On the other hand, Clausewitz argues that each historical era, given its political, social and cultural conditions, has its 'own kind of war' and hence 'its own theory of war'. [593] New conditions may open up new possibilities in war (or close off old ones) as had occurred in his era, making war more dynamic and intense.

> Without the cautionary examples of the destructive power of war unleashed, theory would preach to deaf ears. No one would have believed possible what has now been experienced by all. [581]

Yet this may mean not that principles of strategy have changed, simply that they need to be adapted to new circumstances or that different ones apply. There is constant tension between theory aspiring to be universal and theory focusing on a given historical period Clausewitz leaned toward the latter without abandoning the former.

(ii)   Critical analysis

Once an accurate (and relevant) record of the past is established, critical analysis begins: 'the detailed presentation of a historical event, and the combination of several events, make it possible to deduce a doctrine'. [171] Yet even among campaigns in the same era, each has its particular circumstances, unique episodes and individual personalities. As Clausewitz wrote in an early essay:

> it is exactly the factors that are most important in war and strategy – specifics, pronounced singularities, and local circumstances – that best succeed in evading abstractions and scientific systems.[15]

Neverthelesss, a sufficient number of cases must be found that are sufficiently alike for general conclusions to be drawn.

The problems are apparent even at the tactical level. Clausewitz's discussion of whether the placement of cavalry in relation to infantry affects the outcome of a battle is illustrative. It is insufficient to cite a few defeats where the cavalry was placed on the flanks and a few victories where the cavalry was placed behind the infantry. This is 'clearly a dangerous expedient' since a number of counter-examples can easily be adduced. One must clearly consider cases where, say, cavalry was placed in line with the infantry and victory still achieved. [172]

At the strategic level, matters are even more complex as Clausewitz's discussion of the separate advances by Blücher and Schwarzenberg into France in 1814 and Napoleon's response demonstrates. [162–4] The original decision of the allies to advance with divided forces, he argues, was a 'mistake' even though the campaign eventually proved successful. Napoleon was widely praised for moving his forces rapidly and defeating Blücher and Schwarzenberg in turn. Yet Clausewitz suggests that Napoleon could have halted the allies altogether if he had 'gone on hammering Blücher and pursued him back to the Rhine'. [162] To argue the folly of dividing forces despite its ultimate success, Clausewitz has to show that the strategy might have been defeated. [163] Inevitably this speculative argument turns on certain assumptions and propositions. Even if he is right in this case, moreover, it is only one example, and further examples would be needed to reach a convincing principle of strategy.

This points to fundamental methodological problems for Clausewitz in using history not merely as a source of facts but also as a laboratory in which to develop and test propositions.[16] First, the researcher looking at history may already hold a number of theories and, consciously or unconsciously, simply find evidence to support those theories. Clausewitz is aware of this problem in others but believes he is able to avoid it, claiming that principles are not only derived from history but 'checked against it'. [144] Second, even the most uncommitted theorist who discovers a number of examples of a particular proposition may be doing little more than demonstrating that a hypothesis is plausible. It is never clear whether historical examples are simply illustrating an existing proposition or demonstrating a contested one. The approach of studying a number of cases is always open to the possibility that alternative theories could emerge if different instances were studied.

Clausewitz recognises this when he admits that exceptions are always possible in strategic theory. Aware of the methodological trap, he falls back on the need for judgement in applying strategic theory. What he says of complex defensive campaigns where no decision is sought applies equally well to strategy in general:

> While there may be no system, and no mechanical way of recognizing the truth, truth does exist. To recognize it one generally needs seasoned judgment and an instinct born of long experience. While history may yield no formula, it does provide an *exercise for judgment* here as everywhere else. [517]

Yet the judgement needed to understand and apply strategic principles must itself be based on some theoretical concepts. What alternative is there? The general exercising judgement might claim to rely on experience but in the last analysis this amounts to no more than internalised general propositions about strategy – and is perhaps less reliable for not being exposed to the light of day. If judgement involves the use of theory at least in some measure, we are using theory to test theory.

Perhaps the theorist can rely on genius to point in the right direction: 'what genius does is the best rule, and theory can do no better than show how and why this should be the case'. [136] But this still leaves the problem of explaining why genius works, how its actions match – or do not match – broader propositions. Without some firm theoretical ground from which to start, theory is simply repeating its own assumptions.

Realising there is a problem, Clausewitz adopts an essentially pragmatic position: 'in the art of war experience counts more than any amount of abstract truths'. [164] The best theory is what works best:

> Still, the empirical sciences, the theory of the art of war included, cannot always back their conclusions with historical proofs. The sheer range to be covered would often rule this out; and, apart from that, it might be difficult to point to actual experience on every detail. If, in warfare, a certain means turns out to be highly effective, it will be used again; it will be copied by others and become fashionable; and so, backed by experience, it passes into general use and is included in theory. Theory is content to refer to experience in general to indicate the origin of the method, but not to prove it. [171]

History might 'provide the best kind of proof in the empirical sciences', particularly in the case of war. [170] But it is not irrefutable proof since strategy admits no such thing. We are left with propositions based on experience, common sense and some understanding of their inner workings – not laws, but at best principles, rules and maxims of provisional validity.

What Clausewitz is doing is not searching for scientific propositions but emphasizing the importance of understanding military history. This is not in order to confirm or derive theory. On the contrary, Clausewitz suggests that the role of theory is to help comprehend history.[17] In reading history we will have some broad principles of strategy in mind which will help us understand what happened. For Clausewitz, in other words, theory 'neither summarised nor distilled history, but complemented it'.[18] In the actual conduct of war theory engages not with the past but with the present. What is important to the general is that he should understand from history the nature and limitations of the strategic theory he is employing.

Conclusion

The relationship between history and theory is at the heart of Clausewitz's epistemology of strategy. He is convincing in his discussion of the weaknesses of much strategic theory. Evidence must be selected and events identified that are properly comparable. Propositions must be put forward that are neither too general nor too specific. Similarities must not be overdrawn since generals never conduct the same campaign twice. Differences in the nature of warfare, in armies and in political purpose make each war distinctive. Yet if each war or campaign were genuinely unique, no lesson could ever be taken from one to another. Nor could wars of one era be of any relevance to subsequent eras.

Jomini remarked caustically that *On War* had dismissed the possibility of a theory of war and then gone on to present one.[19] It is fairer to say that Clausewitz asserted the possibility of theory and went on to emphasise the difficulties of achieving it. He recognises that a gap between reality and theory will inevitably exist for a variety of reasons: the complexity of war, reciprocal action between belligerents, the fusion of material and moral elements, and the roles of friction and chance. Strategy is thus more speculative than definitive. As well as studying actual events, the theorist must pursue in the mind battles that were not fought and strategies not followed. The value of strategic theory, Clausewitz concludes, ultimately rests on judgement and expertise.

Definitive propositions about strategy thus appear beyond reach – even given accurate knowledge of the past, relevance to contemporary conditions, and identification of numerous comparable cases. In discussing defence of a theatre where no decision is sought, Clausewitz concedes the point: 'We admit, in short, that in this chapter we cannot formulate any principles, rules, or methods: history does not provide a basis for them'. [516] Only in pure war itself can strategic theory find laws and necessity. *On War* therefore does not offer a substantive, clear and fully developed strategic theory – merely a few general propositions. Those that it offers, moreover, illustrate the dilemma facing any theory of strategy.

Clausewitz's achievement is of a different kind. Until *On War* the character of strategy as an activity was largely neglected. His contribution is, first, to analyse the nature of strategic action and its relationship to tactical and political levels, and to do so with greater clarity than many other thinkers before and since. His identification of the characteristics of strategy – friction, uncertainty, reciprocity, the role of theory and so on – has not been surpassed. Though wars incorporate the spirit of their historical era and each takes on unique character-istics, there exists nonetheless a universal element in war: common and enduring features that escape change and must not be lost from view.[20] For Clausewitz this is the idea of war as contest. It allows for broad principles of strategy to be identified which are relevant across the ages but which take a form shaped by the prevailing character of war in a given era.

Second, Clausewitz tackles some of the epistemological problems that face any attempt to develop a useful theory of military strategy, or for that matter in any field of human endeavour. His qualified success derives from his knowledge of historical method, his accurate under-standing of practical strategy and his own analytical skills. The methodology he proposed yielded solid advances less in the *content* of strategic theory than in the *process* by which to develop it, in particular his demonstration of some of the limitations of that process.[21] As Clausewitz observed in *Strategic Critique of the Campaign of 1814 in France*: 'Not what we have argued but the manner in which we have argued may, we believe, benefit theory'.[22] The task, he concedes, ulti-mately comes down to judgement not science.

Finally, Clausewitz explores not only the relationship between theory and history but that between theory and practice. If strategic theory requires judgement, creativity, inspiration and intellect, it is important to understand how it functions in practice.

15
Praxis

'Theory ... can give the mind insight into the great mass of phenomena and of their relationships, then leave it free to rise into the higher realms of action'. [578]

If Clausewitz's work has any claim to be philosophical, it derives from his attempt to understand the relationship between theory and praxis.[1] Where theory seeks to connect cause and effect in the mind, praxis endeavours to link means and ends in the real world. Where theory deals in categories of cases, praxis focuses on the case in hand. Where theory draws on the practice of the past, praxis may not employ theory at all. Indeed, one might imagine theory and praxis entirely separate. 'Pure theory' would consist of scientific laws applicable to all wars. 'Pure praxis' would mean wars conducted with no conscious or unconscious reliance on theory by the commander – possible only if war is unthinking ritual or sheer passion. In reality, as Clausewitz puts it, '[n]o activity of the human mind is possible without a certain stock of ideas; for the most part these are not innate but acquired, and constitute a man's knowledge'. [145] Strategy, in short, cannot be divorced from ideas and theories in the mind of the commander.

Clausewitz emphasised the constant interaction between theory and practice, regarding the boundary between them as in permanent flux.[2] Theory must be tested against reality – either by applying it to history or by applying it in practice. The latter is the realm of praxis where ideas drawn from the past are tried in the present. Theory influences praxis by offering ideas about how the real world works. In turn, praxis in both past and present provides raw material that can be used to modify existing theories or develop new ones. Theory which is not or cannot be tested against reality is liable to become speculative and unfruitful.[3] In war above all theory must not stray too far from reality:

> Just as some plants bear fruit only if they don't shoot up too high, so in the practical arts the leaves and flowers of theory must be pruned and the plant kept close to its proper soil – experience. [Preface, 61]

Theory and practice, in other words, must never be in contradiction.

Clausewitz's examination of theory and praxis touches on issues found not only in the military sphere but in other fields of endeavour. A central question is what actually occurs in the mind of those making decisions. In the case of strategy Clausewitz distinguishes a general's actual reasoning (why he acted as he did) from judgement by an observer of the rationality or otherwise of his action.[4] The former explains reasons for action, the latter is the basis for evaluation. A second question is whether the conduct of strategy can be regarded as an art or a science – or both, or neither? Third is the problem of how the commander's mind can be prepared for such an activity. Fourth is the relationship between military genius and the theory of war: does the outstanding commander observe or overthrow established principles? Finally, Clausewitz examines the question whether and how generalship can be evaluated – the final stage of *Kritik*. Are there standards by which can we deem this general good, that general bad?

Decisions in war

In almost any art or profession outside the military 'a man can work with truths he has learned from musty books, but which have no life or meaning for him'. [147] The general, by contrast, faces an opponent intent on causing him harm and knows the consequences of failure for himself, his army and his country. With few certainties upon which to rely it is not surprising that commanders often look for simple recipes for success, fall back on routine or lapse into inaction. 'Strength of mind' is needed, but on what basis should the commander employ the knowledge and judgement he possesses?

First, theory works indirectly rather than directly. As Clausewitz stresses, it cannot instruct the commander how to achieve results, nor inspire him to action and decision; rather, it enables him to think more clearly about the situation and the choices open to him. 'Theory exists so that one need not start afresh each time sorting out the material and plowing through it, but will find it ready to hand and in good order'. It provides 'a thinking man with a frame of reference'. [141]

Second, military strategy relies on simple propositions, requiring neither immense or detailed knowledge. Centre of gravity, the strength of the defence, the effects of friction, the relationship between important elements of war are neither abstruse nor complex, but simply part of the commander's intellectual stock-in-trade. 'Knowledge in war *is very simple*, being concerned with so few subjects, and only with their final results at that'. [146] Theory will be simple though its successful application is not.

Third, theory leads to 'close *acquaintance*' with war and, once applied to actual experience, to 'thorough *familiarity*' with it. The greater this acquaintance and familiarity, the more the commander's knowledge 'proceeds from the objective form of a science to the subjective form of a skill'. [141] This knowledge should be 'so absorbed into the mind that it almost ceases to exist in a separate, objective way'. The commander should 'carry the whole intellectual apparatus of his knowledge within him' so that his decisions are natural and intuitive. [147]

Finally, though it may be unconsciously applied, theory can only be developed through judgement and experience.

> This type of knowledge cannot be forcibly produced by an apparatus of scientific formulas and mechanics; it can only be gained through a talent for judgment, and by the application of accurate judgment to the observation of man and matter. [146]

Judgement is necessary because no principles can be laid down which do not have exceptions. Competent commanders never *forget* an established principle but must be prepared to *override* even the apparently most important one.[5] Theory, moreover, constantly develops in the practice of war. The good commander continually reassesses principles he has drawn from the past and is always seeking ideas for the future.

What happens in the mind of the general who reaches a sound decision Clausewitz calls 'the hidden processes of intuitive judgment'. [389] This process is neither easily understood by the outside observer, nor easily explained by the practitioner. Reason and knowledge certainly play a part, but qualities such as intuition and inspiration, judgement and genius, character and experience are also present. The conduct of strategy is an exercise of the human mind; its inner workings are only as knowable as the mind itself.

Art or science?

Does strategy resemble more an art or a science? For Clausewitz science engages in analysis and discovery for its own sake, seeking no particular effect – 'a goal would be nothing more than a pre-conceived opinion, which is entirely alien to science'.[6] For this reason the term 'science', he believed, 'should be kept for disciplines such as mathematics or astronomy' where laws can be identified that confidently predict a particular effect in given circumstances. [148] Arts, on the other hand, usually intend to produce an effect, whether among listeners, readers or viewers, but they lack 'sufficient laws and rules of their own' linking cause and effect. Attempts to formulate such laws have proven 'too limited and one-sided', being constantly 'swept away by the currents of opinion, emotion and custom'. [149]

Yet science and art are never totally divorced in praxis, a view Clausewitz shared with the Enlightenment.[7] Every art requires some measure of scientific knowledge which is essentially mechanical and open to the formulation of laws – such as an architect's calculations of the strength of a building. At the same time, 'no science can exist without some element of art'. [148] Science deals with hypotheses formed by the mind, and hence requires creativity and experience. For Clausewitz 'perception by the mind is already a judgment and therefore an art'. [148] Different activities naturally contain different combinations of science and art.

War is distinctly scientific in areas such as artillery and fortifications, and to some extent logistics and movements, where established formulae can be applied. Tactics and – up to a point – strategy are also susceptible to scientific analysis into cause and effect. But campaign strategy always has a powerful creative element. It applies ideas in situations lacking clear precedents and in often unique circumstances. Like a painter, a general seeks effects on the human mind by using materials with which he is familiar, to create a significantly new outcome. Unlike painting, however, art deals primarily in inanimate objects – paint, musical instruments, words – while war works with human materials – soldiers with all their strengths and frailties. War, moreover, involves an opponent actively seeking to prevent the desired result. 'In war, the will is directed at an animate object that *reacts*'. [149] Those who view paintings may criticise them stridently, but this is not the same kind of resistance encountered by a general.

Clausewitz concludes that war, while sharing elements of both, is 'strictly speaking neither an art nor a science' though both terms are commonly used. If a choice must be made, 'art of war' is preferred to 'science of war'. [149] War is closer to art because of its element of human judgement:

> War is not like a field of wheat, which, without regard to the individual stalk, may be mown more or less efficiently depending on the quality of the scythe; it is like a stand of mature trees in which the axe has to be used judiciously according to the characteristics and development of each individual trunk. [153]

The commander exercises 'an art in the broadest meaning of the term – the faculty of using judgment to detect the most important and decisive elements in the vast array of facts and situations'. [585]

Learning strategy

While strategic principles may be simple, it is not easy to acquire the necessary knowledge. It is certainly not a matter of learning reams of factual material. As early as 1804 Clausewitz criticised military writers who drew up long lists of disciplines – map-making, mathematics, geography, siegecraft and so on – which the general was expected to master.[8] Simply learning of masses of detail could in fact be distinctly 'harmful'. [145] What the commander needs is broad rather than detailed knowledge, a practical rather than professorial understanding of a small number of abstract principles. Such knowledge cannot be quickly taught or learned.

In his youth, Clausewitz admitted, he was attracted by theoretical systems promising to make the student a strategist in a few hours and allow him to pass judgement on great generals. But this was like a child learning rules in school he does not really understand.[9] The very idea that strategic skills could be taught directly – one of the principal aspirations of the Enlightenment – was anathema to Clausewitz.[10] In his view the best teachers were those able to stimulate their pupils to analyse war for themselves. There is a similarity between the military theorist and the swimming teacher

> who makes his pupils practice motions on land that are meant to be performed in water. To those who are not thinking of swimming the motions will appear grotesque and exaggerated. [120]

While nothing can substitute for actually swimming, the student can at least gain some idea of the strokes required before plunging in. The teacher, of course, should have first-hand experience, whether of war or swimming: 'theorists who have never swum, or who have not learned to generalize from experience, are impractical and even ridiculous'. [120]

Education is not a matter of transmitting a fixed body of knowledge but of developing the student's capacity to understand the world and to examine principles for himself. The 'wise teacher guides and stimulates a young man's intellectual development, but is careful not to lead him by the hand for the rest of his life'. Theory is meant 'to educate the mind of the future commander, or, more accurately, to guide him in his self-education'. No doubt recalling his own experience, Clausewitz thought learning strategy to be about study, not doctrine. [141] In that most gregarious of groups – the officer corps – solitary study has often marked the careers of successful generals. And it is doubtful, Clausewitz observes ironically, that they had the advantage of a formal military education.[11]

Military genius

Does the military genius who seems to conduct campaigns with great facility and frequent success simply apply established principles of strategy with consummate skill as an early strand of Enlightenment thinking argued? Or does he break existing rules, perhaps in the process making new ones? By the turn of the century, the Enlightenment, and with it much military thought, had come to stress the freedom and creativity displayed by genius more than its subordination to principles. Clausewitz found difficulty with both approaches.

Following ideas in the theory of art in the late eighteenth century, he emphasised that each war contains elements of novelty, chance and unpredictability. The military genius therefore must be an innovator, devising new strategies or putting old elements together in a new way.[12] 'Genius', Kant had written, 'is a talent for producing that for which no definite rule can be given'.[13] But Clausewitz could not grant arbitrary authority to genius. The idea of Bülow and others that a general simply ignores the rules as he sees fit had to be rejected. Whenever this appears to be the case, either the general is in error or the rules in question are not relevant to the case in hand.[14] This kind of misunderstanding tends to arise, Clausewitz argued, when theorists confine themselves to factors that can be calculated.

> Anything that could not be reached by the meager wisdom of such one-sided points of view was held to be beyond scientific control: it lay in the realm of genius, *which rises above all rules*. [136]

On such a view genius 'needs no theory' and 'no theory ought to be formulated' for it. [145] And since genius is in short supply, the great majority of military leaders must make do with second best: 'Pity the poor soldier who is supposed to crawl among these scraps of rules, not good enough for genius, which genius can ignore, or laugh at'. [136]

If genius is allowed to operate without rules, moreover, the unacceptable corollary follows that 'theory conflicts with practice'. [140] It is one thing for a commander to be unable to rely on existing principles and to have to fall back on 'his innate talent'. [140] It is another to see this as flouting old rules or creating new ones at will. Principles can certainly be broken but, if this occurs sufficiently often, they must be revised since theory and practice cannot conflict indefinitely. Similarly, if new principles are easily created by the actions of a military genius, they belong to the occasion and lack continuing validity. The principles of war must not be reduced to the plaything of genius.[15] The military genius in Clausewitz's view adopts and adapts theory to the occasion, changing it in part and pushing it in new directions. For theory is in a constant state of flux, never finally and completely capturing reality.

Evaluation of military commanders

The third stage of *Kritik* is 'the investigation and evaluation of means employed'. [156] The purpose of evaluating commanders, however, is less to allocate praise and blame than to discover what actually occurred: 'in war more than elsewhere criticism exists only to recognize the truth, not to act as judge'.[16] But the truth about a commander's action, Clausewitz concedes, will usually lead to blame and praise.

> To discover why a campaign failed is not the same thing as to criticize it; but if we go on and show that the causes could and should have been seen and acted on, we assume the role of critic, and set ourselves up above the general. [627]

How, then, is the talent of a general to be assessed?

Merely winning or losing a campaign is no real measure of ability. 'It is legitimate to judge an event by its outcome', Clausewitz says, but 'a judgment based on the result alone must not be passed off as human wisdom'. For one thing, it leads to the illogical situation whereby the same strategy may be either a stroke of genius or an abject failure. As Clausewitz points out:

> Anyone who asserts that [Napoleon's] campaign of 1812 was an absurdity because of its enormous failure but who would have called it a superb idea if it had worked, shows complete lack of judgment. [627]

Again, one general may triumph through luck or possession of overwhelming force, another may fail in impossible circumstances. Nevertheless, we are reluctant to recognise talent in a commander who never wins a campaign. For there is, as Clausewitz put it, 'an obscure sense of some delicate link, invisible to the mind's eye, between success and the commander's genius'. [167]

The Russian campaign illustrates a further problem – judging the commander as opposed to the statesman who sets the objectives of the campaign. Napoleon was both but the distinction is useful in evaluating his actions. Reluctant to criticise Napoleon's political ambitions, Clausewitz is more forthright in judging him as general. The loss of more than half of the French Army was not in itself a sign of military ineptitude. Such losses were to be expected given the extraordinary scale of the enterprise. [629] But Napoleon made obvious mistakes in 'being late in starting the campaign, in the lives he squandered by his tactics, his neglect of matters of supply and of his line of retreat'. [628] Staying too long in Moscow was more political misjudgement of the Tsar's reaction than poor generalship.

Clausewitz found other faults in Napoleon as general, including at Waterloo. [159–62; 252] Though they may be disputed, these judgements demonstrate Clausewitz's insistence that *Kritik* must not simply identify faults but also propose alternative courses of action open to the commander:

> Critical analysis is not just an evaluation of the means actually employed, but of all *possible means* – which first have to be formulated, that is, invented. One can, after all, not condemn a method without being able to suggest a better alternative. [161]

Criticism, like strategy itself, is a creative endeavour since the options a general might have taken must first be imagined and then argued through to their conclusion. Mere assertions of better alternatives without proof are of no value. 'The whole literature on war is full of this kind of thing'. [163]

Good critical analysis, as Clausewitz recognised, is no easy task and is itself equivocal. First, in seeking historical details of a campaign, not all relevant facts will be available. The critic 'will always lack much that was present in the mind of the commander', particularly the 'mass of minor circumstances that may have influenced his decision'. [164] Nor can the critic 'shut off his superfluous knowledge', especially his greater information about the origins and course of the campaign and his awareness of the outcome. [165] The critic will always have both less knowledge and more than the commander.

Second, an important consequence of the unpredictability of strategic interaction must be acknowledged. In a given decision the level of risk which a commander is prepared to take may be critical, and he will be influenced by factors such as his own boldness and the political context in which he operates. To avoid risk is not necessarily a sound principle of strategy so that it is misleading for a critic to 'habitually prefer the course that involves the least un-certainty'. [167]

This leads to a highly problematic element in the passing of judge-ment on a general's decisions in that the critic himself must make use of strategic theory. If a useable and accepted theory exists, the critic is entitled to rely on it to support his judgement against that of the commander in question.

> ... a working theory is an essential basis for criticism. Without such a theory it is generally impossible for criticism to reach that point at which it becomes truly instructive – when its arguments are con-vincing and cannot be refuted. [157]

But theory stands in the same relation to the critic as it does to the commander. It is never totally clear, automatic in its application, or absolute in its conclusions. In judging strategy the 'critic should never use the results of theory as laws and standards, but only – as the soldier does – as *aids to judgment*'. [158] The critic cannot 'check a great com-mander's solution to a problem as if it were a sum in arithmetic'. [165] As Clausewitz put it in an early essay, 'one must not judge generals by mere reason alone'.[17] In the end *Kritik* is only as good as the military theory employed and as good as the judgement of the person undertaking the *Kritik*.

Evaluating one general naturally leads to the question whether he can be adjudged in any sense 'better' than another.[18] Comparison of this kind compounds the difficulties. It requires evaluation of at least two generals as well as criteria for measuring one against the other. Even for contemporaries in the same war, complex variables enter the picture. One theatre of war presents different conditions and different opponents from another; the same theatre differs over time. Comparison across historical eras is still more hazardous – even of Frederick the Great and Napoleon who lived only decades apart. [331] Not even Napoleon's extraordinary military achievements, Clausewitz believed, could provide a standard for all time as Jomini suggested.[19] His campaigns might in future come to 'be considered as brutalities, almost blunders'. [260] Clausewitz can only conclude that 'the events of every age must be judged in the light of its own peculiarities'. [593]

Perhaps the qualities of character and intellect in the commander emphasised by Clausewitz – such as determination, boldness and *coup d'oeil* – will provide a measure. Such traits are usually more evident in great commanders than in lesser but they are difficult to assess and are found in different combinations in commanders. Clausewitz eschews such an approach but does allude to another possible criterion for comparison: 'Only the man who can achieve great results with limited means has really hit the mark'. [573] Frederick the Great is commended more than once for combining increased vigour in his strategy with 'wise limitation in objectives'. [283] Any general who wins great victories with minimal resources is surely to be admired. But by what standards do we judge paucity of resources and greatness of victories? And the attributes of the commander may count for less than the political direction of the war. Frederick's greatness was perhaps more as a statesman than as a general.

Theory's influence on praxis

Theory and praxis are in constant interaction in the mind of the commander. Theory never solidifies into a rigid structure on which to base decisions, but remains an open system of ideas to be employed as the general deems appropriate. What determines appropriateness cannot be laid down. It is neither mere success, nor conformity with existing principles, nor a summary made after the event of the rules that were followed. A combination of science and art, theory is carried 'live' in the mind of the commander.[20] In reality, theory influences praxis less by proclaiming principles to be followed than by testing ideas in the real world through the actions of the general. As Clausewitz puts it, 'in the art of war experience counts more than any amount of abstract truths'. [164]

Any approach to praxis will want to know how to judge the skill of a commander. Clausewitz's process of *Kritik* provides a framework for praise and censure, though this function is less important than identifying actual cause and effect. While it avoids the trap of judgement by results, it cannot overcome the fundamental problem that the evaluation of commanders requires not only the use of strategic theory but also judgement in its application. *Kritik* is a logical approach to the assessment of strategy – and offers a more scientific approach than most of Clausewitz's contemporaries – but it cannot go beyond the limits of theory itself or beyond reliance on the judgement of the critic himself. In the end Clausewitz's *Kritik* is as much an analysis of methodological problems as a solution to them. If it is ultimately unconvincing, it is nonetheless instructive.

Clausewitz's conception of the theory and praxis of war represents a major, if qualified, advance in understanding over the primitive and artificial ideas of many earlier thinkers. It rescued the study of war from those who would reduce it to a scientific exercise and those who saw it as a stage for heroes and geniuses answering to no theory. In the end Clausewitz does more to advance the study of command and leadership than of strategy itself.[21] His development of the idea of praxis, moreover, had value not only in understanding war but in 'its implications for social science in general'.[22] While Clausewitz did not resolve fundamental epistemological problems, he confronted them squarely. It is also fair to say that none of his successors have fully succeeded either.

Part VII
The Political Context

16
Politics and the State

> 'It follows that the transformation of the art of war resulted from
> the transformation of politics'. [610]

On War pays little attention to the political context in which force is
used. For some critics this is a major defect, leaving the work no more
than an abstract 'examination of technique'.[1] Two points can be made
in Clausewitz's defence. First, he focused on the linkages between war
and politics.[2] Discussion of political purposes would distract from his
central theme and cause his work to date quickly. Second, Clausewitz
did have a broad concept of politics which emerges more clearly in
writings other than *On War*. His doctrine was realism, a worldview
by no means original or beyond criticism but one sufficient for his
purposes.

For Clausewitz, quite simply, it is the state around which war and
politics revolve. Above all, the state provides security against external
threats. 'The main notion underlying the state', he wrote to Gneisenau,
'is defense against the external enemy. All else can be, strictly speaking,
regarded as *faux frais*'.[3] This dogma dictates certain principles both in
foreign policy and in internal politics, namely a political and social
system able to create an inner vitality and conduct an energetic external policy. The development of modern, centralised states is thus
the key to understanding European history, including warfare between
them.

Nation and state

Clausewitz's ideas on the origin of the state developed early. In his
essay of 1807 on the French and the Germans he took as given a

natural division of humanity into cultural nations, each with unique qualities and characteristics.[4] Not surprisingly he found more to admire in the Prussian character than in the French but his key point was that every nation is a genuine community bound by psychological and historical ties. It is not some mystical, transcendent entity, as certain philosophers and romantics believed, but a real human group enjoying a degree of unity, a common sense of purpose and the right to develop and to defend itself.

The 'life-principle' of a nation, Clausewitz argued, is to become a state.[5] But not every nation achieves statehood. Those that do not fight for independence deservedly remain little more than slaves.[6] Even Italians and Germans had so far been unable to unite and both remained 'political fossils'.[7] Clausewitz supported unification of the German people who, though lacking national consciousness, still shared a distinct national character. But he was critical of the sentimental aspirations for unity in his time, dismissing popular agitation in the early 1820s as 'illusory' and 'childish'.[8] Rivalry was too strong among the German princes clinging to their sovereignty. Unification was possible only by force of arms 'when one state subdues all others' but there was no certainty about how or even whether it would occur.[9]

For the nation statehood is the only way it can fully express its natural identity and realise its political and moral aspirations. In turn, the state derives vitality and energy from the nation. The state must also be active since inactivity is a recipe for decline. Generations, Clausewitz stated, foreshadowing Marx, 'realize their value only in the work accomplished through them ... they do not exist to observe the world'.[10] But no state can be confident of its ultimate destiny: 'we so often see nations and states achieve unity and independence, only to disappear once again'.[11]

Historical development of the state

One of the most important factors shaping the political life of a state is the rise and decline of social classes which impact on the life of citizens and on the character of armies and war. Underpinning *On War* is Clausewitz's thesis that the nature of war in a given era reflects long-term social and political change within the state. Only from this perspective can the transformation of war in Europe after the French Revolution be understood.

Most warfare in history, Clausewitz argues, has been small scale since few societies possess sufficient wealth to maintain large armies. A notable exception, Rome could afford to maintain numerous legions for several centuries. Alexander the Great was also exceptional through his genius in organising forces and his determination to conquer. The political entities in Europe in the Middle Ages conformed to the general pattern, many of them little more than an 'agglomeration of loosely associated forces'. [588] War was mostly ill-organised, difficult to sustain and resembled more a personal contest among rulers than a clash of state interests. The principal source of fighting power was the knight. When the monarch needed arms nobles rendered personal service in return for status, privilege and political influence. They might enlist peasants as foot soldiers but these were always 'an inconsequential part of the army'.[12] The aristocrat thus acquired a seemingly indispensable role in the defence of the state on which his position and way of life depended.

Over time, however, independent and expanding sources of income allowed monarchs to escape reliance on feudal service. They could now create a standing military force under their control on the basis of 'money and recruitment'. [588] On the battlefield gunpowder challenged the knightly warrior while large and skilful companies of foot soldiers, often mercenaries of various nationalities, undermined the dominance of the aristocratic cavalry. The feudal system – under which the nobility furnished troops as 'a kind of tribute, a human tax' – fell into disuse. [330] Though aristocrats retained rights of patronage and exemption from taxes, power steadily accrued to the monarch.

By the end of the seventeenth century the more advanced states had achieved 'complete internal unity' as the monarch centralised authority, developed a bureaucracy and gained a hold over nobility, church, cities, guilds and other traditional centres of power. Internal cohesion and efficient government permitted more successful states to expand their military capabilities and enhance their security. [588–9] The threefold distinction between government, army and people became firmer and the foundations of modern war were laid. National interest was coming to replace dynastic interests, and the idea grew that armies were to serve as an instrument of national policy.

No longer 'the principal defender of the country' the nobility still 'continued to display a great affinity for the profession of arms'.[13] Yet even here they came under challenge from the middle class. As trade and commerce expanded and towns grew in size, the bourgeoisie concentrated on the activity that came most naturally – increasing 'its wealth through diligence and hard work'. Technical and scientific skills that had once 'more or less belonged to the nobility' now became the property of the middle class'.[14] Growing in number, increasingly equipped with education and filled with ambition, the bourgeoisie looked for a greater role in affairs of state, including the army. By the eighteenth century the middle class could aspire to military careers and were becoming highly valuable, even indispensable, in technical fields such as engineering and artillery.

The poor and labouring classes were also entering the equation. They, too, could accumulate wealth since they 'always contribute somewhat more to the economy than they consume'.[15] They also gained influence as their 'theoretical rights and claims ... gradually emerged from the mists'.[16] Political thinkers began to advocate the rights of the masses in ways that Clausewitz found disturbing:

> These philosophers were neither accustomed nor inclined to view social conditions as a product of historical forces; they proceeded from the abstract concept of a social contract and therefore found only unspeakable injustice and corruption everywhere. Thus they inflamed people's passions.[17]

By one route or another peasant and town worker were becoming important to the economy and to the state.

In France tension among the classes reached such a point that 'a resolution in one form or another became necessary, either gradually through voluntary changes or suddenly by force'.[18] The revolution was thus no accidental phenomenon but arose from fundamental causes:

> Social relationships changed because the different estates progressed along different paths, and they did so because they embodied different principles.[19]

This, together with the manifest abuse, waste and disorganisation in government administration, constituted the two principal causes of the Revolution in France in Clausewitz's view. Privilege and excess might have been remedied, and the army might have stayed loyal to the king. But the underlying cause was failure to adapt to historical trends in France's social structure.[20] The result was that France discovered not only radical political forms but new ways of tapping sources of military power.

Politics after the revolution

Prussia, Clausewitz argued, was less affected than most countries by revolutionary tensions. Abuse of power and excesses had been fewer, and Prussia's monarchs – save for the 'spendthrifts' Frederick I and Frederick William II – had been frugal and responsible. All this created a strong sense of 'internal well-being' and ensured 'the complete domestic peace that prevailed in Germany during the revolutionary wars'.[21] But Prussia could not ignore the French example. Its authoritarian political system and stratified society needed to change in order to broaden the basis of government. Rising social and political forces had to be accommodated without jeopardising stability. The talents of all citizens had to be tapped without opening the path to revolution. Only by these means, Clausewitz and the reformers believed, could Prussia regain its power and ensure its independence.

The disaster at Jena finally shattered any faith in an absolutist state under an enlightened ruler. But the politics of change were not simple. The state, as Clausewitz put it, was not a machine able to drill the citizen for its own purposes. Prussia had to embrace reform – but from above, not below. Three tasks were essential:

- encouraging the population to take a proper interest and an active role in affairs of state;
- reducing or eliminating the privileges of class and other barriers to efficiency and the effective use of citizens' talents; and
- adapting existing institutions, both political and military.

It would not be easy. Prussia was not yet a modern, integrated state. Deep-rooted provincialism still resisted central power. Town government, commercial guilds and the church retained authority and influence, often in opposition to central government. Also troubling was cosmopolitanism inspired by admiration for French philosophy, culture and fashion. Such attitudes cut across the sense of national identity which was based on what Clausewitz called 'healthy prejudices'.[22]

Engaging the wider population in public affairs was particularly problematic. Always suspicious of the motivations and reliability of the masses, Clausewitz wrote in 1807 that a subject's love for his prince is usually nothing more than crude, satisfied interest. For this reason Machiavelli had rightly argued that a prince who cannot inspire both love and fear among his subjects should prefer the latter.[23] Moreover, the emotions of the populace, once given vent, are liable to 'swing back and forth' – for Clausewitz this was 'precisely the problem'.[24]

The middle and upper classes were more reliable partners in national policy since they held a substantial stake in the nation's affairs. But they were often reluctant to commit themselves to the interests of the state, preferring private pursuits or seeking profit from business. Clausewitz agreed with Scharnhorst that 'most people can be floated off the sandbank of their prejudices only by imperceptible levers'.[25] Irresponsible and inflammatory elements were also liable to cause trouble. Clausewitz never had a high opinion of journalists, academics and the like as his comment on public opinion towards France in 1812 reveals: 'We are speaking here of real public concern, not the crackpot opinions of coffeehouse newspaper readers'.[26]

Clausewitz believed the middle and upper classes needed to be educated in political realities and to 'grasp the issues comprehensively'.[27] It was a matter of demonstrating the nation's policies and interests through public discussion and debate. 'If the subject is to be properly linked with the state, he must understand its main interests'.[28] Properly encouraged, public opinion in this limited sense could provide valuable support for government in peace and war. Without it, policy would be more difficult. After 1792, for example, 'public interest in the war [against France] and its objectives faded away'.[29] In war, opinion might also be resentful 'at the fate of the abandoned areas' in the event of a withdrawal though Clausewitz doubted the ability of the people to 'tell the difference between a planned retreat and a backward stumble'. [471]

The second major problem in Prussian society was that of privilege. Clausewitz believed some measure of privilege essential to encourage various classes to support the state. He criticised privilege in France before 1789 because it had become dysfunctional, not because he was a liberal. Prussia needed to remove social and legal barriers hindering the advancement of individual talent – for the benefit of the individual in the first instance but ultimately to assist the state.[30] Reform, already under way before 1806, proceeded with some success: peasants were permitted to own land, equality before the law was established, the nobility lost exemption from taxes and the burden of taxation was more fairly spread, the middle class was given access to all offices of state, and public education supported.[31] But it was a process led by and under the control of the state, always liable to be slowed or halted by conservative elements as occurred after 1809 and 1815.

The third challenge was to create effective political institutions. Calm failed to return after 1815, Clausewitz argued, because 'a part of educated society had set itself two new goals: one was the unity of the German people; the other, constitutions'.[32] He considered both unrealistic. Simplistic political aims and a belief that political agitation could bring about new political institutions were a source of trouble – not because they were wrong in themselves but because they were futile and lacked a solid base. Political systems, he believed, must reflect genuine interests in the community, not abstract doctrines such as democracy or equality.

Clausewitz's actual ideas on internal political arrangements were piecemeal. He did not advocate a purely autocratic form of government for it had clearly failed Prussia in 1806. Nonetheless, he looked to a hereditary monarchy like Prussia's that enjoyed a natural authority and had successfully promoted the nation's interests for much of its history – as opposed to a usurper like Napoleon.[33] The best arrangement in Clausewitz's view was a strong and enterprising king, supported by a cabinet of advisers and ministers. These would not be responsible to a parliament but councillors who support the monarch by keeping aristocratic pretensions in check, promoting moderate reform at home and contributing to wise and consistent foreign policy.[34] But once the monarch loses trust in these advisers and ministers, the latter cease to be influential.[35] It becomes easy for the ruler to prevaricate like Frederick William III before the disaster of Jena. In some circumstances, however, a strong prime minister can provide the leadership and sense of purpose lacking in a monarch.[36]

If an authoritarian system is sometimes weak and inefficient, democratic arrangements are positively dangerous. Clausewitz had no sympathy for representative government. *Agitation* was particularly hostile, describing the idea of popular participation in government as 'a kind of sickness' and 'a true abnormality'.[37] There are attractions for some: 'A constitution calls innumerable petty interests into play in public life, and that in itself [is] a great impetus'. It can revitalise 'political commerce', producing 'hustle and bustle, energy and friction, fear and hope', all of which 'makes for a rich, vital political life'.[38] But popular involvement in politics creates constant turbulence in which

> everyone is constantly thinking about what the state did yesterday, is doing today, will do tomorrow, to the point where the citizen can scarcely close his eyes at night in peace.

The business of government is liable to fall into the hands of cliques with 'the mass of the people remaining spectators in the streets'.[39] It takes an outstanding leader to appeal successfully to the 'few good heads [who] still exist despite the corruption of the electorate'.[40]

Clausewitz's correspondence also reveals an intense dislike for democratic ideas. He believed public criticism of the monarchy highly destabilising and refused to sign a petition to the king concerning a promised constitution, arguing in a letter to Gneisenau in 1817 that the people should have contact with the throne only through the press or through their representatives:

> A direct contact of people and throne is dangerously democratic, and in this sense the mob that gathered before the Tuileries on 10 August [1792] does not differ from the signatories of a popular petition. Their legitimization is identical.[41]

Some of his last letters also pour scorn on liberal thinking and complain of 'factious chambers'.[42] His interest in representative assemblies was based not on any right of citizens but on the need of the state to engage citizens in its affairs.

Clausewitz explored various institutional possibilities. In 1819 he toyed with the idea of limited representative government. If the government feels isolated, then it should

> gather around it representatives of the people, elected from those who share the true interests of government and are known to the people. Let this be the government's main support, friend, and ally, as Parliament has been for a century the support of the king of England.[43]

Clausewitz understood the stability and strength inherent in a representative body such as the English Parliament (still to be transformed by the Reform Act of 1832). But he overlooked the process by which it had steadily accrued power at the expense of the monarch. This was Clausewitz's most radical proposal for political reform, and he did not repeat the idea. At most he supported a limited franchise based on residence, property and professional qualifications. A parliament chosen in this fashion, moreover, should only discuss and advise, not exercise power.

For Clausewitz international circumstances bore directly on the appropriateness of a parliament. Nations such as England or America, favoured by geography with greater external security, could more easily adopt representative assemblies. But even in favourable circumstances Clausewitz doubted this would bolster external policy:

> although one might believe that a certain steadiness, consequentiality, and security in foreign policy should naturally result from a constitution, history – unless we are very much mistaken – does not bear this out.[44]

England had in fact exercised greater power under Elizabeth I and Cromwell when freedom at home had been constrained.[45] The real problem of a popular assembly was not the policies it might favour, but its tendency to suffer deadlock and delay. It was their liberal constitutions, Clausewitz believed, that left the Dutch, Swiss and North Americans – not to speak of the Poles – unable to act decisively or exercise influence in international politics. For Prussia which lay in the middle of the European state-system, the constant external threat required a policy of 'secrecy, resolution, and diplomatic dexterity, and these are not the natural attributes of parliamentary bodies'.[46] Internal political arrangements are to be judged not against ideals but against their contribution to the security of the state.

The nature of politics

For Clausewitz the people are not a source of sovereignty or political power as proclaimed by the French and American revolutions. Politics is the concern of the few rather than the many. For him talk of 'the rights of man' ignored the realities of abuse and exploitation in France.[47] These so-called 'rights' were generalisations produced by philosophers 'whose minds are too distinguished to bother about local conditions and historical experience'.[48] Though railing against doctrinaire approaches to politics, Clausewitz saw no real threat from mere 'disembodied abstractions' like rights and duties. Such thinking amounted to no more than 'a pretentious gobbledegook of accusations'.[49] Ideology is not a force in itself but rather a dependent phenomenon which produces results only if it conforms to deeper social and political forces.[50] Political ideas carry weight and legitimacy only to the extent they reflect real and enduring interests.[51] Clausewitz's view of politics rested on respect for concrete interests and deep-seated historical processes.[52]

Clausewitz was not always content to leave ideological preoccupations to burn themselves out. His essay *Agitation* took opinion and rhetoric seriously enough to go to the trouble of ridiculing the political efforts of university students and their academic mentors. Even schoolmasters 'with a few political slogans learned in the gymnasium or the seminary' could twist impressionable minds, at least temporarily.[53] Agitation and trouble-making of this kind, though never a real danger to the state, had to be kept in check. It might also distract from necessary changes. Demonstrations and violence, such as the assassination of the conservative playwright and political writer Kotzbue in 1819, Clausewitz argued, would provoke unthinking reaction and obstruct rational reform.[54]

Politics for Clausewitz is a traffic in interests rather than opinions – 'a kind of commerce on a larger scale'. [149] The analogy is apt since commerce is largely restricted to the class of merchants and manufacturers while consumers generally remain passive. The function of the state is to manage the political market, developing policies which satisfy diverse concerns as far as possible while guarding the nation's interests:

> It can be taken as agreed that the aim of policy is to unify and reconcile all aspects of internal administration as well as of spiritual values, and whatever else the moral philosopher may care to add. [606]

Many interests are entitled to a voice, including moral and religious values. But Clausewitz's pluralism is constrained by the duty of government to protect state interests and to ensure national cohesion. As with Hegel, the state remains above the struggle between particular interests, embodying unity and serving as ultimate guardian of its political and moral ends.[55]

Policy cannot be left to the free play of domestic forces for one overriding reason. Unity within the state remains a precondition of all defence and security. Internal division is greatly to be feared, above all in time of war, since it prevents vigorous policy and can positively assist an invader. [562–3] As Clausewitz observed in relation to Napoleon's attempted conquest of Russia, only domestic disunity can bring a major European power to ruin. [627][56] Ultimately, internal politics must reflect external demands.

The ideology of the state

The state is central to Clausewitz's ideas about politics. But there is no guarantee that any particular state will be formed or will survive. Each state is responsible for its own internal order and its own defence. This requires leaders who are skilled in the conduct of both domestic politics and foreign policy. External security, above all, relies on a state's ability to mobilise and organise its citizens and their interests in a united and productive fashion. Internal politics takes its cue accordingly.

The state is certainly no vehicle for realising human progress or promoting some ideology. Politics and policies should be driven by national interests, not sentiment or doctrines such as the rights of man, constitutionalism or cosmopolitanism that distract from the goals of order and survival. Citizens had to be taught their obligations towards the state and irresponsible doctrines suppressed if they could not be safely ignored. Clausewitz was no democrat and contemplated reform in government only with caution, favouring an authoritarian system modified by strong counsellors or ministers rather than a genuinely representative body. He did not stray far from the Prussian tradition of absolutism and paternalism. Where the Anglo-Saxon tradition saw the state as the servant of the people, Clausewitz at heart regarded the state as prior to the people.[57]

It is unhelpful to place Clausewitz on the left-right political spectrum which was still to appear. His stance on an issue might coincide with conservative, authoritarian, liberal or progressive views but he can be labelled none of these. He was doctrinaire only in his opposition to doctrines – apart, of course, from realism. His focus was not on ideologies but on the processes and mechanisms of political power, and on their relationship to the fundamental interests of the state. It was this that led him to reject sectional and self-seeking interests, challenge privilege and exploitation, and criticise much conventional wisdom. Clausewitz's political ideas were also tempered by historical perspective, by recognition of diverse interests and by lack of dogmatism. This makes him free of many social and political prejudices, but does not leave him free of ideology in the broader sense – that of realism and the state.

17
External Policy

'In short, at the highest level the art of war turns into policy'. [607]

Clausewitz's belief that the requirements of external security should determine internal political arrangements was inherited from Machiavelli. This *Primat der Aussenpolitik* had been a dominant theme in Prussia from its origins. Despite population and territory far below those of major powers the country began to move into the first rank under Frederick the Great's shrewd and energetic policies. But this 'artificially elevated position' lapsed after his death as Prussia failed to respond vigorously to external challenges, above all from France. In Clausewitz's words, '[t]he energy needed for deceit and cunning, for consequential dishonesty, was lacking'.[1]

Only the ignominy of Jena and occupation by France caused Prussia to fully grasp its predicament and take action to secure its independence. After 1815, too, Prussia needed an energetic foreign policy to secure its place in the international system:

> The Prussian state, with eleven million inhabitants, stands at the same level as the great powers of Europe, which rule thirty or forty million. It lies among them in the middle of the European state system, it is envied by great and small alike because of its rapid development, and it cannot possibly maintain its position without exertions that are uncommon in other states.[2]

Prussia, Clausewitz argued, must be ready for war 'so that she can withstand the two giants who will always threaten her from East and West'.[3] It cannot rely on the goodwill of others or uncertain alliances.[4]

Though intensely concerned with Prussia, Clausewitz sought no privileges for his own country. The right to pursue security and national
interests was common to all states, including Prussia's enemies. Not
even France, Clausewitz wrote in 1803, could be blamed for standing
with its foot on Prussia's neck as it sought to extend its Empire over
the whole of Europe.[5] In one of his last essays in 1831 he recognised
that France and Poland were natural allies and that France had every
right to support Polish independence – precisely because of the threat
to Prussia.[6]

The challenge of foreign policy

At the heart of foreign policy lies the security of the state. In turn,
this rests on two elements. First is the weight and effort which a state
exerts in the international system (another mechanical analogy).
Clausewitz prefers these dynamic terms to static notions of military
strength or power. He rarely speaks of power [*Macht*] in the political
context, using it to refer to a state's potential for military action,
especially in comparing two belligerents.[7] Nor does he see the goal of
the state simply in terms of accumulating power, even military
power.[8] For Clausewitz power is important only for the political ends
it can promote.

The second element of security is a state's honour and dignity (cred-
ibility and prestige in modern terms). In an essay of 1805 Clausewitz
declared that 'the honor of the state' must be regarded as 'sacred', and
that it should prefer a noble defeat to loss of dignity.[9] Looking back
from the early 1820s Clausewitz still maintained that Prussia should
have pursued a more principled policy prior to the inevitable conflict
of 1806 – standing or falling with honour.[10] Indeed, as he observed in
On War, a nation that loses the will to fight has no right to expect
success:

> A government that after having lost a major battle, is only inter-
> ested in letting its people go back to sleep in peace as soon as poss-
> ible, and ... lacks the courage and desire to put forth a final effort ...
> did not deserve to win, and, possibly for that very reason was
> unable to. [483]

The honour of the state includes the personal dignity of the monarch
which cannot be besmirched.[11] But this does not mean he can put
private concerns and scruples before national interest.

While the broad objectives of external policy are easily proclaimed, how is policy to be determined in practice? For Clausewitz the task of foreign policy is to represent the interests found within the state: 'Policy is nothing in itself; it is simply the trustee for all these interests against the outside world'. [606] That policy, moreover, must be 'representative of all interests of the community'. [607] The word 'all' is applied to 'interests' in both quotations; and the original German refers to 'the entire community' in the latter quotation. Foreign policy is simply too important to be left to a particular class or set of interests within the state – as had occurred in pre-revolutionary France. The notion of policy as the representative or advocate [*Sachwalter*] of all interests within a state against the rest of the world may be Clausewitz's 'single brilliant insight' into the nature of politics.[12] It marks the transition from dynastic to national politics, from the state as possession of the monarch to the state as instrument for pursuing the interests of its citizens.

The reconciliation of interests within a state and the determination of national interest, however, cannot be a free or unregulated process, especially with regard to security. Clausewitz was no pluralist, content to accept the outcome of political pushing and shoving. On the contrary, he believed the state must retain control over the determination of policy, promoting the long-term interests of the state rather than the passing moods of its citizens. Two things are necessary: a strong, unified government and the application of reason – conditions increasingly met as the modern European state developed. By the end of the seventeenth century, Clausewitz observed, '[t]he executive had become completely unified and represented the state in its foreign relations' [589]. In contrast to its medieval predecessors the state had gained sufficient control over parochial and cosmopolitan forces that it could be considered 'a personified intelligence acting according to simple and logical rules'. [588]

At the same time reason is required to set a nation's specific objectives beyond security and honour and to select the most effective policies. Clausewitz subscribed to the idea of an objective national interest which it is the task of policy-makers to determine. This requires analysis of a state's situation, its means and its goals in order to reveal its true interests. Controversies over policy are in essence disputes about the correct interpretation of the interests of the state. Clausewitz seemed unaware of the problems inherent in this view. Can there not be genuine disagreement, for example, whether alliance or appeasement will best provide for security? Always confident of his own interpretation of national interest, Clausewitz sometimes failed to understand why others might take a different view.

People and war

Central to sound foreign policy is the temper of the population at large which should take a serious interest in the state's affairs, and above all its security. In the eighteenth century writers had noted that a lengthy peace causes armies to lose proficiency and fighting spirit, and the idea arose that a state needs war to restore its moral and physical strength.[13] The German movement believed that war promoted the development of civilisation, having 'an essential role in strengthening the social body'.[14] As Clausewitz put it, people might feel a sense of well-being, trade and science may flourish and individuals enjoy considerable freedom – but this is not sufficient for a 'great society' that wants to do more than 'live quietly by itself'.[15] Only through vigorous external policy and active preparation for war can a state overcome the self-interest of the individual and set in motion all the energies dormant in society.

Like Kant and Hegel, Clausewitz found in war a nobility and a challenge that rises above the ordinariness of peacetime occupations.[16]

> Today practically no means other than war will educate a people in this spirit of boldness; and it has to be a war waged under daring leadership. Nothing else will counteract the softness and the desire for ease which debase the people in times of growing prosperity and increasing trade. A people and nation can hope for a strong position in the world only if national character and familiarity with war fortify each other by continual interaction. [192]

A government that is strong and far-sighted will inculcate a military spirit into the population as a whole.[17] A genuinely national army will help create and maintain this spirit of war. In turn, a society imbued with such a spirit will fortify the resolve of its leaders.

Clausewitz here opens himself to charges of militarism.[18] In uniform since the age of 12, he naturally contrasted the discipline and self-sacrifice of soldiers with the diverse and self-seeking concerns of civilians. He also believed that compulsory military service both contributed to defence and improved the attitudes of those who served. Without doubt he was deeply imbued with military values like many in his time, and hoped Prussians would adopt at least some of them.

But he was the very opposite of a militarist in that he sought no unearned or unnecessary privileges for the army, and argued that the military must remain subordinate to government in both peace and war. His view was simply that a state must be well prepared for war.

Political-military relations

If war is to be an instrument of policy, the relationship between government and army is critical. *On War* makes several references to political-military relations and Book VIII promises a chapter on 'the structure of the supreme command'. [633] The chapter was never written, perhaps because Clausewitz did not find time, or perhaps because it touched a highly sensitive topic. As we have seen, he frequently disagreed with his political masters over policy and his actions in 1812–13 – leaving Prussian service, negotiating the convention of Tauroggen, and organising the *Landwehr* in East Prussia – clearly ran contrary to the wishes of the king.

The experience of 1789–1815 had demonstrated that rulers who lost the army also lost office – and sometimes even their lives. The French army's desertion in 1789, Clausewitz observed, denied the king his only means of repressing the mob, and both Royal Guards and regulars took part in storming the Bastille. In the 1790s insubordination, mutineering and political activity were rife in the French army.[19] In 1814 Napoleon was deserted by his generals. Throughout the nineteenth century military influence in politics was an ever present possibility and a reality in countries such as Prussia, Spain and Sweden. Only in Britain did the army resolutely stay out of politics.[20] Clausewitz's doctrine of political supremacy, though not always well understood, was highly relevant to the difficult and evolving relationship between governments and armies.

Many contemporaries argued for an autonomous sphere of military action: the government should simply set its objectives at the outbreak of war and give the army a free hand to achieve them. Clausewitz rejected this view unequivocally. Governments must not only shape the planning for war but also exercise overall guidance of military activity. They cannot simply hand matters over to the military:

> Subordinating the political point of view to the military would be absurd, for it is policy that creates war. Policy is the guiding intelligence and war only the instrument. No other possibility exists, then, than to subordinate the military point of view to the political. [607]

Military autonomy could apply only in the hypothetical case of absolute war where policy is absent. In a war driven by 'pure hatred', for example, the political factor would cease to count on the outbreak of hostilities. [607]

For such reasons Clausewitz refused to advise his friend Roeder in 1827 on possible strategies for an exercise concerning a hypothetical war between Austria and Prussia without any indication of the political context.[21] Military and political matters are indissolubly bound together:

> We can now see that the assertion that a major military develop-ment, or the plan for one, should be a matter for *purely military* opinion is unacceptable and can be damaging. Nor indeed is it sen-sible to summon soldiers, as many governments do when they are planning a war, and ask them for *purely military advice*. [607]

In reality there can be no 'purely military point of view'. [607] This also means that the army cannot be held responsible for mistakes in policy. Those who complain about political influence over military action are therefore wrong-headed:

> when people talk, as they often do, about harmful political influence on the management of war, they are not really saying what they mean. Their quarrel should be with the policy itself, not with its influence. [608]

Only if statesmen expect results from military actions that are 'foreign to their nature' can political decisions can be said to 'influence operations for the worse'. [608] As long as policy 'reads the course of military events correctly, it is wholly and exclusively entitled' to determine policy. [607] And by the same token it is fully responsible for that policy.

Here, then, is Clausewitz's model of political-military relations. In practice, as he recognised, matters are more complex. First, the govern-ment cannot and does not control all of the activities of an army. Minutiae can and must be left to the military:

> Policy, of course, will not extend its influence to operational details. Political considerations do not determine the posting of guards or the employment of patrols. [606]

More importantly, the influence of policy will be limited by the violence and uncertainty of war: 'Policy will permeate all military operations and, in so far as their violent nature will admit, it will have a continuous influence on them'. [87] Policy may shape the war and the campaign but cannot run the battle.

Second, policy must take into account what is possible with the military means available.

> War in general, and the commander in any specific instance, is entitled to require that the trend and designs of policy shall not be inconsistent with these means. That, of course, is no small demand; but however much it may affect political aims in a given case, it will never do more than modify them. [87]

If means come to dominate ends, then war is no longer a subordinate instrument. This can legitimately occur only when a lack of means rules out certain ends altogether.

Third, political-military relations are influenced by the knowledge that political leaders have of the army and that military leaders have of political matters. Here the military have an important duty to educate the government. As Clausewitz put it in a letter to Müffling:

> In relation to policy the first duty and right of the art of war is to keep policy from demanding things that go against the nature of war, to prevent the possibility that out of ignorance of the way the instrument works, policy might misuse it.[22]

There are many examples where failure to understand how the military works leads to problems:

> In the same way as a man who has not fully mastered a foreign language sometimes fails to express himself correctly, so statesmen often issue orders that defeat the purpose they are meant to serve. Time and again that has happened, which demonstrates that a certain grasp of military affairs is vital for those in charge of general policy. [608]

This does not mean that civilian leaders require detailed military knowledge or experience:

> We are far from believing that a minister of war immersed in his files, an erudite engineer or even an experienced soldier would, simply on the basis of their particular experience, make the best

director of policy … . Far from it. What is needed in the post is distinguished intellect and strength of character. He can always get the necessary military information somehow or other. [608]

A capable statesman knows how to obtain and use the talents of his subordinates, military and civilian, and is able to distinguish good and bad advice. As with military command, Clausewitz opts for qualities of mind and character rather than detailed knowledge.

For his part the military commander requires some familiarity with political matters since he deals with national leaders at the highest level:

> A commander-in-chief need not be a learned historian nor a political commentator, but he must be familiar with the higher affairs of state and its innate policies; he must know current issues, questions under consideration, the leading personalities, and be able to form sound judgments. [146]

But he must not lose sight of his military responsibilities:

> … a commander-in-chief must also be a statesman, but he must not cease to be a general. One the one hand, he is aware of the entire political situation; on the other, he knows exactly how much he can achieve with the means at his disposal. [111–2]

It is a delicate balancing act so that selection of a commander-in-chief is an important decision for governments.

The political-military relationship is also influenced by institutional arrangements. Clausewitz's analysis reflects Prussia's experience of political and military leaders answering to the king. Senior officers had strong personal links with the monarch by virtue of their commission and their noble status. Rivalry for influence over the monarch often developed between political leaders and the army. This contrasted with the English system where the military were steadily made subordinate to Parliament and hence to the civilian government while the monarch assumed an increasingly ceremonial role in both politics and military affairs. Rather than make common cause with the monarch against civilian leaders, the English army became the impartial servant of the government of the day.

The simplest arrangement, Clausewitz observed, is when the highest political authority and the supreme commander are one and the same person. He prefers a monarch who acts as commander-in-chief, thereby ensuring clear lines of authority and lending royal authority to the conduct of operations. [608] Thus Frederick the Great unified political purpose and military strategy, and enjoyed the advantage of being *'accountable to no one'*. [497] Napoleon also successfully combined soldier and statesman in one person. But such a leader needs to be strong and able to exercise his authority, conditions not always met in Prussia. Even Frederick suffered a heavy penalty in terms of 'isolation and strain'.[23]

More often the government or cabinet rather than the king alone will have responsibility for the conduct of war. Contrary to the views of some, Clausewitz believed this could be an effective arrangement. 'The soul of war', he observed, 'resides in the cabinet'.[24] But there were pitfalls. Under a king prone to doubt or inactivity, cabinets could find it easy to avoid decisions and eschew initiative. To control the conduct of war effectively, cabinets also require effective military input. Here Clausewitz identifies a pivotal role for the commander-in-chief:

> If war is to be fully consonant with political objectives, and policy suited to the means available for war, then unless statesmen and soldier are combined in one person, the only sound expedient is to make the commander-in-chief a member of the cabinet, so that the cabinet can share in the major aspects of his activities. [608]

Though Clausewitz expects the commander-in-chief to have some influence over the cabinet, the emphasis is on the cabinet influencing him. It was this passage which the editor of the second edition of *On War* in 1853, in keeping with the views of his time, changed by one word – *es* to *er* – to imply that the commander-in-chief should influence the major activities of the cabinet rather than vice versa.[25]

Other military influence in the cabinet is undesirable. [609] Conflicting military advice loses one of the principal requirements of effective military action – the vigorous pursuit of objectives. The presence of three commanders-in-chief and two chiefs of staff around the king in 1806 had been absurd. Similar problems arose in 1809 when generals and other commanders resisted the War Department and made use of their historical 'duty relationship' with the king, writing directly to him in criticism of the Department. The king welcomed the division of opinion rather than supporting the Department which consequently lost respect. Clausewitz argued that the Department should be the highest military authority under the War Minister and should be obeyed by the oldest Field Marshal as well as the youngest soldier.[26]

In time of war the geographic location of the political leadership is important. In his history of the campaign of 1799 Clausewitz warns of the difficulty of directing war from afar: 'Ministers and policy advisers never clearly see the effect that their decisions have in the theater of operations'.[27] For '[w]ar resembles a ship contending against storm and waves. One must be aboard to steer it competently, to take advantage of the elements, and so complete the journey as well as may be'.[28] If government is to influence the commander, it cannot follow the old practice of settling strategy in the capital. [177] Moving closer to the army in the field helps the government assert its dominance and avoid long delays in decision making. [608–9]

Clausewitz's discussion of political-military relations in practice is realistic but contains a serious omission, namely failure to discuss political-military conflict rather than mere misunderstanding. How, for example, should military leaders respond to orders that are manifestly foolish or mistaken? How strongly should military leaders urge decisions on a reluctant government? Are there extreme circumstances in which the military might reject the policies of their masters? Clausewitz was not unfamiliar with such problems.

In theory, of course, whatever the political leadership determines must prevail:

> no conflict need arise any longer between political and military interests – not from the nature of the case at any rate – and should it arise it will show no more than lack of understanding. It might be thought that policy could make demands on war which war could not fulfil; but that hypothesis would challenge the natural and unavoidable assumption that policy knows the instrument it means to use. If policy reads the course of military events correctly, it is wholly and exclusively entitled to decide which events and trends are best for the objectives of the war. [607]

This is hardly adequate. In the first place, Clausewitz assumes that policy understands the instrument it intends to use and 'reads the course of military events correctly'. Neither assumption will always be true in practice. On the contrary, both are matters chronically liable to give rise to differences between military and political leaders.

There is a more far-reaching concern, namely Clausewitz's assumption that a state's policy is in line with its true interests. Yet it is quite possible, as he acknowledges elsewhere, that policy may be subordinated to the personal ambitions of a leader or fail to serve national interests. Clausewitz simply assumes that policy promotes those interests. When he grants primacy to policy, it is to 'the political as it should be, not what it necessarily is'.[29] When Clausewitz himself went against the king's wishes in 1812, he firmly believed he was acting for Prussia's honour and true long-term interests. Prussia's ultimate victory over Napoleon does not obviate the question as to who should determine the 'true' interests of the state. Sincerity of belief such as Clausewitz had in 1812 hardly serves as an acceptable reason for disregarding national policy.

Statesmanship

Clausewitz's view of statesmanship owes much to Machiavelli. In an uncertain and hostile environment the leaders of states require both judgement and courage. Lesser nations have little choice but to pursue a policy of caution and cunning, seeking to preserve the status quo and ultimately their very existence. Great states possess immense vitality and energy, and can be more active in pursuing a wide range of goals. Some will rise to the challenge, others will go under, and even the most powerful state may fail after enduring for centuries. Like all creations of society, including the great religions, states carry within them 'the seeds of their own destruction'.[30]

Perhaps inspired by the notion of *fortuna*, Clausewitz stressed the play of probability in war and politics. Human destiny is neither sheer chance and caprice, nor is it merely the playing out of pre-determined historical forces. It can be shaped but not controlled by human action. Just as uncertainty in war challenges the courage and genius of the general, so uncertainty challenges the creativity and commitment of the statesman. Both must focus on the main task, disregard moral niceties, display courage, make bold decisions and take responsibility. Neither great statesmanship nor great generalship have room for timidity and moral qualms.

It is no surprise that Clausewitz enthusiastically endorsed Machiavelli's teaching on foreign policy, recommending *The Prince* as the classic text on statesmanship. 'The twenty-first chapter of Machiavelli's *Prince* ['How a Prince must act to win honour'] is the basic code for all diplomacy – and woe to those who fail to heed it'. Since politics among states is characterised by competition and mistrust '[n]o book on earth is more necessary to the politician than Machiavelli's'. Those who claim to be disgusted at his principles are no more than 'idealistic dilettantes'.[31] Leaders who follow their conscience and 'conduct themselves in high office as they would in private life are true egotists'.[32]

For Clausewitz it was no part of a theory of war to criticise decisions made by political leaders even if they led to national ruin. This pertained to the theory of politics.[33] As with the political-military relationship, Clausewitz remains reluctant to consider the problems of foreign policy going astray: 'That it can err, subserve the ambitions, private interests and vanity of those in power, is neither here nor there'. [606–7] He thus found no reason to criticise Napoleon for his political ambitions on behalf of France. Invasion of Russia was the only means France had of avoiding a war in both East and West and Napoleon pursued the only war plan that might succeed – breaking the nerve of the Russian government:

> Bonaparte may have been wrong to engage in it at all; at least the outcome certainly shows that he miscalculated; but we argue that if he was to aim at that objective, there was, broadly speaking, no other way of gaining it. [628]

Bonaparte as statesman had no choice but to risk his entire army – 'that was the stake in the game, the price of his vast hopes'. [628] At most Clausewitz suggests the invasion was in political terms 'an extravaganza'. [325] To go further in judging Napoleon would require him to state his political values.

Nonetheless, the ambitions of Napoleon or any other statesman could be criticised if they lay beyond the means at his disposal. In many cases, Clausewitz observes, an attacking nation has wisely sought not total defeat of its opponents but 'a state of balance in which it could maintain itself'. [570–1] He finds much to praise in Frederick the Great who, in 'pursuing a major objective with limited resources, ... did not try to undertake anything beyond his strength, but always *just enough* to get him what he wanted'. [179] Napoleon, by contrast, took vast risks and ultimately squandered all he possessed.[34] The verdict was not in the form of political or moral censure but in the fact of failure. Similarly, the statesman fails when, as in Prussia prior to 1806, he does not understand that the means available are inadequate for national defence.

Was Clausewitz's view of statesmanship at heart too nationalistic and militaristic? Certainly, he was an advocate of strong measures to improve Prussia's military capability and of war in the event of threats to its independence. But for the most part his commentaries on international affairs are reluctant to see war as a solution. His view of the war that broke out in 1792 between France and Prussia, for example, was that it was not in the best interests of either state. He thought that some issues such as French actions in Alsace were amenable to negotiation, and that the king's sympathy for the captive royal family should not determine state policy. For its part, 'Prussia had nothing to defend or to conquer in Alsace'. [631] Clausewitz's memoranda on the European situation in 1830–1 also saw him opposing a preventive war against France.[35] Though war might be forced on Prussia, the prevailing balance of forces was unfavourable, including lack of popular support at home.

Like Machiavelli, Clausewitz offered his country a more realistic analysis of the nature of security, arguing the dangers of weakness and neutrality and pointing to security and honour as the principal guides of the statesman. Both spurred on their fellow countrymen to resist foreign domination. Beyond such goals political leaders must determine the nation's interests and how they are to be sought. Legal and moral judgements do not enter the picture and can be left to theorists or 'philosophers' of politics. Nor is the conduct of statesmen subject to judgement save, perhaps, according to the criteria of rationality and prudence. Like Machiavelli, Clausewitz emphasised the difficulties of successful political action against the odds. It is a thoroughly realist, even pessimistic view of foreign policy. It is a philosophy without illusion but not without passion.[36]

18
International Politics

> *'Politics, moreover, is the womb in which war develops – where its outlines already exist in their hidden rudimentary form, like the characteristics of living creatures in their embryos'.* [149]

Clausewitz did not need to present a theory of international politics. He had one ready-made in the form of realism inherited from Machiavelli and others. The state is the most important political actor and by nature pursues its own interests which will periodically clash with those of other states. War is thus a permanent and inevitable feature of international politics, remaining a constant possibility just as combat is a constant possibility in war. 'Peace', Clausewitz observed, 'does not often reign everywhere in Europe, and never throughout the whole world'. [122]

The immediate causes of war are to be found in the relations of states: 'the only source of war is politics – the intercourse of governments and peoples'. [605] War has deep-seated causes and 'never breaks out unexpectedly, nor can it be spread instantaneously'. [78] Its origin 'is not to be sought in slogans but in the sum total of [states'] spiritual and material relationships'.[1] Nor does it result simply from the co-existence of different political systems:

> Suppose the so-called despotism were to disappear completely, so that all peoples were as free and happy as those of Paris are now ... [w]ould an idyllic peace then prevail among the nations, would the clash of interests and passions that has always threatened their security disappear? Obviously not.[2]

France would be a danger to Prussia even if the revolution had not taken place. Nor would war disappear simply because states adopted

223

similar constitutions. Clausewitz could not take seriously Kant's proposal to eradicate war by reconstructing states into peace-loving republics.[3]

While eschewing a theory of international politics, Clausewitz does comment on the (negligible) role of international law and moral principles and he examines in some detail two central features of the international system that bear upon war: alliances and the balance of power. The former is a means of coordinating military power between states for common purposes, the latter a means for preventing domination by a single state.

International law

International law and morality are rarely mentioned in *On War* and then in almost casual fashion. In a discussion of the use of armed force in the first chapter Clausewitz observes bluntly: '[a]ttached to force are certain, self-imposed imperceptible limitations hardly worth mentioning, known as international law and custom, but they scarcely weaken it'. Any limitations derive from voluntary self-restraint by states since, unlike physical force, 'moral force has no existence save as expressed in the state and the law'. [75] While fighting itself might be moderated by chivalry and custom, only fear and prudence can be relied upon to restrain states in their relations with one another. Nor could a supranational body such as the Concert of Europe exercise any authority over its members.

The concept of the just war – principles which govern when a state ought or ought not to resort to war – receives not a single mention in *On War*. The word 'aggression' appears in some translations but carries no moral significance since contemporary usage treated it as a neutral concept.[4] The term Clausewitz actually uses is 'the attacker' which lacks the modern connotations of 'aggressor', referring simply to the state that takes up arms first. *On War* thus contrasts with many earlier studies of war which gave prominence to moral and legal considerations.[5] Like Machiavelli Clausewitz believed that any action necessary for the state is justified. The years after 1789 seemed to vindicate his position when the just war tradition became for all intents and purposes defunct.[6]

For Clausewitz resort to war is simply a question of determining national interests and selecting the right moment to make the first move.[7] On the origins of the Seven Years War, he observes: 'When Frederick the Great perceived in 1756 that war was unavoidable and that he was lost unless he could forestall his enemies, it became a necessity for him to initiate hostilities'. [191] Similarly, with regard to preventive war, Clausewitz suggests that the immediate initiation of hostilities is 'advisable whenever the future affords better prospects to the enemy than it does to us'. [601] Though in these cases resort to force is in part defensive, the same applies to wars of conquest. Considerations of law and morality do not enter the picture save perhaps as convenient pretexts.

Alliances

In the eighteenth century, according to Clausewitz, alliances were commonly entered into with no real intention to make good stated pledges. Though frequently a 'half-and-half affair' and full of reservations, they could not be dismissed as absurd since they were 'deeply rooted in the frailties and shortcomings of the human race'. [603–4] Of real significance, however, were alliances in which the interests of two or more states genuinely converged such that one partner has 'a *substantial interest* in maintaining the integrity of their ally's security'. [373] Even in such cases disagreement among allies was common. Clausewitz had observed the twists and turns of alliances during his career, not least the intense conflicts among the allies in 1813–14.[8] Like war, they had to be understood as an instrument of policy and seen in their political context.

The crux of an alliance is unity of political purpose or at least the degree to which 'the interests and forces of most of the allies are subordinate to those of the leader'. [596] At best, allies agree on a common purpose to defeat an opponent and one of them is able and willing to take a leading role. At worst, a state enters an alliance to weaken or preoccupy its ally or to divert blows away from itself. While these are legitimate purposes that cannot be ruled out on moral grounds, Clausewitz counts this 'a dangerous game' which is better left to more powerful states.[9] The weaker the common interest or centre of gravity within an alliance, the easier it is for an opponent to undermine; the greater the community of interest, the harder the alliance is to disrupt. [596]

It is also true that no state will ever espouse the cause of another as seriously as its does its own. [603] When two states make war against a third 'the affair is more like a business deal' in which each side makes an investment and expects a return. 'Even when both share a major interest, action is clogged with diplomatic reservations' and negotiators are reluctant to commit all their forces to the common cause. [603] Hence

> allies do not cooperate at the mere desire of those who are actively engaged in fighting; international relations being what they are, such cooperation is often furnished only at some later stage or increased only when a balance has been disturbed and needs correction. [79]

Russia was a case in point, always proving slow to meet its obligations. To complain about this, Clausewitz observes, is as pointless as complaining that snow only comes in winter when it is already cold.[10]

Dispute over the command of allied forces is a common symptom of divergent interests. Governments usually insist that forces they contribute should operate under their commander who 'is dependent only on his own government'. [603] However, coordination among different national commanders exercising independent control is difficult to achieve. For example, where an allied force is spread over 250 or 500 miles, or is operating on different fronts, 'cohesion between the parts will usually be very loose, and often completely fictitious'. [486] The worst situation of all is when 'two autonomous generals of different nationality share a theatre as was often the case with Russian, Austrian and Imperial forces in the Seven Years War'. [632] This simply invites intra-alliance conflict.

It is more effective for states to combine their forces, but this requires 'a rare degree of self-effacement' and 'friendliness' on the part of the governments concerned. In 1813 it was '[s]heer necessity' that drove states to combine their forces. [631] Even so, the actions of the Tsar were extraordinarily praiseworthy when the latter 'made no pretension to command an independent Russian force' and placed what was the largest army in the field under Prussian and Austrian generals. [632] Alexander's virtue lay not in his generosity but in his far-sighted understanding of Russian interests. As for Austria, Prussia and the German states, it would be foolish to attempt to set up a united military organisation since 'a federal state is a poor sort of nucleus in war time, lacking unity and vigor, without any rational way of choosing its commander'. [637]

While coalitions face many difficulties, this does not mean success is rare. Clausewitz claims to know of hardly one that totally failed in its objectives apart from the unfortunate alliance against France in 1792. Defensive coalitions, in particular, are least likely of all to fail. They may take time to assemble but they are a natural means of resisting superior power and there is often no alternative.[11] Nor, of course, does a victorious coalition guarantee continued harmony among allies as Clausewitz observed at first hand in Paris in 1815. Temporary alignment of interests in war gives way to the competing interests of peace.

The balance of power

Alliances are also important to the balance of power among states, contributing to what Clausewitz sees as an inherent tendency towards international equilibrium. The origins of this balancing process can be found in fifteenth century Italy where a number of small states, each more or less of the same strength, were situated within a limited geographical area. Trade, art and science expanded, producing much richer and more complex relations among these states than in the rest of Europe.[12] As governments came to understand the complexities of their relationships, a system evolved to balance power among them – a development which Clausewitz thought 'is bound to emerge spontaneously whenever a number of civilized countries are in mutual relations'. [373]

In the following centuries, as foreign policy came under the control of strong central governments, European states developed the capacity to assess their own and others' interests and to evaluate various possible alignments. By the eighteenth century these complex interdependencies produced a stable international political system marked by significant constraints on military activity. 'It was conceivable that two states could fight a major war without, as in former times, involving twenty others'. [589] War could be managed or contained because states had wide and complex interests. 'Political relations, with their affinities and antipathies, had become so sensitive a nexus that no cannon could be fired in Europe without every government feeling its interest affected'. [590]

As a result, Clausewitz argued, any would-be conqueror of Europe faced immense military and political difficulties. Countervailing alliances would have to be avoided so that 'a new Alexander needed more than his own sharp sword: he required a ready pen as well'. [590] Besides, the military means to achieve hegemony did not exist at this time. Louis XIV's ambition was thwarted in part because his methods of waging war were no different from those of his opponents. [590] Given relatively static conditions, understanding of the balance at this time tended to see it as a mechanical, even automatic process in which rules could be deduced by careful examination. Policy required observance of those rules. This view of the international system proved totally inadequate to explain the upheavals after 1789.

Witness to the collapse of the old system, Clausewitz believed that the balance of power needed to be understood in the light of new forces at work.

> the Revolution had thrown the whole weight of the nation and its strengths into a balance that had formerly weighed only small standing armies and limited state revenues. ... To their own and everyone else's surprise, the French learned that a state's natural power and a great simple cause were far stronger than the artificial structure of international relations by which other states were ruled.[13]

Sharing the views of most German thinkers, among whom historians predominated, Clausewitz saw the balance as a harsh and inevitable law based on constant struggle that punished those who failed to observe its dictates. By contrast, an island power like Britain, where statesmen dominated thinking about the balance, could afford to take a more voluntarist view, seeking to adjust and manipulate the balance rather than being fully part of it.[14]

For Clausewitz the key to stability in the system was that states should pursue their own interests and act according to their 'natural weight'.[15] What mattered was not some arbitrary scheme to produce a 'systematically regulated balance of power and of spheres of influence' but the natural interaction of forces. [373–4] The balance in Europe derived from the totality and complexity of relations among states:

> major and minor interests of states and peoples [are] interwoven in the most varied and changeable manner. Each point of intersection binds and serves to balance one set of interests against the other. The broad effect of all these fixed points is obviously to give a certain amount of cohesion to the whole. [373]

Here was no delicate game played by cabinets but a more dynamic, more natural set of relationships among states pursuing their own interests 'without noticeable distortion or moral exertion'. Given these conditions, 'there is no question of a balance of power *system*; the balance simply exists in itself'.[16]

Despite a natural tendency to stability among states, this condition is not immune to challenge or breakdown. Inevitably, attempts to upset the balance will occur:

> one should not be surprised that diseases occur in a loosely consti-
> tuted polity such as a multitude of states of various sizes; after all,
> they also occur in the marvelously structured organic whole of all
> living nature. [374]

What might be called 'deviations, hyperactivity of individual states, actual cases of disease' are in fact normal occurrences. [374] In many instances challenges to the balance are successfully dealt with – 'prevented or reversed by the more or less overt reaction of the other states'. [375] In other cases the balancing process is slow to operate and states have effected radical changes 'without the slightest effort by the rest to hinder them. There have even been cases in which a single state has become so powerful that it could virtually dictate to the rest'. [374]

Yet this 'does not disprove the tendency on the part of common interests to support the existing order'. [374] Sooner or later states naturally resist hegemony. Hence '[t]he balance of power *system* only reveals itself when the balance is in danger of being lost'.[17] Clausewitz never doubted this inherent tendency towards equilibrium – though some might 'laugh at these reflections and consider them utopian dreams'. [374]

The chief reason for collapse of a balance in the short and medium term lies in the failure of statesmen to understand the nature of the challenge and to concentrate their efforts, pursuing instead 'fifty different small objectives'. [636] After 1789 few grasped the unprecedented political forces at work and the dramatic changes in warfare, but in the end states reacted because they came to comprehend their own interests: 'Only in recent times did the extreme danger emanating from Bonaparte, or his own unlimited driving power, force people to act in a natural manner'. [603] Upholding the balance is thus not a matter of observing rules but the result of a proper understanding of self-interest.

Three processes assist states to restore the balance. One is the military burden on the attacker which increases as he is compelled to defend the gains he has made. The other factors relate to international politics. On the one hand, states seeking hegemony find it difficult to win and retain allies. The attacking state usually acts alone but any allies are likely to grow anxious and detach themselves if the attacker's success grows too great. [525, 569] Nor will the conqueror easily win allies among those he conquers. Napoleon's practice of seizing booty, imposing levies, living off the land and restricting trade provoked resistance more often than cooperation.

On the other hand, attempts to overthrow the balance of power create a common interest among others in restoring stability:

> Most states will certainly assume that the collective interest will always represent and assure their stability. It is thus also certain that in defending itself every individual state whose relations with the rest are not already strained will find it has more friends than enemies. [374]

Hence 'as a rule the defender can count on outside assistance more than can the attacker'. [376] Preserving the independence of a state under attack is another shared concern. The more the survival of the defender 'matters to the rest – that is, the sounder and more vigorous his political condition – the more certain he can be of their help'. [376] At the same time, resentment of the state seeking hegemony grows. Thus France's invasion of Russia prompted widespread support for the latter since '[a]t heart, all Europe was opposed to Bonaparte'. [615] They wanted France 'brought to her knees and taught a lesson any time she chooses to resume that insolent behavior with which she has burdened Europe for a hundred and fifty years'. [636] Support does not accrue to the weaker state or against the stronger in mechanical fashion but as a consequence of political calculation and sentiment. The process works

> thanks to the laws of psychology rather than those of dynamics. Envy, jealousy, anxiety, and sometimes perhaps even generosity are the natural advocates of the unsuccessful. They will win new friends for him as well as weaken and divide his enemies. [597]

The overall working of the system is further assisted by a power such as England which, without ambitions of its own on the continent, plays the role of balancer. Whenever France threatened to achieve preponderance, Clausewitz noted, England opposed her at sea and in Europe. But too great a reliance cannot be placed on the balancer since England 'has too little direct involvement on the continent to be the main counterweight, and from the moment Europe relies primarily on England it will be ruined'.[18] Another cause for concern about England

was that popular sentiment – for example, in favour of Polish independence – might undermine sound policy though Clausewitz thought
it absurd that its leaders might actually assist France.[19]

In sum, the nation that seeks to destroy the European balance,
Clausewitz wrote, takes 'a burden on its shoulders that it cannot carry
forever'. '[V]iolent political oscillations will result' as each part of the
system reacts, not according to 'a rational will', but simply by following 'its own momentum wherever it may lead'. A new and different
equilibrium will be the result.[20] The balance of power had served
Europe well over several centuries, containing attempts at hegemony
despite the sometimes slow responses of states. Prussia had benefited as
had a number of smaller nations in Italy, Holland and Germany whose
independence was preserved by balancing alliances.[21] But on occasion
the system seemed to require the sacrifice of a state as the case of
Poland demonstrated.

The partitions of Poland

Successive partitions by Russia, Austria and Prussia between 1772 and
1795 caused Poland to disappear entirely from the map of Europe. As
Clausewitz put it, a state of eight million inhabitants 'fell prey' to some
of the most powerful states without any others lifting a sword to
prevent this shift in the distribution of power. [375] For this reason
Poland

> is always trotted out by those who ridicule the very idea of a polit-
> ical balance – because it seems to be an extremely relevant example
> of how a harmless, unaggressive country perished without any other
> coming to its assistance. [375]

In defending the partitions, Clausewitz first points out that even if
they did breach the system, 'a single case, however striking, cannot
vitiate a general principle'. [375] He then presents arguments to the
effect that the partitions were in fact consistent with the balance of
power.

Clausewitz first raises doubts about Poland's status as a full member
of the European comity of nations: 'Could Poland really be considered
a European state, an equal among equals in the European community
of Nations? She could not'. Poland was in fact a 'Tartar state' located in
the midst of the European order. Clausewitz claims he is not criticising
Poland by these observations. 'In saying this we do not wish to slight
the Poles or justify the partition of their country. Our only concern is

to face the facts'. [375] The balance of power is for advanced European states and Poland's relative lack of civilisation necessitates different treatment.

The second problem with Poland is its negative impact on the stability of Europe. 'Poland had not really played a political part for a century or so; she had merely been a cause of dissension among other states'. [375] This was due primarily to her internal condition and her constitution which made for a 'chaotic public life' and 'boundless irresponsibility'. [375] Unable to maintain her independence and having ceased to be 'an independent state with meaningful frontiers', Poland

> had lost the character of a private home and had become more like a public highway on which foreign armies could disport themselves whenever and however they pleased. [375–6]

Poland's own failings, in short, caused it to be 'swallowed up by the abyss'. [375]

Clausewitz, finally, dismissed the claim that Poland could contribute to stability by acting as a buffer state. This could never occur since it required Poland to be well-disposed towards the Germans. In reality, Poland had more permanent conflicting interests – over territory, language and trade – with Prussia than with any other state. Worse still, Poland had for centuries been a natural ally of France.[22] To undo the partitions would aid France and undermine Austria and Prussia. 'Can any reasonable man believe this to be in the interest of Europe?'[23]

Clausewitz's discussion of Poland contains much special pleading. But neither France nor England protested at all vigorously against partition even though both failed to gain. It is also true that the partitioning states were united only temporarily, posing no long-term threat to the balance. For Clausewitz the European system neither could nor should protect the boundaries of every state:

> if collective security [*Schutz des Ganzen*] has not always sufficed to maintain the integrity of each individual state, the fact should be ascribed to irregularities in the life of the system as a whole which instead of destroying were absorbed into it. [374–5]

It is simply 'asking too much [of the international system] when a state's integrity must be maintained entirely by others'. [375] In this case 'nothing was surer than that Poland would have become a Russian province if she had not been partitioned'. [375] Far from substantively upsetting the balance, the partitions merely ensured a more even distribution of power.

War in international politics

While war is an instrument of state policy, it can also serve the international community in important ways. Clausewitz recognises the existence of common values among the European powers and refers on occasion to a community of states [*Staatenrepublik*] in Europe. One of the more enduring common interests is the desire to avoid hegemony by one state by maintaining a balance of power. This may require war which, though sometimes slow to be set in motion, usually succeeds in restoring a balance of some kind. As a citizen of the weakest of the major powers Clausewitz had good reason to focus on the long term workings of the balance.

War also serves the international community as a means of settling disputes among states. The transition from war to peace at the end of hostilities, Clausewitz suggests, is generally marked by a treaty which signifies for the time being that 'the purpose of the war has been achieved and its business is at an end'. [91] The treaty extinguishes 'a mass of sparks that might have gone on quietly smoldering' while 'tensions are slackened and lovers of peace (and they abound among every people under all circumstances) will then abandon any thought of further action'. [90] Of course, as Clausewitz emphasises, war does not settle disputes once and for all. States may regard defeat as merely 'a transitory evil, for which a remedy may still be found in political conditions at some later date'. [80] In the constant struggle that is international politics war promises at least a temporary measure of security, if successfully waged.

Part VIII
The Relevance of *On War*

19
Clausewitz to 1945

'Mahdi of mass and mutual massacre'[1]

Since the publication of *On War* between 1832 and 1834 Clausewitz has become a key figure in understanding war – at times ignored, condemned or canonised, his ideas sometimes merely misunderstood, sometimes deliberately distorted. His actual influence over strategy, whether for good or ill, has also been debated, though the topic is so elusive that scholars have preferred to focus on his 'reception' – the ways in which others have understood his ideas and reacted to them.[2] The relevance of his ideas to evolving modern warfare and to nuclear strategy has been much discussed while in recent years his irrelevance to sub-national warfare and terrorism has been argued. This part of the book can only touch lightly on Clausewitz's contribution to the understanding of war since his time.

At the outset *On War* attracted some immediate criticism, not least from Jomini whose reputation as an analyst of military affairs outshone that of Clausewitz for much of the century. In his *Summary* published in 1838 Jomini aimed numerous barbs at his rival, while adjusting many of his ideas to Clausewitz's analysis.[3] *On War* also won ardent supporters who sensed that it was a work of intellectual significance. Engels came across Clausewitz around mid-century and recommended him to Marx who read some of the military histories and became familiar with the main ideas of *On War* without reading the text itself.[4] But with the initial print-run of 1500 copies still not fully sold it is fair to say that Clausewitz had fallen into 'respectful oblivion'.[5]

Nonetheless, the publishers of *On War*, Dümmler of Berlin, produced a second edition in 1853 with support from Clausewitz's brother-in-law.[6]

In Prussia the book was taken up in earnest from around the 1860s by leading military theorists and generals. Their interest was less in Clausewitz's broad theory of war than in winning military conflicts within existing political and technological constraints.[7] Moltke, in particular, was an avowed follower of Clausewitz, admiring his apparent advocacy of 'Napoleonic' war with its emphasis on mass, morale, patriotism and leadership.[8] His decisive victories against Austria in 1866 and France in 1870–71 helped promote the view that war was a practical, proper and glorious instrument of national policy. No matter that Moltke fundamentally misread Clausewitz's idea of picking up the sword in place of the pen to mean that soldiers should take over from politicians in wartime. He initially refused Bismarck's demands to bombard Paris in the war of 1870–71 – on tactical military grounds rather than moral – but the Chancellor, who knew little of Clausewitz, insisted on and eventually won political control.[9]

Reprints of *On War* appeared in 1857 and 1867 followed by a third edition in 1880. Clausewitz now enjoyed a strong following, even reverence, in Germany, though many readers complained of his obscure philosophy.[10] Clausewitz's wider reputation also grew. A French translation had appeared in 1849–51 and an English version followed belatedly in 1873.[11] Military colleges in Europe and North America adopted *On War* as a major text. Many soldiers found congenial Clausewitz's focus on battles and campaigns – operational strategy – and his general disregard for logistics and technology.[12] But many were unhappy with the idea that defence is the stronger form of war and found the Prussian too abstract and heavy-going. By and large, practical soldiers preferred Jomini who remained more widely read. Whether liked or disliked, *On War* earned the attribute 'classic' and became a common source for quotation in military writings inside and outside Germany.[13]

The British army took a particular interest in Clausewitz after their failure against irregular forces in the South African war of 1899–1902. Once their semi-regular forces were defeated, the Boers resorted to guerrilla tactics. Exploiting mobility, small 'commando' units and support from the population, they launched a campaign of sabotage and harassment against slow-moving British forces. In time Britain found effective counter-measures – burning crops, establishing concentration camps and increasing troop numbers until the Boers gave up the struggle. The principal message Britain found in Clausewitz, however, was not the value of guerrilla war but the need for popular militarism and mass armies. The nations of continental Europe seemed intent on building powerful armies and fleets, and it was easy to link Clausewitz with these developments. Introducing an English edition of *On War* in 1908, Colonel F.N. Maude declared that 'it is to the spread of Clausewitz's ideas that the present state of more or less readiness for war of all European armies is due'.[14] By 1914 Clausewitz and Prussia had become synonymous with militaristic policies.

The 'Great War' epitomised modern war as Clausewitz understood it. Fought between armies on battlegrounds largely remote from the civilian population, it was structured according to battles and campaigns and it was intended to serve national objectives. It also embodied new developments that were misunderstood, in this case the impact of technology on the battlefield. Many still believed that the 'moral' factor, rightly stressed by Clausewitz, remained decisive, and for much of the war soldiers were sacrificed to the new weaponry on a profligate scale. The bloody tactical impasse was matched by strategic deadlock. Both sides improvised defensive lines that ran 'from sea to sea', as Clausewitz had speculated, a situation that offered little freedom of choice and 'no convergent attack'. [367] Where innovation had marked Napoleon's campaigns from the outset, new strategic ideas were applied only in the last year or two of this war.

The war also resembled a large-scale industrial operation with armies requiring a large, disciplined and trained workforce, a constant supply of materiel, and complex systems of management. The 'machine-gun' symbolised this connection between industry and warfare. Whole societies and economies became engaged. National passions and the interaction of the belligerents overcame any friction due to the resistance of soldiers or public reaction to the carnage. The cost to both sides in blood and treasure careered out of all proportion to the issues at stake. Political leaders might control the military but they did not control the war which appeared less and less like a rational instrument of policy.

Once the slaughter stopped, governments and citizens alike hoped for a new order in which war would no longer be necessary. The League of Nations was set up to control and limit future resort to war. In the 1920s and early 1930s states also entered negotiations for disarmament and arms limitations. In 1928 a total of 65 countries subscribed to a General Treaty for the Renunciation of War as an Instrument of National Policy (the Kellogg-Briand Pact), formally abandoning war as 'an instrument of national policy in their relations with one another'. Clausewitz might have appreciated the reference but not the lack of realism in these solemn attempts to remove force from international politics.

At the same time, popular fears of Prussian militarism helped produce a Treaty of Versailles designed to punish and permanently weaken Germany. Strategic thinkers also sought to apportion blame for the war and its appalling costs. Clausewitz was a promising target. In Britain views propounded by Captain Basil Liddell Hart and General J.F.C. Fuller helped demonise the author of *On War*. Though Liddell Hart read Clausewitz carefully, he was determined to paint him as 'the apostle of total war' and the antithesis of his own strategic nostrum, the indirect approach to victory.[15] The concept of absolute war, he argued, encouraged a focus on mass and battle to the exclusion of all else. In the Great War military leaders blindly followed this 'ill-omened prophet of mass'.[16] What is worse, 'the fighting impulse' took over from reason so that 'the end is pursued, regardless of what lies beyond'.[17] *On War* and its theory of unlimited war, Liddell Hart proclaimed, had 'gone far to wreck civilization'.[18]

General Fuller picked up the theme of obscurantism, dismissing *On War* as 'little more than a mass of notes, a cloud of flame and smoke' and Clausewitz himself as outmoded, an obsolete 'general of the agricultural period of war'.[19] But how could such a work be so influential? For both Fuller and Liddell Hart, Clausewitz had failed to distinguish the moderating elements in his philosophy from inflammatory ideas such as absolute war and the importance of mass. Ordinary soldiers could not be expected to follow a text that was 'too metaphysical' and whose 'generalizations made more impression than his careful qualifications'.[20] Not even generals could understand his subtle logic and 'philosophical jugglery'.[21] To fully grasp *On War* required 'a mind already developed by years of study and reflection'; it simply 'befogged the plain soldier'.[22] In a continent arming for war Clausewitz's ideas had simply been too dangerous.

Another British officer writing at this time, Captain T.E. Lawrence, likewise rejected the mindlessness of the Great War and 'the ritual [in which] two nations professing incompatible philosophies put them to the test of force'.[23] Focusing on the Arab revolt against the Turkish Empire in 1916–18 when he led the insurgents in a campaign that brilliantly exploited their advantages of range, mobility, popular support and political cause, 'Lawrence of Arabia' wrote a classic analysis of guerrilla tactics and strategy. Yet he was a great admirer of *On War*, finding it 'logical and fascinating', and considered Clausewitz the intellectual master of all writers on war.[24] Lawrence shared his emphasis on the political and social context of military action. Conflict is ultimately settled in the minds and hearts of people –

combatants on both sides, their societies, and neutral states, 'circle beyond circle'.[25]

In Germany the defeat of 1918 prompted a search for a deeper understanding of war. Several popular versions of *On War* appeared as well as new scholarly editions in 1933 and 1937. Clausewitz, who had helped turn the humiliation of 1806 into the triumph of 1815, offered hope for a revival of national fortune. Not surprisingly, in the 1930s the National Socialists adopted him as a patriot and a nationalist.[26] There is little evidence that Hitler actually read *On War*.[27] Clausewitz's reputation as a proponent of 'absolute war' sufficed for most Nazis. Some Germans did understand Clausewitz but disliked what they saw. Field Marshal Ludendorff believed that war must take priority over politics since it was more fundamental to national survival:

> The nature of war has changed, the character of politics has changed [both towards totality], and now the relations existing between politics and the conduct of war must also change. All the theories of Clausewitz should be thrown overboard. ... warfare is the highest expression of the national 'will to live', and politics must, therefore, be subservient to the conduct of war.[28]

War, in short, had to be total and totalitarian, subordinating the entire political and social system to the nation's struggle.[29]

Other military leaders, including Seeckt (Chief of the Army Command, 1919–1926) and Beck (Chief of the General Staff, 1933–1938), understood enough of Clausewitz to challenge this assertion.[30] As Hitler determined on a European war, such level-headed Germans looked to Clausewitz's doctrine that war should remain subordinate to political goals and be used with prudence and caution.[31] Many likewise rejected the view that the state should always maximise its efforts, employ the totality of its resources and see war as a matter of either victory or defeat. The reckless call for 'total war' – a term Clausewitz does not use – made the war plan merely a matter of tactics.[32]

The leaders of the new Soviet Union also took an interest in Clausewitz. Lenin, who grasped the linkage between war and politics better than most, urged senior officers of the Red Army to study the Prussian general.[33] Three themes struck a chord in communist ideology. First was Clausewitz's historicism, his belief that war reflected changing social and material conditions.[34] Second was Clausewitz's rejection of war as a subject that would yield to scientific analysis. Struggle – whether in war or revolution – could not be reduced to mere technique. Third was Clausewitz's insistence that policy must control military action. All Soviet leaders were fearful of military coups and military adventurism. Though Stalin later dismissed Clausewitz's ideas as relevant only to the 'hand-tool period of warfare' rather than the machine age, more serious thinkers in Russia argued for recognition of the progressive features in his work.[35]

Clausewitz's appeal lay primarily but not exclusively with those nations in the 'continental' rather than the 'Anglo-Saxon' tradition of warfare.[36] For Germany – like Prussia before it – war always loomed since it constantly faced threats across land borders from both East and West. Russia, too, felt permanently threatened by invasion. The need for large armies was self-evident. Britain could afford a less fatalistic view. Thanks to geography and a powerful navy, it could avoid war by astute diplomacy; employ seapower as a political and military lever in place of large armies; form coalitions as required; and, if war became necessary, raise armies for the occasion. Britain, in Francis Bacon's phrase, could take 'as much or as little of the war' as it chose.[37]

Germany's invasion of Poland in September 1939, however, left Britain with no real choice. War now demanded full mobilisation of human and material resources by the belligerents who conscripted citizens, mobilised popular support and harnessed science, industry, agriculture, communications and much of the rest of the economy to the war effort. The concept of total war, foreshadowed in World War I, was realised in World War II. Not only was it a war of total effort but logic made each nation's assets and resources into targets, including factories, transport systems and merchant shipping. Anything contributing to the enemy's war effort, it was argued, should be attacked by all available means. Ultimately, the enemy's morale, even the people in their homes and cities, were legitimate targets. In this sense World War II was the first true 'people's war'.

The war of 1939–45 was a protracted and bloody struggle. The so-called 'strategic bombing' of cities did not bring the rapid victory promised by its advocates; even its indirect contribution to allied victory is much debated. In the end the war against Germany was won by defeating armies on the ground and was still recognisable as 'modern' in the Clausewitzian mould. At each level reciprocal relationships existed between belligerents: war plans were agreed, campaign strategies were devised and revised, soldiers killed and died. In the end Germany was invaded and signed a surrender in traditional fashion but Japan's fate was different. In August 1945 a radically new weapon – the atomic bomb – brought about surrender in a matter of days. Japan was coerced by military force to yield to the will of another state but everything else seemed different. Nuclear weapons promised an unprecedented revolution in military and political affairs. Clausewitzian war, already stretched beyond the battlefield, might finally lose its relevance.

20
Hypermodern War

'a kind of war by algebra' [76]

Only two nuclear weapons have ever been used in anger yet they dominated military thinking between 1945 and the end of the Cold War.[1] Some believed Clausewitz's relevance lost once and for all since nuclear war would be so destructive it could never serve as an instrument of policy. Through a massive increase in destructive capacity modern war had reached its 'logical extreme', its hypermodern form. But others, focusing on the ends of policy, argued that Clausewitz's importance had increased since the need to understand the linkages between war and policy was greater than ever. In either case nuclear weapons promised a radical impact on strategy and international politics.

The nuclear revolution

The striking parallel between Clausewitz's concept of absolute war and nuclear war was soon noticed. A nuclear war could be 'an isolated act' which 'breaks out unexpectedly', arising through a single irrational decision, a simple miscalculation or a mechanical accident. Fought only with weapons constructed before hostilities began, 'preparations would tend toward totality, for no omission could ever be rectified'. It could take the form of 'a single short blow', consisting 'of one decisive act, or of a set of simultaneous decisions' determined in advance. Nuclear war could 'be spread simultaneously', engulfing not only belligerents but also third parties fearing for their survival. And the outcome might well be 'final' with the annihilation of the states involved and even civilisation itself. [78–9]

For Clausewitz. of course, absolute war could not exist in the real world. Extreme effort is a 'fantasy' while the nature of military resources 'means that they cannot all be deployed at the same moment'. [78–9] Nuclear war, however, seemed to have overcome all the modifying factors in real war – from human frailties to political constraints. Maximum destruction was possible with minimal effort. But while Clausewitz's absolute war was a theoretical construct unachievable in practice, nuclear war seemed all too possible.

Some strategists, notably in the US Air Force, initially saw nuclear weapons as simply an extension of World War II 'strategic bombing'. As early as 1946, however, Bernard Brodie argued that the role of the military establishment could no longer be to win wars: 'From now on its chief purpose must be to avert them. It can have almost no other useful purpose'.[2] A new field of inquiry, sweepingly labelled 'strategic studies', arose to tackle the problems of war in the nuclear age, examining options for nuclear arsenals, scenarios for employing nuclear weapons, and ways of deterring nuclear attack. As Clausewitz had observed with absolute war, so it was with nuclear war: 'the inquiring mind can never rest until it reaches the extreme'. [78] But it was a field of inquiry lacking something he considered essential to strategy – historical experience. Weapons could be tested in the real world but strategies for their employment could not. Nuclear war remained war on paper.

This is not the place to examine nuclear strategies of the Cold War. The aim is rather to set out ways in which nuclear weapons challenged Clausewitz's four levels of war – fighting, contest, national strategy and politics. All seemed totally confounded by the nuclear arsenal yet in each case some of Clausewitz's ideas appeared more relevant than ever.

Fighting and friction

Most fundamentally, nuclear war seemed to have abolished fighting in the sense of an encounter between military forces on the battlefield with outcomes shaped by traditional soldierly virtues like courage, endurance, experience and leadership.[3] An enemy's will to resist, indeed his entire country, could be destroyed without meeting and defeating his armed forces in battle. Where modern war sought to isolate fighting on a battlefield, hypermodern war made entire societies into targets, abolishing traditional distinctions between soldier and civilian, and between front and rear. Rather than a clash of arms nuclear war would be simply 'a process of mutual destruction without any combat'.[4] Or, if one state prevailed by some good fortune, a unilateral campaign of devastation. Since fighting had disappeared the term 'nuclear exchange' was sometimes preferred to 'nuclear war'.

At the same time nuclear arsenals promised to eliminate friction. For Clausewitz friction normally slowed down action, a burden to be carried by the efforts and endurance of armies. But now all the internal restraints that shackled war and prevented realisation of the extreme were thrown off.[5] Where conventional war operates in a resistant medium, nuclear weapons had created a condition of superconductivity.[6] Given adequate preparations, a nuclear attack could be easily launched and as easily met with a counter-attack. A rapid, virtually instantaneous rise to extremes was the likely result. Technology, in short, had taken the brakes off war – if national leaders chose to employ it.[7]

But friction remained in Clausewitz's strict sense – the difference between war on paper and war in reality. In the nuclear context it might lead to greater violence than intended or speed up the process of destruction – or it might retain its usual sense of degrading performance. Orders to fire missiles might be misunderstood or disobeyed, missiles might fail to work as intended, and targets might be missed. Nuclear war, like all war, could not escape mistakes, malfunctions and miscalculations. Aware of these dangers, nuclear powers cooperated to avoid such eventualities as mechanical accident, misreading radar screens and misunderstanding an opponent's intentions.[8]

Campaign strategy

Nuclear weapons also transformed campaign strategy, causing it merge with both tactics and national strategy. A nuclear campaign would no longer take the form of generals manoeuvring forces to threaten and give battle in a defined theatre of war. The use of even a single nuclear weapon was a matter for national leaders, not for the military alone. Efforts were made to restore campaign strategy by deploying 'tactical' (low-yield) nuclear weapons and delegating authority for their use to commanders in the field. This strategy promised effective deterrence, and effective war-fighting if deterrence failed.[9] But few were confident that initial use of tactical nuclear weapons would not be followed by rapid escalation, controlled or uncontrolled, to the global level.

The function of the military became instead to develop, maintain and deploy the nuclear arsenal in peacetime for use as required by government. Generals ceased to be commanders with a degree of independence in their own theatre of operations. The army consisted not of fighting soldiers, but of technicians and experts skilled in targeting and despatching weapons against military and non-military targets alike. The role of the people had also changed. Where in modern war they contributed numbers, skills and spirit to the nation's military effort before and during hostilities, now they were required to serve as hostages to the other side's nuclear missiles in time of peace – and as targets once war has broken out. The army had lost its normal function of protecting civilians from attack and being the principal object of enemy attack. Nuclear weapons had taken war from both the people and the army, placing in the hands of the political leadership.

National strategy – the unusable instrument of policy?

Nuclear weapons immediately prompted the question whether war could any longer serve as an instrument of policy. To some, they had decisively overturned the balance between offence and defence, promising a first strike that left the opponent with no capacity to strike back, even if the blow was expected. Clausewitz's ideal of rendering the enemy completely 'defenceless' appeared achievable and in the late 1940s some American strategists advocated a knock-out blow against the Soviet Union. At no stage, however, did either the US (even when it held a nuclear monopoly) or USSR convince themselves that a first strike with nuclear weapons would yield lasting military or political advantage.

The new weapons, it turned out, offered more to the defender than to the attacker. No first strike could be totally confident of eliminating all capacity to hit back. Even a small number of surviving enemy missiles posed credible and frightening threats of retaliation. The defender thus enjoyed an 'assured destruction capacity' that was reinforced by the construction of more or less invulnerable nuclear arsenals – greater numbers of missiles, deployment in underground silos and on submarines, and multiple nuclear warheads. As both the US and USSR acquired such forces, the result was a situation of 'mutual assured destruction', aptly abbreviated to MAD. In Clausewitz's terms, defence still consisted not in passively absorbing blows but in preparing and delivering well-directed blows against the attacker. Now such preparations apparently sufficed to deter war altogether. Defence seemed once and for all the stronger form of war in military and political terms.[10]

Finding a way to use nuclear weapons for positive purposes proved elusive.[11] Even during major conventional conflicts no state has used nuclear weapons against either a nuclear or non-nuclear opponent. Nuclear war, many concluded, might be a continuation of politics arising from political rivalries or miscalculations, but could never be a rational continuation of policy. For others, however, the point was to apply Clausewitz's formula while taking into account the changed values in the equation. The costs and risks of initiating nuclear war are manifestly enormous while prospective gains are dubious or simply illusory. The formula still applies – even, or especially, at the extreme. It effectively rules out nuclear war since the costs have risen beyond all reason.

Supporters of the formula also argue that it can accommodate the idea of using the *threat* of nuclear war as an instrument of policy. While actually fighting a nuclear war is 'devoid of sense', creating a finite risk of nuclear war to bolster deterrence can be rational policy.[12] The means is not actual use of nuclear weapons but maintaining the possibility of nuclear retaliation whether through cold calculation, blind fury or desperate confusion. The rationality lies in making careful use of a 'threat that leaves something to chance' such that a prospective attacker cannot be sure the victim will not respond.[13] Even simple possession of nuclear weapons, for example, without explicit threats or doctrines – 'existential deterrence' – can be a rational and effective instrument of policy.

International politics

The advent of nuclear weapons changed two central features of international politics. First, it undermined the traditional pecking order of great, middle and minor powers. The US and USSR created for themselves a new category of 'superpower', building nuclear arsenals that enjoyed global reach and remained invulnerable against any attack. But for the first time in history even the strongest state was vulnerable to devastation by a lesser power – if the latter possessed nuclear arms. Like the Colt .45 in the West nuclear weapons were the 'great equaliser', making irrelevant traditional criteria of military strength such as population, resources and industry. It would not surprise Clausewitz that rather than rely on deterrence alone the US has repeatedly shown interest in developing the capacity for physical protection against nuclear attack.

Second, nuclear weapons challenged war as a means of settling disputes between major powers. For Clausewitz war served to resolve clashes among states by creating new political relationships. But nuclear war offered little such prospect, threatening instead the total destruction of one or both belligerents. Where formerly a defeated major power could expect to regain a place in the international arena following a peace settlement, in the nuclear age it could hardly be confident even of surviving.

Some strategists, not all, came to believe that states would recognise the futility of putting their disputes to the test of war and resolve their differences by negotiation. Clausewitz had anticipated this in theory:

> so that in the end one would never really need to use the physical impact of the fighting forces – comparative figures would be enough. That would be a kind of war by algebra. [76]

In reality it took some time before major nuclear powers could rule out the possibility of war amongst themselves. During the Cold War a series of crises and proxy wars occurred in which states hurled threats against one another, uncertain whether a compromise would be reached or mutual annihilation ensue. After the tensest confrontation of all, the Cuban missile crisis of 1962, both superpowers took great care to avoid another such showdown.

The new system sought to operate without resort to force. Clausewitz had seen that battles offered but not actually fought were part of strategy but he believed that states would sooner or later have to fight real battles – like cash payments in a banking system. By contrast, the nuclear-armed superpowers were like gamblers who do not pay their debts in cash and must therefore guard their credit with care.[14] The underlying assumption of the nuclear system was that no state would press another so far that it felt compelled to use its nuclear forces.[15] It was the prospect of common calamity – akin to the collapse of a banking system – that allowed the system to survive. For Clausewitz, however, the threat of war alone could not serve as a permanent guarantee of peace. Policy must be backed by a capability and readiness to fight since war would come sooner or later.

Nor could Clausewitz accept the view that in the second half of the twentieth century the clear distinction between war and peace familiar to him and his contemporaries had disappeared. In an ironic twist of the formula, it was suggested that peace was now a continuation of war by other means. But for Clausewitz war and peace are distinct: 'What remains peculiar to war is simply the peculiar nature of its means'. [87] The Cold War was not true war – merely normal political struggle.

Clausewitz and hypermodern war

Nuclear weapons threatened to abolish Clausewitz's structure of war – as fighting, campaigning and an instrument of policy. For some the new means of war meant his relevance had been lost. Anatol Rapoport, for example, dubbed 'neo-Clausewitzians' those who continued to believe that war remained normal in international relations and could be managed as a rational means of policy.[16] Critics argued that even to consider war and its attendant risk of nuclear escalation was to accept its legitimacy and the risk of catastrophe.[17] Policy could not and should not be conducted with an admixture of military means.

But for others Clausewitz's formula still provided wise counsel to statesmen. It meant the careful tailoring of war to meet the ends of policy and hence a natural reluctance to resort to force when its consequences were unknowable and potentially catastrophic. Though Clausewitz had said little about deterrence, he had pointed to the risks of escalation. His principle of political supremacy over the military reinforced the importance of ends over means. Like pure war, the idea of nuclear war might serve as a reference point for those concerned with national security – but as an extreme to be avoided, not an ideal to be pursued.

21
Anti-Modern War

'War is not the continuation of policy by other means' [1]

If nuclear war fortunately remained a hypothetical exercise and major conventional war occurred infrequently, war within states did neither. Throughout history most political violence has taken place outside the framework of modern war. What might be called anti-modern war – because it operates on contrary principles – originates when a non-state group decides to use irregular force against a government or another non-state group.

The origins of such a conflict may be ethnic or tribal rivalries, communal antagonisms, 'warlordism', ideology, religious fanaticism and so on, often in combination. War of this kind is open to all-comers since the entry price is low. Weapons and explosives are readily obtained, no uniform or insignia is necessary, and targets are everywhere. Ambushes and raids are preferred to armed confrontation. Everyday criminal activities – robbery, extortion, kidnapping and the like – may be embraced to secure money and resources. [2] Though methods are usually low-tech, lethality can be high, extending to ethnic cleansing, mass slaughter and genocide.

All this makes it very difficult for states to deal with anti-modern warriors. They make no clear distinction between combatant and civilian, and usually lack the controls of modern war – political primacy, chain of command, disciplined formations and laws of war. They generally do not possess territory and visible assets, making serious retaliation difficult without hurting bystanders. Military victories against them, even if achievable, may not lead to the customary political concessions. There may be no leader willing to negotiate or able to ensure that agreements stick. Malcontents and factional elements disrupt cease-fires or revive hostilities with little effort. Not only are such wars easy to begin, they are hard to end.

Are Clausewitz's ideas at all relevant to anti-modern war? Though his focus was squarely on war between states, he was well acquainted with the phenomenon. In Spain, Portugal, Calabria and Tyrol French forces met armed resistance from local populations driven in part by national enthusiasm but also parochialism, threats to religion and popular culture, and the impositions and brutality of the occupiers. Familiarity with guns and violence also facilitated resistance.[3] Clausewitz's insights into the tactics of anti-modern war drew primarily on reports of the Spanish *guerrillas* and on his own observation of Russian partisans harassing Napoleon's army. Like all professional soldiers, he was uneasy with this form of war. At best, it was a necessary evil that, as in Prussia, should be made subordinate to regular warfare.

Clausewitz was also familiar with rebellion against established governments, not least the momentous revolution in France. He dismissed the prospect of revolution in Prussia while noting that rebellion could weaken an opponent in wartime. But in general he paid little attention to it as a form of war, largely ignoring the revolts in the 1790s in the Vendée and in Britanny where the Chouans relied heavily on terror. He made no reference to the American War of Independence of 1775–83 (though it was fought largely by regular armies which also used irregular tactics). Nor did he have much interest in or sympathy for the nationalist rebellions that from the 1820s sought freedom from Russian, Austro-Hungarian and Turkish rule. If Clausewitz was to contribute to later ideas about national liberation and revolutionary war, it would be in indirect fashion.

Revolutionary war and terrorism

The Boer War and the Arab revolt led by T.E. Lawrence prompted interest in Clausewitz. But more significant in the history of anti-modern war after Clausewitz was its alliance with communist ideology to form the doctrine of 'revolutionary war'. The idea of Mao Zedong in China in the 1930s, Che Guevara in Cuba and Vo Nguyen Giap in Vietnam in the 1940s and 50s was to combine irregular tactics with a political movement. Avoiding direct clashes with government forces, revolutionaries sought to win the hearts and minds of the people and establish a parallel government. Clausewitz's doctrine of political supremacy and his discussion of guerrilla tactics contributed to their theory of revolutionary war – mostly through Lenin.[4] Mao Zedong read *On War* in translation early in 1938.[5] In his own work *On Protracted War* written in the same year, he approvingly cited Clausewitz's argument (without naming him) that war is a continuation of politics.[6] The term 'people's war' was also used though not in Clausewitz's principal sense.

Where modern war focuses on armed forces and the will of the government, revolutionary war aims at the population. All objectives are defined in political terms, and strategy and tactics are directed at winning the loyalty of individuals. Where modern war recognises activities at the lowest level that are purely military, revolutionary war emphasises the political significance of every action.[7] Institutional distinctions also disappear as army and political party fuse in a single revolutionary movement, and the people are enlisted in direct support of military activities – providing, as Mao put it, the water in which guerrilla fish can freely swim. The theory of revolutionary war also saw conflict primarily in terms of social classes rather than states. As Lenin wrote in the spring of 1917: 'War is the continuation of the politics of one particular class'.[8] For Clausewitz war was a clash among states, not classes.[9]

The practice of revolutionary war, nonetheless, gave some support to the Clausewitzian paradigm. Mao, Giap, Castro and others made maximum use of popular nationalism directed against an alien or alienated regime as did the national liberation movements that sought independence from European colonists after 1945. Some revolutionary theorists accepted that conventional battle was necessary alongside guerrilla tactics, and even that a final military campaign might be required – the *coup de grâce* once a government is politically defeated. Some colonial territories were granted independence with little or no violent confrontation, the result of far-sightedness and lack of means for repression on the part of European powers. Elsewhere bitter struggles ensued, particularly when they were seen as clashes between the West and communism.

The first and second Vietnam Wars illustrate these patterns. The former engaged only France which found no means of using its conventional forces effectively against the guerrilla methods of the Viet Minh. The latter war drew in the United States and other Western powers, turning into a test case in the Cold War – a clash between communism and democracy and between methods of waging war. Vital precedents for the rest of Asia and the Third World were seen to be at stake. But the US proved unable to bring its opponent to fight on the battlefield where its conventional advantage could be exploited. Using a combination of regular and irregular forces and with some outside assistance, a people poorly equipped but highly motivated and fighting on its own soil defeated the world's greatest military power.

Just as the failure of British forces in the Boer War caused a sudden burst of interest in Clausewitz, so defeat in Vietnam caused the US military to look for a more political understanding of war after 1975. There was a need to link fighting and policy more effectively, and Clausewitz offered the means of doing so. A new translation of *On War* by Michael Howard and Peter Paret published in 1976 'made Clausewitz accessible for the first time to the generation of officers returning from the wreckage of Vietnam'. What appealed was his emphasis on the role of political judgement, his insistence that moral forces lie at the heart of war, and his diagnosis of war as 'inherently unpredictable, uncertain and ambiguous at every level'.[11] The concept of friction was eagerly embraced and written into the US Army Field Manual 100–5 and US Marine Corps doctrine.[12] US military schools and colleges adopted *On War* with enthusiasm.[13] Here was a philosophy of war that seemed relevant to the experience in Vietnam.

In an aptly titled work, *On Strategy*, Colonel Harry Summers adopted explicitly Clausewitzian principles to criticise America's direction of the war – as a failure of policy to understand the political basis of the war rather than as a failure of arms.[10] The US military had failed to convey the nature of the war to their political leaders who in turn had failed to win public support for the war. But would better understanding of the political character of the war have led to success? To see a conflict in political terms is no guarantee of effective policy, let alone victory on the ground. A better grasp of the political and social realities might have helped the US avoid entering the war in the first place or prompted withdrawal at an early stage.

Among policy-makers the desire to avoid 'another Vietnam' encouraged the formulation of guidelines to help determine the wisdom of future entanglements with irregular forms of warfare. There was a sense that such wars were different, less predictable and less controllable than modern wars. The Weinberger, Clinton and Powell doctrines, amongst others, proposed criteria such as clear objectives, public support and exit strategies. Particularly after the Cold War, when national interests in fighting anti-modern wars were often unclear, leaders were reluctant to 'take the first step without considering the last'.

The terrorist attacks of 11 September 2001 brought home the unpredictability and uncontrollability of anti-modern war. Before then most terrorism had been national – grounded in the politics of one state, and confining its violence and ambition to that state, even when actions and rhetoric extended to the international scene, as in the case of the IRA and PLO. The attacks by al-Qaida, by contrast, demonstrated that terrorism could draw support and membership from many countries, attack targets anywhere in the world, and badly hurt even a superpower. Just as many areas of political and social life are globalised, so too anti-modern war in one of its manifestations enjoys global reach. To counter it requires resolute action not just by one state but by many in cooperation.

September 11 also revived concerns that anti-modern warriors could acquire the weapons of hyper-modern war. Normally reliant on simple arms and incapable of operating complex weapons, some irregular forces may see nuclear, radiological, chemical or biological weapons as offering immediate and substantial means of harming target states. Their capacity for credible *threats* of mass destruction is also high on account of their ruthlessness, fanaticism and suicidal tactics and the difficulty of retaliating against them. Threats to destroy entire cities, poison large populations or spread lethal disease – or actual resort to such an action – might cause governments to capitulate and societies to collapse.

Whether against their own home-grown terrorism or against the global terrorism of groups like al-Qaida, however, governments have not crumbled easily. National leaders instinctively resist terrorist action and rarely succumb to blackmail, stiffening their resolve as they consider the consequences of surrender or appeasement. States also have a wide range of capacities for response, notably restrictions on civil liberties and use of police and intelligence services which improve in effectiveness as they learn to collaborate across national borders. Most importantly, perhaps, modern societies are remarkably robust and resilient. Despite periodic mayhem and continuing anxiety, communities persist in their daily occupations. Wealthy societies also benefit from immense redundancy. Destruction of one target – an aircraft, building, railway station, embassy and so on – leaves innumerable others unscathed. Terrorism has so far achieved little in political terms against modern states except to provoke strong responses.

Clausewitz and anti-modern war

If anti-modern war in its many manifestations is the dominant form of conflict in the future Clausewitz loses much of his relevance: fighting is among civilians not between soldiers, 'campaigns' are conducted by political leaders not generals, factional or ideological interests are pursued not state policy, and clashes take place internally or transnationally rather than between states. Violence, in other words, is not seen as a rational instrument of policy in the hands of states within the shared framework of modern war. This, many argue, is the future of warfare, especially in those parts of the world that lack the robust institutions necessary to keep violence under state control and to ensure it remains separate from civilian life. While advanced states have the wherewithal to resist anti-modern war, many less capable states have become chronic victims of irregular violence, and others have collapsed altogether into anarchy and civil war.

Clausewitz's focus, by contrast, was clearly on the state as the dominant political organisation with specialised and professional armies. Though aware of societies differently organised – referring, for example, to the Tartars where 'people and army had been one' [589] – he felt no need to theorise about them.[14] It may be argued, nevertheless, that his institutional framework – the division between government, army and people – still exists even in conditions of anti-modern war.

> In any conflict organized enough to be called war, there will be some kind of leadership organization, some group of fighters, some kind of population base – if not people, army, and government *per se*, then people, army, and government analogs.[15]

The distinction may be primitive in the case of, say, a war of national liberation using guerrilla tactics, but is sufficient to make the Clausewitzian framework relevant. Even global terrorism may be said to have leaders, followers and a population who are to be won over.

Against this, it can be suggested that although the distinction may hold up analytically – even a bank robbery must have people who plan it, people who carry it out and people who put money in the bank – it may not capture the essence of what is going on. Those engaged in anti-modern war do not necessarily see it in terms of objectives, political or otherwise, to be secured by military activity. For them it may be a passion, a personal realisation or a way of life. Alternatively, a more appropriate concept may be that of criminality against which police and intelligence agencies are deployed rather than military force. In terms of counter-measures a 'war on terrorism' is comparable to a 'war on crime'. In terms of legitimacy, however, whether anti-modern warriors should be regarded as criminals or as political actors often remains the very issue at stake.

22
Modern War since 1945

'We are all Clausewitzians now'[1]

If nuclear weapons seemed to make conventional forces and modern war redundant, this was an illusion. States were not confident that the simple threat of nuclear response to conventional attack would successfully deter. An opponent might disbelieve the threat, be prepared to try his luck or simply act irrationally. Conventional forces were necessary, strategists argued, to allow a response in kind to conventional attack. This would provide the state under attack with a viable option and make a barely credible nuclear threat more persuasive by creating a risk of escalation. Much debate focused on the appropriate level of conventional forces. Should it be just enough to initiate hostilities with a prospect of early escalation, or sufficient to fight an extended conventional war if required? The former presented a greater deterrent to potential aggressors, the latter a more reassuring option to the defender.

Fear of escalation has inhibited nuclear powers from initiating conventional war amongst themselves – apart from minor Sino-Russian border clashes in 1968–9. Instead, the US and USSR engaged in confrontations (Berlin and Cuba) or conducted proxy wars (notably Korea) in which each carefully avoided provoking the other into rash responses. Strategists paid much attention to ways of creating limits in such wars regardless of how ferociously they might be fought on the ground. Nuclear powers, of course, did not refrain from fighting conventional wars against weak, non-nuclear powers when it seemed necessary – for example, Britain against Egypt in 1956 and Argentina in 1982, the US against Iraq in 1991 and 2003. The superpowers also used conventional forces to intervene in weak states, finding success in their own backyards on several occasions but failing badly in more adventurous undertakings – the US in Vietnam and the USSR in Afghanistan. Conventional armed forces thus had their uses for major powers: engaging the nuclear deterrent and policing spheres of influence. Certain middle powers also found them useful in acquiring territories to which they had some claim, genuine or otherwise – such as China and Tibet, India and Goa, and Indonesia and East Timor.

But conventional inter-state wars have rarely led to positive results for the state initiating them. North Korea's attack on the South in 1950 was driven back by an alliance under the UN banner. Britain and France were compelled to withdraw from Egypt in 1956 by diplomatic and economic pressure. Israel made spectacular gains in 1967 but found holding on to all of its captured territory too costly. Iran and Iraq fought from 1980 to 1988 with no significant territorial change. Argentina was driven from the Falklands in 1982, Iraq from Kuwait in 1991. Though the first use of force often achieved major surprise, the initial gains were usually reversed. The one-sided wars against Afghanistan in 2001 and Iraq in 2003, while producing clear military victory, may likewise find political success elusive.

The value of modern war as a instrument of policy has seemed in question. Not only the risk of nuclear escalation but other factors are at work. Notable has been the increasing cost of equipment – especially in navies and air forces – and of recruiting and retaining soldiers, particularly since the abandonment of conscription in most Western countries. In an interdependent global economy war also harms a state's trade, financial relations, communications and tourism whatever its political system. Nor can the degree of restraint on governments exercised by the international community and the UN be discounted. Two additional factors – domestic politics and technology – can be explored in more detail.

The domestic political context

Clausewitz did not foresee the way in which the peoples of Western Europe would steadily acquire an effective say in government. Beginning in England in 1832, political reform slowly and unevenly gave the masses greater influence in policy-making. Many viewed it with suspicion and some opposed it root and branch. Clausewitz would have been deeply concerned by universal adult suffrage, the growth of representative institutions, the proliferation of sectional interest groups, and the need for governments to keep mass opinion on side. The people had a role in war, not policy.

The Cold War might have heartened Clausewitz for its inculcation of a military spirit among entire societies and the adoption of universal conscription in many countries. As in his time, some critics worried about too great a militarisation of society.[2] The period after 1989, however, would have troubled Clausewitz with widespread expectations of a 'peace' dividend, reductions in armed forces and defence budgets, and abolition of compulsory military service, actual or planned, in many states. Sustaining defence spending became more difficult as the cost of weapons systems and personnel steadily increased. A public reluctance to accept casualties, particularly where national interests are not obviously engaged, added to the difficulties of waging war for democracies. Yet September 11 and the initiation of the 'war on terrorism' has revived the willingness of most Western democracies to contribute blood and treasure to this new struggle.

Since Clausewitz's time both politics and war have become far more specialised, making his argument for mutual understanding between soldier and politician even more important and more difficult to realise.[3] His doctrine of political supremacy is, however, unchallenged. All political systems – whether democratic, communist, liberal or autocratic – have insisted on maintaining political control over the military. As ever, this depends not simply on governmental structures but on a complex of laws, conventions, attitudes and traditions that are not easily created, if sometimes easily destroyed.

The impact of technology

War, it can be argued, follows the economic system and its means of producing wealth.[4] Earliest human society survived on hunting and gathering and later on agricultural production. Communities were thus unable to produce sophisticated weapons or afford large armies. Their style of fighting was simple and crude, taking the form of raids on neighbouring communities to plunder crops, property, women and other booty. This 'pre-modern' warfare remained ill-organised and endemic, reflecting both its simple economic basis and the traditional social structures that conducted it.

The emergence of the sovereign state from around 1500, as Clausewitz observed, brought a degree of order and control to warfare and the French Revolution added immensely to its scale and power. But it was the industrial revolution under way from the mid-1700s that transformed warfare again after Clausewitz's death. Where population (a factor he mentioned frequently) had been a major factor in determining military capacity, now a state's manufacturing, scientific and technological base came to the fore. Where *On War* assumed stable technology with advances adopted at more or less the same rate, it came to matter whether a country had more and better rifles, machine guns, artillery, capital ships and the like. Armies resembled factories, relying on specialised equipment, planning and logistics, and employed large numbers of trained and disciplined 'workers'. This was the industrial age of warfare which possessed 'an appetite for innovation as much as for blood – an appetite which calls out for continually new forms of destructiveness'.[5] By 1945 science and technology had presented modern war with weapons capable of unprecedented destruction.

At the turn of the third millennium the economic basis of the wealthiest societies is changing yet again in fundamental fashion – from industry to information. A transition is under way to economic productivity based on knowledge and the exploitation of communications technology and electronic systems. In turn, advances in electronics, communications, information technology, surveillance and related fields have produced weapons systems of unprecedented precision, range and lethality that are transforming how war is organised and fought in radical fashion. This is the so-called Revolution in Military Affairs (RMA).

The impact of technology on war since Clausewitz's time is too complex to cover here. Two critical themes – strategic doctrine and generalship – must suffice together with speculation about the future directions of war.

Strategic doctrine

Driven by technology unfamiliar to Clausewitz intense competition resulted between offence and defence after 1830. At the tactical level the balance swung freely as a result of uneven technological advances allied with failure to grasp the implications of new weapons such as the machine gun, the tank and the aircraft. In the campaign technology shared its favours more evenly between offence and defence. Rapid transport of troops by rail, for example, granted the attacker speed in deployment, re-supply and reinforcement. But it also gave the defence mobility to concentrate forces quickly against an attack and to throw in reserves as necessary. Clausewitz's argument that defence is inherently the stronger form of warfare remains contentious but not yet discarded.

A key issue has been the capacity for surprise attack. In theory, technology enables the offence to concentrate forces more rapidly and control them more effectively. Yet the defence is better able to forestall surprise through improved surveillance and intelligence and the use of long-range weapons to disrupt an impending attack. In practice, attacking armies more than once achieved the strategic surprise which Clausewitz considered decidedly advantageous but difficult to realise. Most cases of surprise, however, resulted from failure at the political level to read the signs of a forthcoming attack. As noted, gains secured by surprise have mostly been reversed in the longer term through both political factors and military action. Again, the proposition that defence is the stronger form of war retains at least *prima facie* validity.

Generalship

Generalship has also changed. As the accuracy of rifle fire grew, the range of artillery multiplied and fronts stretched from a few miles at most to dozens and ultimately hundreds of miles, it became increasingly difficult for the general to remain on or near the battlefield.[6] It was also less important since battles lasted much longer than the one or two days common in the Napoleonic era. Individual bravery among commanders counted for less, while victory and defeat were not so dependent on command decisions made on the spot. At the same time, the greater geographical spread of forces demanded strategic skills of a high order. Generals came to dispose of bombers, cruise missiles and even artillery that could be brought to bear from great distances. Battles might be decided by forces located anywhere within the theatre or brought in from outside. The term operational art was coined to embrace developments in campaign strategy Clausewitz could never imagine.

Communications and surveillance also presented new challenges as the collection and analysis of information became more extensive, specialised and organised. In the course of the nineteenth century intelligence became a formal discipline and a military specialisation. The small staff supporting a commander in Clausewitz's era steadily expanded into major branches of military formations.[7] In the twentieth century and especially in recent decades the speed of collection, variety of sources, range of subjects, computerised management of information and sheer volume of data have transformed intelligence in quantity and quality. The commander is promised an instant, accurate and comprehensive view not just of the battlefield but the entire theatre of war. The mental capacity to 'see the other side of the hill', as

Wellington put it, became less important. Some commentators concluded that the fog of war had lifted altogether.[8]

Yet the revolution in intelligence and surveillance has produced
counter-weights. If today – contrary to Clausewitz – most information
is true, it is often 'trivial in quality and overwhelming in quantity'.[9]
Rapid and extensive data collection from multiple sources brings information overload, making separation of wheat and chaff, signal and
noise extremely difficult. More than ever, knowledge that better information is around the corner may induce the general to postpone decisions until the final piece of the jigsaw is found – a problem Clausewitz
had observed. The speed with which intelligence can be gained and
can lose its currency still places a premium on rapid decision-making.[10]
Friction also ensures that the smartest system breaks down at the
wrong moment, malfunctions or is misread by operators.

In sum, commanders still require Clausewitz's qualities of mind and
temperament – determination in an uncertain environment, ability to
comprehend rapidly changing situations, sound judgement, as well as
understanding of the wider political context in which politicians may
seek to exercise detailed and continuing control. Genius may perhaps
be less essential when intelligence can provide 'adequate grounds' for
decision.[11] But personal bravery and endurance may be in demand
again to cope with long-range precision attacks and the stress of
24-hour battles. In modern war, despite its many changes, generals
have not escaped Clausewitz's fog and friction.

The RMA and future war

One consequence of the new technology may be to make modern war
'safe' to wage once more if armies are able to direct highly accurate
weapons against each other while avoiding civilian populations.
Military targets may be as discrete as a single radar facility or a communications centre. The idea of a campaign fought primarily between
armies again seems feasible. Such a clash of arms, indeed, could take
place not only on the battlefield but also away from it – the so-called
'empty battlefield'. Modern war, it might be thought, remains still possible albeit more intense, more destructive and more costly than ever.
Iraq in 2003 demonstrated the scope for this form of war, albeit against
a third-rate military force. Unlike hypermodern war and anti-modern
war, it is a mode of fighting with which military people feel familiar
and comfortable.

Technology, however, has not stopped at this point. The United
States has demonstrated the potential for what might be called 'war

without fighting'. The Gulf War of 1991 showed how long-range precision weapons could undercut an enemy's fighting strength, leaving relatively little to be done in the form of combat on the ground. In the Kosovo campaign of 1999 Serbia could barely put up any resistance against attacks by bombs and missiles launched by NATO against selected targets. Aircraft flew above the ceiling of anti-aircraft fire, facing risk of mechanical failure or accident rather than enemy action. In this case no 'combatants' met in battle. It was a 'campaign', not in the traditional military sense but a political campaign of coercion against a recalcitrant government. It was, in effect, war without fighting between soldiers.

There are important limits to war without fighting. Few states will possess an arsenal with the necessary accuracy and the up-to-date intelligence required. War of this kind also requires opponents that have sufficient modern infrastructure to suffer from its destruction but are not advanced enough to fight back in serious fashion. Serbia was unfortunate enough to belong to this intermediate category – as was to some extent Iraq in 1991 and 2003. War without fighting would have been irrelevant in, say, Somalia or Afghanistan (where friendly troops were needed on the ground), and too dangerous against, say, North Korea or China. The defence can also do what it normally does – harden, disperse, disguise and duplicate its vital assets. War without fighting remains so far more of an aspiration than a reality – but a vision which will continue to attract strategic planners.

Beyond 'war without fighting' lies 'war without weapons'. The increasing reliance of states on computer and communications systems renders them vulnerable to attacks in cyber-space. A state's economy and society may be debilitated by 'hacking' into electronic networks, destroying or paralysing systems of finance, trade, power distribution, transport, communications, social security, law enforcement, and so on. Enormous pain and loss may be inflicted with little or no visible, physical destruction. The damage may be unilateral or mutual but in neither case do armed forces inflict physical harm on things or people. It is also a form of war with virtually no entry requirements as individual hackers have demonstrated. In Clausewitzian terms, however, it hardly deserves the name 'war'.

The continuing relevance of Clausewitz

Some writers suggest that technology has rendered Clausewitz outmoded or in need of qualification. Michael Handel, for example, argues

that a fourth element – the material realm of technology and economics – should be added to 'square the triangle' of reason, passion
and chance.[12] Certainly, technology is now critical in modern war and
the fascination with it may mean that Clausewitz loses favour, including his place in American military colleges.[13] But war is a chameleon
and the means employed can be seen as simply changes in colour –
dramatic but not so far altering its fundamental nature as a fight
among soldiers. Centres of gravity and modes of destruction may
change but they do not replace the contest. Only if radically new forms
of war such as 'war without fighting' or 'war without weapons'
triumph over traditional forms will technology render Clausewitz
redundant.

From the wars that have occurred and from the endless rehearsal of
wars, it is clear that modern war is immensely more complex than in
the past and is pressing in new directions. Weapons, communications
and surveillance are far more capable than anything dreamed of in
Clausewitz's time or even up to 1939. Politics has also changed as
populations in western countries and increasingly elsewhere have
acquired greater influence in national politics. Significantly, too, the
readiness of citizens to support military effort and sacrifice has varied
markedly – a problem not unfamiliar to Clausewitz.

The skills required of generals have changed though in the last
analysis temperament and judgement remain central. The qualities
needed by soldiers have likewise altered – for example, the demands of
complex equipment, communications and 24-hour fighting – but
much remains the same in terms of courage, discipline and endurance
in the face of personal danger. As long as armies still fight armies, or at
least seriously armed opponents, the key qualities expected of soldiers
do not change – a continuity that reaches back before modern war is
shared with anti-modern war.

23
A Farewell to Clausewitz?

'War is therefore liable to eternal reinvention' [1]

Clausewitz's interpretation of war has retained at least some relevance in the face of hyper-modern war, anti-modern war and the technological and political transformations of modern war. Can it survive other challenges which are yet more fundamental? Three in particular are worth examining: the contemporary challenge to realism; the possible decline of the state; and the assumption of rationality in war. All three seek to knock away the underpinnings of Clausewitz's theory of war – indeed, of all theories of modern war.

The challenge to realism

Underlying much thinking about war since 1945 has been an unease that calls on earlier pacifist and anti-war traditions. World War I convinced many of the futility of war though this did not prevent another global conflict within a generation. The advent of nuclear weapons in 1945 brought a dramatic increase in the destructiveness of war – to an absolute level in that it could destroy all humankind. This realisation has so far helped dissuade states from even a single use of nuclear weapons in anger in over fifty years. War in the twentieth century – modernised, industrialised, unprecedentedly destructive – lost much of the glory and glamour it once had. Modern psychology probed more deeply the damage caused to survivors of war, soldier and civilian alike. Many societies seemed less willing to recognise the virtues of the warrior or to tolerate casualties. War, in short, got something of a bad name.

In this atmosphere Clausewitz has come under attack for his failure to bring moral judgement to the idea of war as an instrument of policy. (See chapter 9) Perhaps this was justified in his day but war, critics argue, should be seen differently now. It is too damaging, too destructive, too counterproductive in an interdependent world to continue as a social institution. Clausewitz and his followers are accused of exhorting statesmen 'to be ready and willing to go to war if the prize [is] worth it'.[2] The purposes (and conduct) of war must be subject to moral standards and cannot be left, as he proposed, to the judgement of history. A better way of pursuing policy and settling disputes must be found. Having lost its rationale and traditional function, war should be abandoned like other redundant social institutions such as slavery and the duel.

This challenge to Clausewitz, of course, is the challenge to realism. His defence is the defence of realism: readiness for war remains the best practicable guarantee of security for a nation and for ensuring peace among states. A peaceful world is an ideal to be admired but for the time being abandoning readiness for war will create more dangers than it prevents. A credible military force will also serve to deter war. Of course, when war is employed as an instrument of policy, this must be done more prudently and judiciously than ever in the light of added costs and risks. War may have become a less common feature of contemporary state relations but has not been abolished. Even lengthy periods of relative peace, as Clausewitz knew, can be followed by violent cataclysms.

War without the state

The state was central to the development of modern war, furnishing it with resources, goals and a degree of rationality in linking means and ends. If contemporary political, social and economic changes displace the state from centre stage, Clausewitz loses his relevance. Several arguments predicting the decline of the state have been put forward.[3] Here it suffices to note that the key element would be a shift in control over military force away from the state to: (i) global regimes of some kind, whether a world government with comprehensive and effective powers or a set of regimes managing different aspects of global affairs; or (ii) non-state groups, based on ideology, ethnicity, religion, economic activity or any principle other than territorial sovereignty. Either development would signify the end of the process of concentration of military power in the hands of state that began in Europe some 500 years ago. If the state disappears, war can no longer serve as an instrument of state policy.

In the meantime three current trends – each alien to Clausewitz's thinking – may indicate that armed force is being increasingly directed toward globally determined rather than national purposes. First are efforts to regulate the resort to war. States no longer freely claim, as they did in the nineteenth century, a sovereign prerogative to decide when and how to employ military force. Where Clausewitz believed international law had little or no relevance to national decisions about war and peace, the twentieth century after 1918 saw increasing efforts to restrain states from using war for purposes not approved by the international community. The United Nations Charter prohibited the resort to force by states – with the significant exception of self-defence – while proclaiming the organisation's right to employ and authorise military means. Of course, states retain the physical capacity to resort to war unilaterally but need to pay increasing attention to the political drawbacks of lack of international approval. Perhaps only a superpower or a rogue state will feel free to ignore this trend.

Second is the growth of international peacekeeping. The UN and regional organisations have made extensive use of national armed forces for peacekeeping within and between states. States do not abandon command and control of their armed forces but do become deeply entangled in multinational operations where their political room to manoeuvre is constrained. Particularly after the Cold War international action to keep the peace became more possible and more frequent. Internal conflicts, above all, have demanded attention from the international community on account of humanitarian tragedies and massive abuse of human rights. Several operations have been authorised to use force to deal with such calamities under Chapter VII of the Charter. Peacekeeping has grown in its depth of involvement in the internal affairs of states and in the breadth of activities taken on by the UN. A few countries see peacekeeping as the primary function of their armed forces, but this is not a policy widely adopted.

Third is the rise of law enforcement tasks undertaken by armed forces. Since Clausewitz's time security has become significantly more complex as a result of a more diverse range of threats.[4] Global terrorism, transnational crime, people trafficking, drug smuggling as well as more diffuse threats such as the spread of disease and environmental hazards all raise the question whether the state is best adapted to deal with such challenges in the long run. Populations in many countries seem less concerned with future military attack than with immediate 'non-traditional' threats to their safety and security. Many such challenges can be effectively countered only by serious and sustained cooperation between states taking a law enforcement approach involving military forces along with police and security organisations.

These developments, however, are taking place within the framework of a system of more or less sovereign states, causing it to work rather more effectively rather than transforming it. Nor are they totally new – Clausewitz's last posting was to establish a *cordon sanitaire* against the spread of cholera. For the state to lose its independence and for armed forces to lose their traditional role in national security would require far more extensive political change than we have seen so far.

War without reason

Some critics of Clausewitz have argued that we fundamentally misunderstand the character of war by placing it in a framework of reason. Whether we are talking about modern or anti-modern war, we cannot ignore the psychology underlying most major violence which resists subordination to reason. Thus Martin van Creveld, echoing Nietzsche, argues that all war remains at heart non-rational and uncontrollable because men – as distinct from women – love fighting for the psychological satisfaction it brings. Why else would they risk or even embrace their own death? War is psychologically sustained, he adds, because women love warriors.[5] On this view war is not an instrument of policy, but an expression of deep-seated internal drives such as love of fighting, the need to face and overcome challenge or the desire for social or sexual esteem. War is no more a calculated instrument of policy than sex is merely a rational means of producing offspring.

This can be seen even in those European societies that appear to have subordinated war to reason. In response to foreign invasion, for example, resort to guerrilla methods is a natural, almost automatic response. Partisans do not calculate their chances of success but simply fight for their nation, often with great bravery and self-sacrifice. Legal restraints on violence are often abandoned. There is no assessment of costs and benefits except in extreme terms – honour or death, national pride or eternal disgrace. The issues are not negotiable, no compromises can be made. Interpreting such violence in rational, instrumental terms is misleading. Perhaps most wars have origins too deep within the human psyche to make them amenable to interpretation in terms of rational action. The superficial instrumentality of war should not be mistaken for the deep-seated human mentality of war.

Others critics such as John Keegan emphasise the socio-cultural origins of war, arguing that it is based primarily on social ritual and tradition. This is most apparent in non-European cultures which see war and violence as part of, rather than separate from, the rest of life. There is no specialised group for fighting, since all adult males, unless too old or unfit, are regarded as warriors. Violence is part of the way in which authority is exercised in society. National interests are not separated from religious or cultural norms, and politics remains little more than 'an embryonic, subordinate and despised activity'.[6]

War is not an instrument but more of an institution, a practice or custom built into human society. The warrior spirit is ingrained not so much in human nature as in human society which sustains the warrior ethic and pays homage to the demands of war. Culture encourages warriors to sacrifice their lives for their fellow soldiers, for their unit or for their nation in a way no 'rational' man would. War is further encouraged by the propensity of societies to distinguish between insiders and outsiders, to be fearful of strangers and to make much of minor differences such as tribal or national identity.[7] Hence warfare is at heart 'apolitical' – neither fully managed nor significantly moderated by states or any political organisation.[8] In short, 'in warmaking it is culture that counts, a perception that escaped Clausewitz'.[9]

The Clausewitzian paradigm

Clausewitz offered a paradigm, a way of thinking about war. Though inherent in human society and brimming with passion and chance, war can be shaped to human ends. This is best done by keeping control of war in the hands of states and its conduct as a matter between armies – the concept of modern war. It is not an easy task, nor one free of cost in blood and treasure, but it offers two principal benefits. First, it limits violence against the civilian population and the social order. As a matter of principle fighting ought to be limited to armies on the battlefield, albeit practice sees it readily spill over into the civilian arena. Second, it provides a way of reaching a decision in disputes between states, or at least a result accepted by the contending parties as final for the time being. Belligerents share some idea of what constitutes success in battles and campaigns, and of what this signifies for winner and loser.

The consequences of abandoning this paradigm are evident in antimodern war. Whether in the context of revolutionary war, national liberation or terrorism, violence is among and about civilian society rather than the exclusive business of soldiers. Anti-modern war is less an instrument of policy wielded by government on behalf of the people than a violent activity that engages all elements of society, armed or unarmed. Violence is more endemic than instrumental. Those engaging in it often value it for its own sake rather than what it can realistically achieve. Most anti-modern warfare, moreover, is chronically persistent and indecisive. It lacks 'waypoints' such as battles after which hostilities can be halted by agreement. No conventions for reaching finality exist save physical destruction or psychological exhaustion of the opponent. The only decisive means are genocide and massacre. If such wars end, they usually peter out as societies weary of constant fighting; or they persist at such a low level as to be hardly noticed by the rest of the world.

Of course, modern war has its faults. Clausewitz recognised that passion and chance would always be present, that leaders might embark on wars out of personal ambition, that generals may seek to take over policy. Like any instrument of policy, war could be used in unthinking or incompetent fashion. Risks may be misjudged, costs and benefits miscalculated, opponents underestimated. More than once the first step into war is taken without considering the last. Political leaders (and now public opinion) might demand of war what it cannot guarantee such as bloodless victory. Nor is modern war necessarily decisive, as Clausewitz recognised, often failing to settle political questions in the long-term. There is simply no guarantee that states will treat war in a rational fashion, as a means to an end.

Modern war has a further drawback which Clausewitz indicated without foreseeing the end result. If war carries great significance as a means of settling disputes, participants are encouraged to fight with maximum effort and unlimited means. In Clausewitz's time modern war began to see increasing mobilisation of society to provide manpower; after his time mobilisation of science and industry provided weapons of increasing destructiveness. This competitive approach to war, Gallie suggests, has in an important sense got out of hand.

> For several thousand years that culture has instilled the belief that there are no lengths of destructiveness to which a government is not entitled – and, more, is not obliged – to go in preserving and advancing the interests of its people.[10]

By the second half of the twentieth century war in its hyper-modern form demonstrated its potential to deliver destruction far beyond the battlefield into whole societies, even perhaps the entire planet.

Yet Clausewitz's trust in reason remains arguably the best practical response. The sheer dangers of hyper-modern war have caused governments to understand that weapons of mass destruction are not useful as positive instruments of policy. Even the most simple or cynical of minds can recognise the logic of avoiding their use. The costs and risks of conventional war are self-evidently high and perhaps increasing. Even if norms against resort to force are very weak, states have calculated their interests in ways that have kept them from another global war and, in most cases, from lesser wars. Where war has been initiated, it has mostly been unsuccessful or subsequently reversed. Indeed, it is anti-modern war that has killed more people than wars between states since 1945. Modern war, used cautiously and carefully as an instrument of policy, avoids the worst though it does not promote the best.

Other times and other societies may treat war as a way of life, a ritual activity, a pastime for the warrior, a personal feud between individuals or even as an enduring social institution. No paradigm of war is right or wrong. It is a matter of how humanity collectively 'chooses' to interpret war. Clausewitz offered a powerful interpretation of war based on the state and its capacity for rational pursuit of national interests that became the dominant – though not undisputed – paradigm for understanding war in Europe and much of the rest of the world. Any future paradigm will likewise reflect prevailing intellectual, cultural, social, economic and technological currents. Whether the Clausewitzian canon will retain its preeminence in the long term remains unknown and unknowable. It is a question that, like Clausewitz, we must 'leave to the philosophers'.

Notes

Preface

1. Brodie, 1973, p. 291.
2. For a comparison of Clausewitz and Sun Tzu see Handel, 2001.
3. Perlmutter, 1988, pp. 9–12.
4. Maude, 1940, p. v.
5. Luvaas, 1986, p. 205.
6. Brodie, 1976, p. 52.
7. Atkinson, 1981.
8. Strachan, 1983, p. 6.
9. Cited Handel, 2001, p. 25.
10. Howard, 1976, p. 28.
11. Aron, 1976, I, p. 30.
12. Skinner, 1969.
13. Lider, 1977, p. 313.
14. Howard, 1976, p. 44.
15. Paret, 1976 and 1992; Gat, 1989; Aron, 1976.
16. Howard, 1983.

Chapter 1   Soldier

1. Letter to Marie, 18 September 1806, Schwartz, 1878, I, p. 219.
2. Schössler argues that Clausewitz was born on 1 July and that the earlier date was used to increase his apparent age and assist entry into the army. 1991, pp. 9–10.
3. 'Observations on Prussia in her Great Catastrophe', p. 40. Unless otherwise indicated, references to Clausewitz's writings other than *On War* are taken from the translations in Paret and Moran, 1992.
4. Letter to Marie, 28 January 1807, Schwartz, 1878, I, pp. 240–1.
5. Paret, 1976, pp. 52–3.
6. 'Observations', p. 40.
7. 'Observations', pp. 40–41.
8. Paret, 1976, p. 55.
9. White, 1989, chapter 2. Lieutenant von Clausewitz became member number 50. Hahlweg, 1980, p. 27n.
10. 'Bemerkungen über die reine und angewandte Strategie des Herrn von Bülow' in the journal *Neue Bellona*, reprinted in Hahlweg (ed.), 1979, pp. 63–88.
11. 'Considérations sur la manière de faire la guerre à la France', reprinted in Hahlweg (ed.), 1966, I, pp. 58–63.
12. 'Observations', p. 77.
13. Rothenberg, 1980, p. 189.
14. Schwartz, 1878, I, p. 225; Paret, 1976, p. 124n.

15. Schwartz, 1878, I, p. 226.
16. Paret, 1976, p. 125.
17. Chandler, 1987, p. 124. See also Weigley, 1991, pp. 394–8. Battle figures are notoriously variable.
18. Rothenberg, 1980, p. 190.
19. Schwartz, 1878, I, pp. 53, 61.
20. 'Historische Briefe über die grossen Kriegsereignisse im Oktober 1806', reprinted in Niemeyer (ed.), 1977.
21. Paret, 1976, p. 131.
22. Paret, 1976, p. 183.
23. 'The Germans and the French', pp. 250–62.
24. 'Observations', esp. pp. 63–66.
25. Paret, 1976, p. 67.
26. Paret, 1966, esp. ch. 4.
27. Paret, 1968, p. 405.
28. Letter to Gneisenau, 8 February 1810, Hahlweg (ed.), 1966, I, p. 620.
29. Paret, 1976, p. 144.
30. 'Observations', pp. 73–5.
31. 'On the Life and Character of Scharnhorst', p. 95.
32. Schramm, 1976, pp. 27–8.
33. Paret, 1976, p. 436.
34. Letter of 24 June 1810, cited Paret, 1976, pp. 187–8.
35. Paret, 1976, p. 201.
36. 'Meine Vorlesungen über den kleinen Krieg', Hahlweg (ed.), 1966, I.
37. Schramm, 1976, p. 28. Only one letter survives from the period 1816–30. Paret, 1976, p. 266n.
38. 'Political Declaration', p. 303. Clausewitz sent it to Gneisenau, asking him to keep it 'under lock and key'. Hahlweg (ed.), 1966, I, p. 682.
39. Paret, 1966, p. 171.
40. *Principles of War*, Gatzke (trans. and ed.), 1942.
41. Letter to Marie, 12–24 August 1812, Linnebach, 1917, p. 294.
42. 'The Campaign of 1812 in Russia', p. 114.
43. Schwartz, 1878, I, p. 493. Translation from Parkinson, 1970, p. 194.
44. Brodie, 1976a, p. 643.
45. 'Campaign of 1812', pp. 188–200; Paret 1966, pp. 191–5.
46. Letter to Marie, 18–30 December 1812, Schwartz, 1878, I, p. 539. Even more painful was the thought that one of them might be taken prisoner. 'Campaign of 1812', p. 184.
47. Paret, 1976, p. 232; *Laus* has the same connotations as *louse* in English.
48. Paret, 1976, p. 220.
49. Paret, 1976, p. 250; Schramm, 1976, p. 23. By this time his brother Friedrich had received the Pour le Mérite and Wilhelm both the Iron Cross First Class and the Pour le Mérite with cluster.
50. Letter to Marie, 12 July 1815, Schwartz, 1878, II, pp. 161–4.

Chapter 2   Scholar

1. Letter to Marie, 3 July 1807, Schwartz, 1878, I, p. 283.

2. 'Agitation', pp. 365–6.
3. 'Scharnhorst', pp. 88–109.
4. Parkinson, 1976, p. 295.
5. 'On the Political Advantages and Disadvantages of the Prussian *Landwehr*', p. 333.
6. 'Our Military Institutions', p. 328.
7. Schramm, 1976, pp. 517–9.
8. Paret, 1976, pp. 319–323; Hahlweg, 1980, p. 33; Paret, 1992a.
9. Paret, 1976, p. 436.
10. On the problems of interpreting this essay, see Paret, 1976, pp. 298–306.
11. Paret, 1976, pp. 85–7.
12. 'Observations', p. 65. It was finally published in 1888.
13. Paret, 1976, p. 364.
14. Paret, 1976, p. 15.
15. One study was *The Campaign of 1815 in France* of which the Duke of Wellington wrote a respectful critique. Bassford, 1994, pp. 41–45.
16. Aron, 1977, p. 1259.
17. 'Gedanken zur Abwehr', Hahlweg (ed.), 1979, pp. 493–530.
18. Paret, Moran (eds), 1992, pp. 377–8.
19. Paret, 1976, p. 430.
20. Schwartz, 1878, II, p. 441.
21. Hahlweg, 1980, p. 163n.
22. Paret, 1976, pp. 431–40 is closer to the latter view; Brodie, 1973, pp. 299–305, is closer to the former, suggesting that Clausewitz suffered from a 'neurosis'. See also Steiner, 1991, esp. pp. 217–23.
23. Letter, 18 September 1806, Schwartz, 1878, I, p. 219.
24. 9 April 1807, Schwartz, 1878, I, p. 266.
25. Schwartz, 1878, II, pp. 448–9. Quotations from Brandt's memoirs are from Graham, 1940, p. xxxvii.
26. Paret, 1976, p. 211.
27. Paret, 1976, p. 323.
28. Schramm, 1976, p. 34.
29. Cited Paret, 1976, p. 431.
30. Paret, 1976, pp. 281–2.
31. Gallie, 1978a, p. 167.

Chapter 3   On Warfare

1. 'Scharnhorst', p. 103.
2. Bond, 1998, p. 16.
3. Duffy, 1987, p. 6.
4. Rothenberg, 1980, p. 61.
5. 'Bekenntnisdenkschrift' ('Political Declaration'), Hahlweg (ed.), 1966, I, p. 750 [own translation]. See also Marshal Foch: 'The wars of Kings were at an end, the wars of peoples were beginning'. Foch, 1918, p. 29.
6. Moran, 1989, p. 198.
7. Best, 1982, p. 31.
8. 'Observations on the Wars of the Austrian Succession', p. 27.
9. Best, 1982, pp. 78–9.

10. Cited Porter, 1994, p. 131.
11. Porter, 1994, p. 131.
12. At Hochkirch in October 1758 Frederick the Great was defeated decisively but not disastrously by Austrian forces.
13. Cited Best, 1982, p. 81.
14. Esdaile, 1995, p. 49.
15. Esdaile, 1995, p. 56.
16. McNeill, 1983, p. 194.
17. Esdaile, 1995, p. 248.
18. Esdaile, 1995, pp. 248–9.
19. Paret, 1970a, p. 4.
20. Esdaile, 1995, pp. 276–7.
21. Holmes, 1991, p. 69.
22. Rothenberg, 1980, p. 194.
23. Cited Esdaile, 1995, p. 265.
24. Esdaile, 1995, p. 267.
25. Esdaile, 1995, p. 246.
26. 'Our Military Institutions', p. 324.
27. 'Our Military Institutions', p. 327.
28. Cited Paret, 1976, pp. 290, 291.
29. 'Our Military Institutions', p. 328.
30. 'Prussian *Landwehr*', p. 332.
31. 'Prussian *Landwehr*', p. 332.
32. 'Our Military Institutions', p. 328.
33. Paret, 1976, p. 235.
34. Paret, 1976, p. 291.
35. Cited Esdaile, 1995, p. 136.
36. Jomini, 1992, pp. 29–35.
37. The term *Kleinkrieg* also means 'small war'. Clausewitz's extensive lectures on this topic at the War Academy in 1810–11 covered many guerrilla-type tactics for detachments of between 20 and 400 men such as ambush, capture of patrols and destruction of bridges. Hahlweg, 1966, I, pp. 208–599. The focus, however, was not partisan warfare but instructing regular soldiers in the use of such tactics as part of normal operations. Paret, 1976, p. 190n.
38. Best, 1982, p. 178.
39. Esdaile, 1995, p. 138.
40. Esdaile, 1995, p. 137.
41. Esdaile, 1995, p. 139.
42. Esdaile, 1995, p. 252.
43. Best, 1982, p. 162.
44. Paret, 1976, p. 227.
45. Weigley, 1993, p. 195.
46. Best, 1982, p. 94; see also Rothenberg, 1980, pp. 120–23.
47. 'Our Military Institutions', p. 318.
48. 'Agitation', p. 344.
49. 'Our Military Institutions', pp. 319–322.
50. 'Our Military Institutions', p. 319.
51. 'Observations on the Wars of the Austrian Succession', p. 27.

52. 'Political Declaration', p. 292.
53. Porter, 1994, p. 135.
54. Esdaile, 1995, p. 53.
55. See chapter 16.
56. 'Scharnhorst', p. 102.

Chapter 4   On Armies

1. Esdaile, 1995, p. 42.
2. Duffy, 1987, p. 245.
3. 'Agitation', p. 343.
4. McNeill, 1983, p. 173.
5. McNeill, 1983, p. 164.
6. Palmer, 1986, p. 92.
7. van Creveld, 1991a, p. 143.
8. Esdaile, 1995, p. 59.
9. Esdaile, 1995, p. 56.
10. McNeill, 1983, p. 164.
11. McNeill, 1983, p. 188.
12. Best, 1982, p. 34; Esdaile 1995, p. 54.
13. Esdaile, 1995, p. 64.
14. Esdaile, 1995, p. 63.
15. Esdaile, 1995, p. 65.
16. Best, 1982, p. 154.
17. Koch, 1978, p. 156.
18. 'Observations', pp. 39–40.
19. Esdaile, 1995, p. 206.
20. Esdaile, 1995, p. 207.
21. Cited Paret, 1966, p. 133.
22. Rothenberg, 1980, p. 191.
23. Koch, 1978, p. 181.
24. McNeill, 1983, p. 217.
25. Scharnhorst, cited Koch, 1978, p. 181.
26. McNeill, 1983, p. 159.
27. McNeill, 1983, p. 163.
28. van Creveld, 1985, p. 61.
29. Esdaile, 1995, p. 62.
30. McNeill, 1983, p. 162.
31. Bond, 1998, p. 38.
32. Rosello, 1991, p. 107.
33. See chapter 13.
34. Rosello, 1991, p. 108. See also Kahn, 1986.
35. Rosello, 1991, pp. 110–12.
36. van Creveld, 1985, p. 100.
37. Wilkinson, 1992.
38. Dupuy, 1977, ch. 5.
39. Duffy, 1987, pp. 95–6.
40. McNeill, 1983, p. 165.
41. Posen, 1993, p. 90.

42. Posen, 1993, p. 90.
43. Esdaile, 1995, pp. 45–6.
44. Esdaile, 1995, p. 45.
45. Best, 1982, p. 51.
46. Duffy, 1987, p. 258.
47. Esdaile, 1995, p. 68.
48. 'Scharnhorst', p. 102.
49. For a critical view of Clausewitz see van Creveld, 1977, pp. 36–9.
50. Best, 1982, pp. 103–4.
51. Howard, 1983, p. 102.
52. Howard, 1983, p. 4.
53. Schramm, 1976, pp. 38–9; McNeill, 1983, p. 173.
54. Clausewitz points out the difficulty of comparing the three arms (infantry, artillery, cavalry) each of which has a different basis in the national economy (human, equine, finance) and, in an allusion to cost-benefit analysis, refers to 'the only ascertainable factor: the monetary cost'. [286].
55. McNeill, 1983, p. 220.
56. Best, 1982, pp. 298–99.
57. Best observes that this insularity was as great as that which afflicted the British with regard to war on land, 1982, p. 122.
58. Arndt, 1980, p. 203.
59. Arndt, 1980, p. 205; Tashjean 1986, pp. 53–4.
60. This stratagem has not been lost; witness General Schwarzkopf's use of the marines in the Gulf War of 1991.
61. 'Europe since the Polish Partitions', p. 375.
62. Howard, 1984, p. 184.
63. Gat, 1992, pp. 216–221.
64. Best, 1982, p. 69.
65. Esdaile, 1995, p. 99.
66. Posen, 1993, pp. 121–22.
67. Porter, 1994, p. 124.
68. Strachan, 1983, p. 61; Esdaile, 1995, pp. 295–6.

Chapter 5   The Intellectual Provenance of *On War*

1. Author's Preface, 'To an Unpublished Manuscript on the Theory of War, Written between 1816 and 1818', *On War*, 1976, p. 61.
2. For a comparison of Adam Smith and Clausewitz see Perlmutter, 1988.
3. Hinsley, 1963, chs. 2–4.
4. Paret, 1976, p. 84.
5. Gat, 1992a, p. 370.
6. Koch, 1978, p. 175.
7. Gat, 1989, pp. 25–6.
8. Niemeyer, 1977, p. 18; Gat, 1989, pp. 64–6.
9. Gat, 1989, pp. 55–56.
10. Mentally unbalanced, von Bülow was eventually jailed by Prussian authorities. *On War* contains several references to his elder brother, General Friedrich Wilhelm von Bülow.
11. Howard, 1970, p. 25.

12. Palmer, 1986, p. 117.
13. Paret, 1976, p. 92.
14. Palmer, 1986, pp. 118–9.
15. Gat, 1989, pp. 75–7.
16. Shy, 1986, p. 149.
17. Howard, 1970, p. 23.
18. Howard, 1970, p. 25.
19. Howard, 1970, p. 26; King, 1977, pp. 6–7; Strachan, 1983, p. 5.
20. Gat, 1989, p. 153.
21. Gat, 1989, p. 154.
22. For biographical details see Elting, 1964.
23. Gooch, 1980, p. 27.
24. Howard, 1970, p. 31.
25. Shy, 1986, p. 184.
26. Shy, 1986, p. 152.
27. Shy, 1986, p. 159.
28. Elting, 1964, p. 25.
29. Gat, 1989, p. 160.
30. Cited Gat, 1989, p. 154.
31. Paret, 1976, pp. 173ff.; 'Letter to Fichte', 11 June 1809, pp. 280–4.
32. Delbrück, 1990, pp. 103–5.
33. 'Notes on History and Politics', p. 269.
34. Perlmutter, 1988, p. 13; see also chapter 16.
35. Gat, 1989, p. 176.
36. Kant, 1976, pp. 130–132 (Part I, Book I, Chapter I, §1); see also Echevarria, 1995, p. 231.
37. Gat, 1992, pp. 241–48.
38. Croce, 1935, p. 248n.
39. Paret, 1976, p. 150.
40. Van Creveld, 1986, pp. 37–8.
41. Paret, 1976, p. 151.
42. Paret, 1976, p. 162.
43. Paret, 1976, p. 149.

Chapter 6   *On War*

1. Author's Comment, 'On the Genesis of his Early Manuscript on the Theory of War, Written around 1818', *On War*, 1976, p. 63.
2. Author's Preface, 'To an Unpublished Manuscript on the Theory of War, Written between 1816 and 1818', *On War*, 1976, p. 61.
3. Paret maintains that this Author's Preface was inappropriately included with first edition of *On War* and retained thereafter. 1976, p. 360.
4. Paret, 1976a, p. 3.
5. 'Unfinished Note', *On War*, 1976, pp. 70–71. Gat presents convincing argument that this Note was written in 1827, possibly before the Note of 10 July, not in 1830 as commonly assumed. 1989, pp. 255–63.
6. Gat, 1989, p. 213.
7. Gallie, 1978, pp. 48ff; 1978a, p. 152.

8. Aron, 1983, p. 89 refers to Schering's description of Book VIII in these terms.
9. Paret, Moran (eds), 1992, p. xii.
10. Cited Brodie, 1976, p. 48.
11. Brodie, 1976, pp. 45, 58.
12. Brodie, 1976, p. 45.
13. Gat, 1992, p. 231.
14. Aron, 1983, p. 1.
15. Aron, 1983, pp. 1–2.
16. Paret, 1965, p. 26.
17. Paret, 1976a, p. 12; see also Paret 1992b.
18. Handel, 1986a, pp. 1–2.
19. Gat, 1989, p. 253.
20. Gat, 1989, pp. 178–83.
21. Brodie, 1976, p. 57.
22. Rapoport, 1968, p. 14.
23. Kitchen, 1988, p. 31.
24. Gallie, 1978, pp. 42–3.

Chapter 7   War as Fighting

1. Best, 1983, pp. 63–67; Weigley, 1993, p. 195.
2. Rothenberg, 1994, p. 88.
3. van Creveld, 1997, pp. 13–14.
4. Gibbs, 1975, pp. 16–17.
5. Gat, 1989, pp. 153–4.
6. Paret, 1976, pp. 157–8.
7. The phenomenon of 'cannon fever' (later known as 'shell shock') was identified in the eighteenth century. Duffy, 1987, p. 253. Goethe accompanied a detachment from Weimar on campaign in 1792 in order to conduct experiments on the psychological effect of cannon fire on troops. Davies, 1997, p. 721.
8. Paret, 1986a, p. 204; Aron, 1983, p. 117.
9. 1942, p. 61.
10. *Principles of War* lists eight specific causes of friction which fall under these headings. 1942, pp. 62–67.
11. *Principles of War*, 1942, p. 64.
12. Paret, 1976, p. 124.
13. See, for example, *Campaign of 1812*, 1970, p. 185.
14. Bassford, 1994, p. 25.
15. 'Letter to Fichte', p. 282.

Chapter 8   War as Contest

1. Clausewitz's phrase is *ein erweiterter Zweikampf*. The word *Zweikampf* is correctly translated as 'duel' by Howard–Paret [75] but for reasons outlined below 'contest' reflects Clausewitz's meaning more closely.
2. Walzer, 1978, p. 25n.
3. Hepp, 1978a, p. 403.

4. Gallie, 1991, p. 63.
5. 'Strategie aus dem Jahr 1804', Hahlweg (ed.), 1979, pp. 20–1.
6. Howard, 1983, p. 47.
7. See also the letter to Roeder, 22 December 1827, 'Gedanken zur Abwehr', Hahlweg (ed.), 1979.
8. 'Gedanken zur Abwehr', Hahlweg (ed.), 1979, pp. 497–8.
9. On this idea among states see Gallie, 1988, p. 22.
10. Scarry, 1985, p. 101.
11. Walzer, 1978, pp. 24–5. Walzer, however, argues that Clausewitz denied the element of convention, p. 25n. This is true only of Absolute War.
12. Hanson, 1989, ch. 2.
13. van Creveld, 1991b, p. 423.
14. Scarry, 1985, especially chapter 2.
15. Scarry, 1985, p. 69.
16. Gallie, 1991, p. 50.

Chapter 9   War as an Instrument of Policy

1. Hepp, 1978a, pp. 411–2, 415–6.
2. Duffy, 1987, p. 154.
3. Cited Gat, 1989, p. 242.
4. Paret, 1976, p. 94.
5. Cited Paret, 1976, p. 315.
6. See Gallie, 1978, pp. 50–51.
7. 'Gedanken zur Abwehr', Hahlweg (ed.), 1979, p. 498.
8. King, 1977, pp. 30–31.
9. Cited Paret, 1976, p. 338.
10. Walzer, 1978, p. 79.
11. Scarry, 1985, p. 77.
12. Rapoport, 1968, pp. 411, 77.
13. Hepp, 1978a, p. 417.
14. Brodie, 1976a, p. 647.
15. van Creveld, 1997, pp. 19–20.

Chapter 10   Pure War and Real War

1. Weber's later use of 'ideal types' follows in this path.
2. The Howard-Paret translation runs together violence, hatred and enmity whereas the German suggests that hatred and enmity give rise to violence.
3. Suganami, 1997, p. 409 who notes J. David Singer's argument that all social events result from 'a concatenation of some deterministic, stochastic, and voluntaristic elements'.
4. Aron, 1972, p. 602.
5. Meinecke, 1984, p. 7.
6. Paret, for example, observes that Napoleon's passion for conquest carried more weight than any hatred the French people had for the rest of Europe, while in the last years of the Empire 'common sense, that particularly

impressive form of rationality, rested more with the war-weary people than it did with Napoleon'. 1986a, p. 202. See also Aron, 1983, p. 398.

Chapter 11   The Nature of Strategy

1. 'Gedanken zur Abwehr' (1827), Hahlweg (ed.), 1979, p. 495; translation from Paret, 1976, p. 379.
2. On real and perceived differences see Handel, 2001, ch. 11.
3. Clausewitz put forward this idea in an essay 'On Progression and Pause' in 1817. Paret, 1976, p. 377.
4. Thus Clausewitz asks whether France could defeat a European coalition. With Russia neutral a coalition of states with 75 million people between them could put a force of 725,000 troops in the field, more than matching anything that France could do with a population of only 30 million. This disparity is the 'main consideration' that would ensure a French defeat. [633].
5. Horne, 1996, p. 375.
6. Gilbert, 1981, p. 12.
7. Paret, 1976, p. 333.
8. Clausewitz's 'war plan' [*Kriegsplan, grosse Kriegführung*] is now commonly referred to as strategy, grand strategy, national strategy or national policy. For the conduct of a campaign Clausewitz used various terms, including 'strategy' [*Strategie*] which was coming into fashion. Today this is generally referred to as the operational level of war or command. Clausewitz's terminology is retained here though 'campaign strategy' is used where necessary to avoid ambiguity. See also Echevarria, 1995, p. 230.
9. Paret, 1976, p. 91.
10. Palmer, 1986, p. 107.
11. Delbrück, 1985, p. 388.
12. To be distinguished from 'decisive point' [*entscheidender Punkt*] which Clausewitz uses in a tactical context. [194–7, 204].
13. Echivarria draws attention to passages in the Howard-Paret translation which imply that a centre of gravity is a source of strength. 2002, p. 9.
14. *Historische Briefe*, p. 58.
15. *Campaign of 1812*, p. 184.
16. Echivarria, 2002, p. vii.
17. Delbrück, 1985, pp. 378–81, 421–39; see also Craig, 1986, pp. 341–44.
18. Bond, 1998, p. 24.
19. Aron, 1983, pp. 77–8.

Chapter 12   The Conduct of the Campaign

1. van Creveld, 1977, ch. 1.
2. See Delbrück, 1985, pp. 371–2 on ideas about the 'normal' size of armies based on the need for control and manoeuvrability.
3. O'Connell, 1989, p. 181.
4. Tashjean, 1992, p. 169.
5. *Campaign of 1812*, p. 254. See also pp. 185, 193.

6. Cited van Creveld, 1977, p. 28.
7. Delbrück, 1985, p. 393.
8. 'The Campaign of 1812 in Russia', p. 166.
9. Strachan, 1983, p. 96.
10. Aron, 1983, p. 151.
11. Gat, 1988, p. 24.

Chapter 13   Command

1. 'Über den Zustand der Theorie der Kriegskunst' (1808–9), cited Paret, 1976, p. 155.
2. 'Strategic Critique of the Campaign of 1814 in France', p. 207.
3. Duffy, 1987, p. 140.
4. *Principles of War*, p. 19.
5. Brodie, 1976a, p. 643.
6. Duffy, 1987, p. 142.
7. 'Strategie aus dem Jahr 1804', Hahlweg (ed.), 1979, p. 10; trans. from Gat, 1989, p. 179.
8. 'Strategie aus dem Jahr 1804', Hahlweg (ed.), 1979, p. 10.
9. Gat, 1989, p. 179.
10. Gat, 1989, p. 180.
11. See Herbig, 1986, pp. 98–9; Gallie, 1978, p. 45.
12. Paret, 1976, p. 349.
13. It is surprising Clausewitz does not once mention Wellington whose genius was arguably decisive at the battle of Waterloo. See Keegan, 1987, ch. 2.
14. Handel, 2001, p. 185.

Chapter 14   Theory

1. Machiavelli, 1990, pp. 122, 202–4.
2. Paret, 1976, p. 349.
3. 'Scharnhorst', p. 102.
4. 'Abstract Principles of Strategy' (1808–9), cited Paret, 1976, p. 152.
5. See 'Strategie aus dem Jahr 1808', Hahlweg (ed.), 1979, p. 46.
6. 'Strategie aus dem Jahr 1809', Hahlweg (ed.), 1979, p. 60; trans. from Paret, 1976, p. 155.
7. Paret, 1976a, p. 14.
8. Trans. and ed. Lewis White Beck, 1949, pp. 130–66. See also Echevarria, 1995, p. 231.
9. Hahlweg, 1980, p. 18.
10. For a discussion with reference to Clausewitz see Beyerchen, 1992–93.
11. 'The Campaign of 1812 in Russia', p. 165.
12. Cited Paret, 1976, p. 334.
13. Duffy, 1987, pp. 52–3.
14. This excludes the Napoleonic wars. Paret, Moran (eds), 1992, p. 19.
15. 'Strategie aus dem Jahr 1809', Hahlweg (ed.), 1979, pp. 60–1, trans. from Paret, 1976, p. 155.

16. This is the thrust of Reynolds, 1978 and Gooch, 1980.
17. Paret, 1976a, p. 23.
18. Sumida, 2000, p. 70.
19. Aron, 1972, p. 603.
20. 'Strategie aus dem Jahr 1808', Hahlweg (ed.), 1979, p. 47.
21. See Gallie, 1978, pp. 43–4.
22. 'Campaign of 1814', p. 208.

Chapter 15   Praxis

1. Aron, 1972, p. 600.
2. Hahlweg, 1980, pp. 12–3.
3. Hahlweg, 1980, p. 13.
4. Reynolds, 1978, p. 187.
5. Gallie, 1978, p. 44.
6. 'Notes on History and Politics', p. 265.
7. See Gat, 1989, p. 165.
8. 'Strategie aus dem Jahr 1804', Hahlweg (ed.), 1979, pp. 6–8.
9. 'Bülow', Hahlweg (ed.), 1979, pp. 87–8.
10. Gat, 1989, p. 181.
11. *Principles of War*, 1942, p. 60.
12. van Creveld, 1986, p. 38.
13. Cited Gat, 1989, p. 175.
14. 'Bülow', Hahlweg (ed.), 1979, pp. 80–1.
15. See Crocé, 1935, pp. 248–9.
16. 'Campaign of 1815', cited Paret, 1976, p. 341.
17. 'Strategie aus dem Jahr 1808', Hahlweg (ed.), 1979, p. 49; trans. from Gat, 1989, p. 180.
18. King, 1977, p. 17.
19. Paret, 1976a, p. 11.
20. Gallie, 1978, p. 44.
21. Sumida, 2000, p. 72; see also Sumida, 2001.
22. Gallie, 1978, pp. 42–3.

Chapter 16   Politics and the State

1. Reynolds, 1978, p. 189.
2. Weil, 1955, p. 293; Paret, 1976, p. 439.
3. Letter of 9 September 1824, Hahlweg (ed.), 1990, p. 456. *'faux frais'* means incidental expenses or small change.
4. 'The Germans and the French', p. 252ff.
5. Cited Rothfels, 1920, pp. 75–6.
6. 'History and Politics', pp. 240–1.
7. 'History and Politics', p. 248.
8. 'Agitation' pp. 349, 359
9. 'Agitation', p. 350.
10. 'In Reference to Well-Meaning German Philosophers', p. 270.
11. 'Polish Partitions', pp. 372–3.

12. 'Agitation', p. 342.
13. 'Agitation', p. 342.
14. 'Agitation', pp. 340–41.
15. 'Agitation', p. 340.
16. 'Agitation', p. 344.
17. 'Agitation', p. 345.
18. 'Agitation', p. 344.
19. 'Agitation', p. 339.
20. This interpretation of the French Revolution was admired by Delbrück who saw Tocqueville's major ideas in Clausewitz. Aron, 1977, p. 1260–1.
21. 'Agitation', pp. 346–7.
22. 'Germans and the French', p. 258.
23. 'Bemerkungen und Einfälle', Rothfels, 1920, p. 223.
24. 'Agitation', p. 353.
25. 'Scharnhorst', p. 107.
26. 'Observations', p. 73.
27. 'Germany's Existence', p. 383.
28. 'Agitation', p. 353.
29. 'Observations', p. 73.
30. Paret, 1968, p. 395.
31. 'Agitation', p. 349.
32. 'Agitation', p. 349.
33. 'Gedanken zur Abwehr', Hahlweg (ed), 1979, 496–7.
34. 'Observations', p. 36; see also 'Agitation', p. 352.
35. 'Observations', p. 34.
36. 'Observations', pp. 35–6.
37. 'Agitation', p. 353.
38. 'Agitation', p. 352.
39. 'Agitation', p. 353.
40. 'Notes on History and Politics', p. 273.
41. Letter of 12 November 1817, Hahlweg (ed), 1990, pp. 303–4. Trans. from Paret, 1976, p. 262.
42. Linnebach, 1917, pp. 445, 465, 473.
43. 'Prussian *Landwehr*', p. 333.
44. 'Agitation', p. 351.
45. 'Agitation', p. 351.
46. 'Agitation', p. 352.
47. 'Agitation', p. 346.
48. 'Agitation', p. 347.
49. 'Agitation', p. 355.
50. Moran, 1989, pp. 190–1.
51. Paret, Moran (eds), 1992, p. 337.
52. Paret, Moran (eds), 1992, pp. 228–9.
53. 'Agitation', p. 366.
54. 'Agitation', pp. 354, 358.
55. Gat, 1989, pp. 247, 215.
56. See also 'Campaign of 1812', p. 165.
57. See the discussions in Behrens, 1976 and Paret, 1980a.

Chapter 17   External Policy

1 'Observations', pp. 63–4.
2. 'Our Military Institutions', p. 317.
3. 'Our Military Institutions', p. 328.
4. 'Ueber die künftigen Kriegs-Operationen Preußens gegen Frankreich', Hahlweg (ed.), 1966, I, p. 89.
5. 'Historisch-Politische Aufzeichnungen', Rothfels (ed.), 1922, p. 2; see also 'Notes on History and Politics', p. 239.
6. 'Germany's Existence', p. 382.
7. Aron, 1972, p. 612.
8. Aron, 1972, pp. 611–2.
9. 'Notes on History and Politics', p. 245.
10. 'Observations', p. 42.
11. 'Notes on History and Politics', pp. 272–3.
12. Gallie, 1978, p. 61; see also Schramm, 1958, pp. 709–10.
13. Duffy, 1987, pp. 146, 147.
14. Gat, 1989, pp. 242–3.
15. 'Observations', p. 41.
16. Gat, 1989, pp. 243–4; Ritter, 1969, p. 51.
17. 'Our Military Institutions', pp. 317–8.
18. Behrens, 1976, p. 42; Rapoport, 1968, p. 64.
19. Best, 1982, p. 75.
20. See Esdaile, 1995, p. 313.
21. 'Gedanken zur Abwehr', Hahlweg (ed.), 1979, pp. 495–6.
22. Cited Paret, 1976, p. 369; see also 'Gedanken zur Abwehr', p. 499.
23. Duffy, 1987, p. 151.
24. Cited Hahlweg, 1980a, p. 70 from an unpublished manuscript.
25. Howard, Paret (eds and trans.), 1976, p. 608n.
26. Letter to Gneisenau (1809), Hahlweg (ed.), 1966, I, p. 677.
27. Cited Paret, 1976, p. 338.
28. Cited Paret, 1976, p. 338.
29. Aron, 1983, p. 267.
30. 'Notes on History and Politics', p. 264; see also the letter to Marie, 5 October 1807, Linnebach, 1917, p. 142.
31. 'Notes on History and Politics', pp. 268–9.
32. 'Notes on History and Politics', p. 242.
33. Paret, 1976, p. 365.
34. Aron, 1972, p. 620.
35 Paret, 1976, pp. 402–3.
36. Aron, 1976, p. 33.

Chapter 18   International Politics

1. 'Polish Partitions', p. 375.
2. 'Polish Partitions', pp. 374–5.
3. Gallie, 1978, p. 63.

4. 'Aggression' was often used with other terms that imported a moral or legal element e.g. 'unjust' aggression and 'unprovoked' aggression. Brownlie, 1963, p. 351.
5. This was an attraction for some. Ritter, 1943, p. 58n.
6. Scheuner, 1980, p. 161.
7. Weil, 1955, p. 306.
8. Ritter, 1969, p. 67.
9. 'On Coalitions', p. 242.
10. 'Ueber die künftigen Kriegs-Operationen Preußens gegen Frankreich', Hahlweg (ed.), 1966, I, p. 76.
11. 'On Coalitions', p. 242.
12. 'On Coalitions', p. 243.
13. 'Observations', p. 76.
14. Holbraad, 1970, pp. 152–3 .
15. 'On Coalitions', p. 244.
16. 'On Coalitions', p. 244.
17. 'On Coalitions', p. 244.
18. 'Notes on History and Politics', p. 241.
19. 'Polish Partitions', pp. 374–5.
20. 'Notes on History and Politics', p. 249.
21. 'On Coalitions', p. 242.
22. 'Germany's Existence', pp. 381–2.
23. 'Polish Partitions', pp. 373–4.

Chapter 19   Clausewitz to 1945

1. Liddell Hart, 1933, p. 120.
2. Bassford, 1994, p. 6 and *passim*. See also Heuser, 2002.
3. Bassford, 1996, p. 267.
4. Hahlweg, 1980a, pp. 91–4; Gat, 1992a, pp. 366–7.
5. Gat, 1989, p. 129.
6. Hahlweg, 1980a, p. 121; Dümmler remain the publishers of *On War*, now in its 19th edition (1980).
7. Echevarria, 2000, p. 7.
8. Bond, 1998, p. 78.
9. Dupuy, 1977, pp. 107–8.
10. Shy, 1986, p. 177.
11. Bassford, 1994, pp. 69–70.
12. Howard, 1979, p. 976.
13. Paret, 1965, p. 23.
14. 1940, p. ix.
15. Bond, 1977, pp. 37–8, 80–1.
16. Liddell Hart, 1933, pp. 101–2, 21.
17. Liddell Hart, 1933, p. 143.
18. Liddell Hart, 1941, p. 357.
19. Cited Bassford, 1994, p. 138.
20. Liddell Hart, 1933, p. 105.
21. Liddell Hart, 1933, p. 125.

22. Liddell Hart, 1933, pp. 133, 123.
23. Lawrence, 1935, p. 190.
24. Lawrence, 1935, p. 188.
25. Lawrence, 1935, p. 195.
26. Baldwin, 1981, p. 10.
27. Hahlweg, 1980a, pp. 107–8.
28. 1936, pp. 23–4.
29. Strachan, 2000, p. 349.
30. On the clash between Beck and Ludendorff, see Müller, 1986, pp. 242–9.
31. Baldwin, 1981, p. 17.
32. Howard-Paret's translation of *ganz Krieg* as 'total war' [605] rather than, say, 'pure war' is misleading.
33. Hahlweg, 1960, p. 223.
34. Gat, 1992a, pp. 376–7.
35. Cited Gat, 1992a, p. 377.
36. Rothfels, 1943, p. 94.
37. Howard, 1984, p. 200.

Chapter 20   Hypermodern War

1. On the scholarly reception of Clausewitz since 1945 see Bassford, 1994, ch. 21; Heuser, 2002, ch. 7.
2. Brodie, 1946, p. 76.
3. Handel, 1986b, pp. 83–4.
4. Lider, 1977, pp. 163–4.
5. Howard, 1983, p. 70.
6. Echevarria, 1995/96, p. 79.
7. Strachey, 1967, pp. 75–6.
8. See Bell, 1971, p. 78.
9. Kissinger, 1969, ch. 6.
10. Aron, 1983, pp. 330–1.
11. Nardulli, 1982, p. 503.
12. Moody, 1979, p. 419.
13. Schelling, 1963, ch. 8.
14. Aron, 1983, p. 344.
15. Aron, 1983, p. 338.
16. Rapoport, 1968, pp. 64–5.
17. Rapoport, 1968, pp. 412–3.

Chapter 21   Anti-Modern War

1. Keegan, 1993, p. 3.
2. van Creveld, 1991, p. 59.
3. Esdaile, 1995, ch. 4.
4. Hahlweg, 1980a, pp. 161–2.
5. Schössler, 1991, p. 129.
6. Hahlweg, 1980a, pp. 161–2.
7. Aron, 1983, p. 302.

8. Cited Hahlweg, 1960, p. 222.
9. Aron, 1983, pp. 313, 295.
10. Summers, 1982; Heuser, 2002, pp. 168–72.
11. Murray, 1997, p. 61.
12. Murray, 1997, p. 61.
13. Bassford, 1994, pp. 204–5.
14. van Creveld, 1997, p. 9; Keegan, 1993, p. 23.
15. Villacres, Bassford, 1995, pp. 15–16.

Chapter 22   Modern War since 1945

1. Howard, 1976a, p. 755 (in relation to political control over the military).
2. Lasswell, 1977, ch. 3.
3. Handel, 1986b, pp. 74–5; Roxborough, 1994, p. 631.
4. Toffler and Toffler, 1993.
5. Gallie, 1991, p. 56.
6. Keegan, 1987, p. 331.
7. Rosello, 1991, p. 113.
8. Orme, 1997–98, pp. 145–56; Owens, 2000.
9. Ferris, Handel, 1995, p. 49.
10. Ferris, Handel, 1995, p. 48–9.
11. Ferris, Handel,1995, pp. 43–4.
12. Handel, 1986b, pp. 58–9. Roxborough proposes the 'mundane' i.e. economics, science, technology and logistics as the fourth element. 1994, p. 628.
13. Murray, 1997, pp. 62–4.

Chapter 23   A Farewell to Clausewitz

1. Bassford, 1994a, p. 329.
2. Rapoport, 1968, p. 411.
3. See, for example, van Creveld, 1999.
4. Buzan, 1991.
5. van Creveld, 1991, ch. 6; see also van Creveld, 2001, ch. 16.
6. Keegan, 1993a.
7. Ignatieff, 1997.
8. Keegan, 1993, p. 58.
9. Keegan, 1993a.
10. Gallie, 1988, p. 26.

Bibliography

Adams, Thomas K. 'LIC (Low-Intensity Clausewitz)', *Small Wars & Insurgencies*, vol. 1, no. 3 (December 1990).

Arndt, Hans Joachim 'Clausewitz und der Einfluß der Seemacht' in Wagemann, Niemeyer (eds), *Freiheit ohne Krieg?*, 1980.

Aron, Raymond 'Reason, Passion, and Power in the Thought of Clausewitz', *Social Research*, vol. 39, no. 4 (Winter 1972).

Aron, Raymond 'Clausewitz's Conceptual System', *Armed Forces & Society*, vol. 1, no. 1 (November 1974).

Aron, Raymond *Penser la Guerre, Clausewitz*, vol. I: *L'âge européen*, vol II: *L'âge planétaire*, Gallimard, Paris, 1976.

Aron, Raymond 'Note Critique: *Clausewitz et L'Etat'*, *Annales* (November–December 1977).

Aron, Raymond 'Verdächtiger Anwalt: Bemerkungen zu Robert Hepps Rezension', *Zeitschrift für Politik*, vol. 26, no. 1 (1979).

Aron, Raymond 'Zum Begriff einer politischen Strategie bei Clausewitz' in Wagemann, Niemeyer (eds), *Freiheit ohne Krieg?*, 1980.

Aron, Raymond 'Staaten, Bündnisse und Konflikte' in Wagemann, Niemeyer (eds), *Freiheit ohne Krieg?*, 1980a.

Aron, Raymond *Clausewitz: Philosopher of War* (translation of *Penser la Guerre* by C. Booker, N. Stone), Routledge & Kegan Paul, London, 1983.

Atkinson, Alexander *Social Order and the General Theory of Strategy*, Routledge & Kegan Paul, London, 1981.

Baldwin, P.M. 'Clausewitz in Nazi Germany', *Journal of Contemporary History*, vol. 16, no. 1 (January 1981).

Ball, Desmond *Can Nuclear War be Controlled?*, Adelphi Paper no. 169, International Institute for Strategic Studies, London, 1981.

Bassford, Christopher 'Jomini and Clausewitz: Their Interaction', Clausewitz homepage www.clausewitz.com/CWZHOME/Jomini/JOMINIX.htm, 1993.

Bassford, Christopher *Clausewitz in English: The Reception of Clausewitz in Britain and America 1815–1945*, Oxford University Press, New York, 1994.

Bassford, Christopher 'John Keegan and the Grand Tradition of Trashing Clausewitz: a Polemic', *War in History*, vol. 1, no. 3 (November 1994a).

Bassford, Christopher 'Landmarks in Defense Literature: *On War*', *Defense Analysis*, vol. 12, no. 2 (1996).

Behrens, C.B.A. 'Which Side Was Clausewitz On?', *New York Review of Books*, vol. XXIII, no. 16 (14 October 1976).

Bell, Coral *The Conventions of Crisis: A Study in Diplomatic Management*, Oxford University Press, London, 1971.

Best, Geoffrey *War and Society in Revolutionary Europe, 1770–1870*, Fontana, London, 1982.

Best, Geoffrey *Humanity in Warfare*, Methuen, London, 1983.

Beyerchen, Alan 'Clausewitz, Nonlinearity, and the Unpredictabilty of War', *International Security*, vol. 17, no. 3 (Winter 1992–93).

Bond, Brian *Liddell Hart: A Study of his Military Thought*, Cassell, London, 1977.

Bond, Brian *The Pursuit of Victory: From Napoleon to Saddam Hussein*, Clarendon Press, Oxford, 1998.

Boulding, Kenneth *Conflict and Defense: A General Theory*, Harper & Row, New York, 1962.

Brandt, General Heinrich von 'Brief Memoir of General Clausewitz' in J.J. Graham (trans.), *On War*, 1940.

Brodie, Bernard *The Absolute Weapon*, Harcourt Brace, New York, 1946.

Brodie, Bernard 'On Clausewitz: A Passion for War', *World Politics*, vol. 25, no. 2 (January 1973).

Brodie, Bernard 'The Continuing Relevance of *On War*' in Clausewitz, *On War*, Howard, Paret (eds), 1976.

Brodie, Bernard 'A Guide to the reading of *On War*' in Clausewitz, *On War*, Howard, Paret (eds), 1976a.

Brodie, Bernard 'In Quest of the Unknown Clausewitz', *International Security*, vol. 1, no. 3 (Winter 1977).

Brownlie, Ian *International Law and the Use of Force by States*, Clarendon Press, Oxford, 1963.

Butterfield, H. and Wight, M. (eds) *Diplomatic Investigations*, Allen & Unwin, London, 1966.

Callwell, Charles *Small Wars. Their Principles and Practice*, 3rd edition, HMSO, London, 1906.

Chandler, David (ed.) *The Dictionary of Battles*, Ebury Press, London, 1987.

Cimbala, Stephen J. *Clausewitz and Escalation: Classical Perspectives on Nuclear Strategy*, Frank Cass, London, 1991.

Clausewitz, Carl von *On War*, translated by Colonel J.J. Graham, revised edition, 3 volumes, Kegan, Paul, Trench, Trubner & Co., London, 1940.

Clausewitz, Carl von *On War*, edited and translated by Michael Howard, Peter Paret, Princeton University Press, 1976.

Clausewitz, Carl von *Historische Briefe über die großen Kriegsereignisse im Oktober 1806*, edited by Joachim Niemeyer, Dümmler, Bonn, 1977.

Clausewitz, Carl von *Vom Kriege*, edited by Werner Hahlweg, 19th edition, Dümmler, Bonn, 1980.

Clausewitz, Carl von *The Campaign of 1812 in Russia* (London, 1843), reprinted by Academic International, Hattiesburg, 1970.

Clausewitz, Carl von *Principles of War*, edited and translated by Hans W. Gatzke, Military Service Publishing Company, Harrisburg, Pennsylvania, 1942.

Craig, Gordon A. 'Delbrück: The Military Historian' in Paret (ed.) *Makers of Modern Strategy*, 1986.

Crocé, Benedetto 'Action, succès et jugement dans le "Vom Kriege" de Clausewitz', *Révue de métaphysique et de morale*, vol. XLII (April 1935).

Danchev, Alex *Alchemist of War: The Life of Basil Liddell Hart*, Weidenfeld & Nicolson, London, 1998.

Davies, Norman *Europe: A History*, Pimlico, London, 1997.

Delbrück, Hans *The Dawn of Modern Warfare: History of the Art of War*, Vol. IV, University of Nebraska Press, Lincoln, 1985.

Dill, Günther (ed.) *Clausewitz in Perspektive: Materialen zu Carl von Clausewitz: Vom Kriege*, Ullstein, Frankfurt-am-Main, 1980.

Duffy, Christopher *The Military Experience in the Age of Reason*, Routledge & Kegan Paul, London, 1987.

Dupuy, T.N. *A Genius for War: The German Army and General Staff, 1807–1945*, Macdonald and Jane's, London, 1977.

Echevarria, Antulio J., II 'Clausewitz: Toward a Theory of Applied Strategy', *Defense Analysis*, vol. 11, no. 3 (1995).

Echevarria, Antulio J., II 'War, Politics, and RMA – The Legacy of Clausewitz', *Joint Forces Quarterly*, no. 10 (Winter 1995/96).

Echevarria, Antulio J., II *After Clausewitz: German Military Thinkers Before the Great War*, University Press of Kansas, Lawrence, Kansas, 2000.

Echevarria, Antulio J., II *Clausewitz's Center of Gravity*, US Army War College, Carlisle, PA, September 2002.

Elting, John R. 'Jomini: Disciple of Napoleon?', *Military Affairs*, vol. XXVIII, no. 1 (Spring 1964).

Esdaile, Charles J. *The Wars of Napoleon*, Longman, London, 1995.

Fuller, J.F.C. *The Conduct of War: 1789–1961*, Da Capo Press, New York, 1992.

Ferris, John and Handel, Michael I. 'Clausewitz, Intelligence, Uncertainty and the Art of Command in Military Operations', *Intelligence and National Security*, vol. 10, no. 1 (January 1995).

Foch, Ferdinand *Principles of War*, Chapman & Hall, London, 1918.

Gallie, W.B. *Philosophers of Peace and War*, Cambridge University Press, 1978.

Gallie, W.B. 'Clausewitz Today', *Archives européennes de sociologie*, vol. XIX, no. 1 1978a.

Gallie, W.B. 'Power politics and war cultures', *Review of International Studies*, vol. 14, no. 1 (January 1988).

Gallie, W.B. *Understanding War*, Routledge, London, 1991.

Gat, Azar 'Clausewitz on Defence and Attack', *Journal of Strategic Studies*, vol. 11, no. 1 (March 1988).

Gat, Azar *The Origins of Military Thought from the Enlightenment to Clausewitz*, Clarendon Press, Oxford, 1989.

Gat, Azar 'Clausewitz's Political and Ethical World View', *Political Studies*, vol. XXXVII, no. 1 (March 1989a).

Gat, Azar *The Development of Military Thought: The Nineteenth Century*, Clarendon Press, Oxford, 1992.

Gat, Azar 'Clausewitz and the Marxists: Yet Another Look', *Journal of Contemporary History*, vol. 27, no. 2 (April 1992a).

Gibbs, Norman H. 'Clausewitz on the Moral Forces in War', *Naval War College Review*, vol. XXVII, no. 4 (January–February 1975).

Gilbert, Felix 'From Clausewitz to Delbrück and Hintze: Achievements and Failures of Military History', *Journal of Strategic Studies*, vol. 3, no. 3 (1980); also in Amos Perlmutter and John Gooch (eds), *Strategy and the Social Sciences: Issues in Defence Policy*, Frank Cass, London, 1981.

Gilbert, Felix 'Machiavelli: The Renaissance of the Art of War' in Paret (ed.), *Makers of Modern Strategy*, 1986.

Goerlitz, Walter *History of the German General Staff: 1657–1945* (trans. Brian Battershaw), Praeger, New York, 1953.

Gooch, John 'Clio and Mars: The Use and Abuse of History', *Journal of Strategic Studies*, vol. 3, no. 3 (1980).

Graham, J.J. 'Brief Memoir of General Clausewitz' in *On War*, translated by Graham, revised edition, 3 volumes, Kegan, Paul, Trench, Trubner & Co., London, 1940.

Haffner, S. 'Mao und Clausewitz' in G. Dill (ed.), *Clausewitz in Perspektive*, 1980.

Hahlweg, Werner 'Clausewitz, Lenin, and Communist Military Attitudes Today', *Journal of the Royal United Services Institution*, vol. CV, no. 618 (May 1960).

Hahlweg, Werner (ed.) *Carl von Clausewitz: Schriften-Aufsätze-Studien-Briefe*, vol. I, Vandenhoeck & Ruprecht, Göttingen, 1966.

Hahlweg, Werner *Clausewitz: Soldat-Politiker-Denker*, Musterschmidt-Verlag, Göttingen, 1969.

Hahlweg, Werner (ed.) *Carl von Clausewitz: Verstreute kleine Schriften*, Biblio Verlag, Osnabrück, 1979.

Hahlweg, Werner 'Das Clausewitzbild Einst und Jetzt' in *Vom Kriege* (19th edition), Dümmler, Bonn, 1980.

Hahlweg, Werner 'Clausewitz and Guerrilla Warfare' in Handel (ed.), *Clausewitz and Modern Strategy*, 1986.

Hahlweg, Werner (ed.) *Carl von Clausewitz: Schriften-Aufsätze-Studien-Briefe*, vol. II, Part 1, Vandenhoeck & Ruprecht, Göttingen, 1990.

Hahlweg, Werner (ed.) *Carl von Clausewitz: Schriften-Aufsätze-Studien-Briefe*, vol. II, Part 2, Vandenhoeck & Ruprecht, Göttingen, 1990a.

Handel, Michael I (ed.) *Clausewitz and Modern Strategy*, Frank Cass, London, 1986.

Handel, Michael I. 'Introduction' in Handel (ed.), *Clausewitz and Modern Strategy*, 1986a.

Handel, Michael I. 'Clausewitz in the Age of Technology' in Handel (ed.), *Clausewitz and Modern Strategy*, 1986b.

Handel, Michael I. *Leaders and Intelligence*, Frank Cass, London, 1989.

Handel, Michael I. *Masters of War: Classical Strategic Thought* (3rd edition, revised), Frank Cass, London, 2001.

Hanson, Victor D. *The Western Way of War*, Oxford University Press, 1989.

Hepp, Robert 'Der harmlose Clausewitz (I)', *Zeitschrift für Politik*, vol. XXV, no. 3 (1978).

Hepp, Robert 'Der harmlose Clausewitz (II)', *Zeitschrift für Politik*, vol. XXV, no. 4 (1978a).

Herbig, K.L. 'Chance and Uncertainty in On War' in Handel (ed.), *Clausewitz and Modern Strategy*, 1986.

Heuser, Beatrice *Reading Clausewitz*, Pimlico, London, 2002.

Hinsley, F.H. *Power and the Pursuit of Peace*, Cambridge University Press, 1963.

Holbraad, Carsten *The Concert of Europe*, Longman, London, 1970.

Holmes, Richard *Nuclear Warriors: Soldiers, Combat and Glasnost*, Jonathan Cape, London, 1991.

Horne, Alistair *How Far from Austerlitz?: Napoleon 1805–1815*, Macmillan, London, 1996.

Howard, Michael 'War as an Instrument of Policy' in Butterfield, Wight (eds), *Diplomatic Investigations*, 1966.

Howard, Michael 'Jomini and the Classical Tradition in Military Thought' in Howard, *Studies in War and Peace*, Temple Smith, London, 1970.

Howard, Michael 'The Influence of Clausewitz' in Clausewitz, *On War*, Howard, Paret (eds), 1976.

Howard, Michael 'The Military Philosopher', *Times Literary Supplement*, 25 June 1976a.

Howard, Michael 'The Forgotten Dimensions of Strategy', *Foreign Affairs*, vol. 75, no. 5 (Summer 1979).

Howard, Michael *Clausewitz*, Oxford University Press, 1983.

Howard, Michael *The Causes of Wars*, Unwin, London, 1984.

Huntington, Samuel P. *The Third Wave: Democratization in the Late Twentieth Century*, University of Oklahoma Press, Norman, 1991.

Ignatieff, Michael 'The Narcissism of Minor Difference' in Ignatieff, T*he Warrior's Honor*, Metropolitan Books, New York, 1997.

Jomini, Baron Antoine de *The Art of War*, reprinted Greenhill Books, London, 1992.

Kahn, David 'Clausewitz and Intelligence' in Handel (ed.), *Clausewitz and Modern Strategy*, 1986.

Kant, Immanuel *Critique of Practical Reason*, edited by Lewis White Beck, Garland Publishing, New York, 1976.

Kaplan, Robert D. *The Coming Anarchy: Shattering the Dreams of the Post Cold War*, Vintage Books, New York, 2000.

Keegan, John *The Mask of Command*, Penguin Books, Harmondsworth, 1987.

Keegan, John *A History of Warfare*, Hutchinson, London, 1993.

Keegan, John 'On Clausewitz', Letters, *Times Literary Supplement*, 23 April 1993a.

Kennedy, Paul M. *The Rise and Fall of the Great Powers: Economic and Military Conflict from 1500 to 2000*, Unwin Hyman, London, 1988.

Kessel, Eberhard 'Zur Entstehungsgeschichte von Clausewitz' Werk *Vom Kriege*', *Historische Zeitschrift*, vol. 152 (1935).

Kessel, Eberhard 'Zur Genesis der modernen Kriegslehre', *Wehrwissenschaftliche Rundschau*, vol. 3, no. 9 (1953).

Kessel, Eberhard 'Die doppelte Art des Krieges', *Wehrwissenschaftliche Rundschau*, vol. 4, no. 7 (1954).

King, James E. 'On Clausewitz: Master Theorist of War', *Naval War College Review*, vol. XXX, no. 2 (Fall 1977).

Kissinger, Henry A. *Nuclear Weapons and Foreign Policy*, Norton, New York, 1969 (first published 1957).

Kitchen, Martin 'The Political History of Clausewitz', *Journal of Strategic Studies*, vol. 11, no. 1 (March 1988).

Klein, Bradley S. *Strategic Studies and World Order: The Global Politics of Deterrence*, Cambridge University Press, 1994.

Koch, H.W. *A History of Prussia*, Longman, London, 1978.

Lasswell, Harold 'The Garrison State' in Lasswell, *Essays on the Garrison State*, ed. and intro. Jay Stanley, Transaction Publishers, New Brunswick, 1977.

Lawrence, T.E. *Seven Pillars of Wisdom: a triumph*, Jonathan Cape, London, 1935.

Lebow, Richard Ned 'Clausewitz and Nuclear Crisis Stability', *Political Science Quarterly*, vol. 103, no. 1 (Spring 1988).

Liddell Hart, Basil *The Ghost of Napoleon*, Faber & Faber, London, 1933 (repr. Greenwood Press, Westport, CT, 1980).

Liddell Hart, Basil *Strategy: The Indirect Approach*, Faber & Faber, London, 1941 (3rd revised edition, 1954).

Lider, Julian *On the nature of war*, Saxon House, Farnborough, UK, 1977.

Linnebach, Karl (ed.) *Karl und Marie von Clausewitz: Ein Lebensbild in Briefen und Tagebuchblättern*, Martin Warneck, Berlin, 1917.

Luvaas, Jay 'Clausewitz, Fuller and Liddell Hart' in Handel (ed.), *Clausewitz and Modern Strategy*, 1986.

Machiavelli, Niccolo *The Art of War*, Da Capo Press, New York, 1990.

Marwedel, Ulrich *Carl von Clausewitz: Persönlichkeit und Wirkungs-Geschichte seines Werkes bis 1918*, Harald Boldt Verlag, Boppard am Rhein, 1978.

Maude, F.N. Col. 'Introduction', reprinted in Carl von Clausewitz, *On War*, translated by Colonel J.J. Graham, revised edition, 3 volumes, Kegan, Paul, Trench, Trubner & Co., London, 1940.

McNeill, William H. *The Pursuit of Power: Technology, Armed Force, and Society since A.D. 1000*, Basil Blackwell, Oxford, 1983.

Meinecke, Friedrich *Machiavellism*, Routledge, Kegan Paul, London, 1984.

Moody, P.R. Jr. 'Clausewitz and the Fading Dialectic of War', *World Politics*, vol. 31, no. 3 (April 1979).

Moran, Daniel 'Clausewitz and the Revolution', *Central European History*, vol. 22, no. 2 (June 1989).

Müller, Klaus Jürgen 'Clausewitz, Ludendorff and Beck: Some Remarks on Clausewitz' Influence on German Military Thinking in the 1930s and 1940s', in Handel (ed.), *Clausewitz and Modern Strategy*, 1986.

Murray, Williamson 'Clausewitz Out, Computer In', *National Interest*, no. 48 (Summer 1997).

Nardulli, B.R. 'Clausewitz and the Reorientation of Nuclear Strategy', *Journal of Strategic Studies*, vol. 5, no. 4 (December 1982).

Niemeyer, Joachim (ed.) 'Einleitung' in Clausewitz, *Historische Briefe über die grossen Kriegsereignisse im Oktober 1806*, Dümmler, Bonn, 1977.

O'Connell, Robert L. *Of Arms and Men*, Oxford University Press, New York, 1989.

O'Neill, Robert 'Insurgency and Subnational Violence' in O'Neill, Horner, D.M. (eds), *New Directions in Strategic Thinking*, Allen & Unwin, Sydney, 1981.

Orme, John 'The Utility of Force in a World of Scarcity', *International Security*, vol. 22, no. 3 (Winter 1997–98).

Osgood, Robert E. *Limited War: The Challenge to American Strategy*, University of Chicago Press, 1957.

Owens, William A. *Lifting the Fog of War*, Farrar, Straus & Giroux, New York, 2000.

Palmer, R.R. 'Frederick the Great, Guibert, Bülow: From Dynastic to National War' in Paret (ed.), *Makers of Modern Strategy*, 1986.

Paret, Peter 'Clausewitz and the Nineteenth Century' in Michael Howard (ed.), *The Theory and Practice of War*, Cassell, London, 1965.

Paret, Peter 'Clausewitz: A Bibliographical Survey', *World Politics*, vol. 17, no. 2 (January 1965a).

Paret, Peter 'On Clausewitz', *Military Review*, vol. 45, no. 7 (1965b).

Paret, Peter *Yorck and the Era of Prussian Reform 1807–1815*, Princeton University Press, 1966.

Paret, Peter 'Education, Politics, and War in the Life of Clausewitz', *Journal of the History of Ideas*, vol. 29, no. 3 (1968).

Paret, Peter 'An Anonymous Letter by Clausewitz', *Journal of Modern History*, vol. 42, no. 2 (June 1970).

Paret, Peter 'Nationalism and the Sense of Military Obligation', *Military Affairs*, vol. 34, no. 1 (1970a).

Paret, Peter *Clausewitz and the State*, Clarendon Press, Oxford, 1976.

Paret, Peter 'The Genesis of *On War*' in Clausewitz, *On War*, Howard, Paret (eds), 1976a.

Paret, Peter 'Raymond Aron, *Penser la guerre*' (Review), *Journal of Interdisciplinary History*, vol. 8, no. 2 (Autumn 1977).

Paret, Peter 'Gleichgewicht als Mittel der Friedenssicherung bei Clausewitz und in der Geschichte der Neuzeit', *Wehrwissenschaftliche Rundschau*, no. 3 (1980).

Paret, Peter 'Die politischen Ansichten von Clausewitz' in Wagemann, Niemeyer (eds), *Freiheit ohne Krieg?*, 1980a.

Paret, Peter 'Clausewitz' Politische Schriften' in Dill (ed.), *Clausewitz in Perspektive*, 1980b.

Paret, Peter (ed.) *Makers of Modern Strategy: Machiavelli to the Nuclear Age*, Princeton University Press, 1986.

Paret, Peter 'Clausewitz' in Paret (ed.) *Makers of Modern Strategy*, 1986a.

Paret, Peter *Understanding War: Essays on Clausewitz and the History of Military Power*, Princeton University Press, 1992.

Paret, Peter '"A Proposition Not a Solution" – Clausewitz's Attempt to Become Prussian Minister at the Court of St. James' in Paret, *Understanding War*, 1992a.

Paret, Peter 'Clausewitz as Historian' in Paret, *Understanding War*, 1992b.

Paret, Peter and Moran, Daniel (editors and translators) *Carl von Clausewitz: Historical and Political Writings*, Princeton University Press, 1992.

Parker, Geoffrey *The Military Revolution: Military innovation and the rise of the West 1500–1800* (2nd edition), Cambridge University Press, 1996.

Parkinson, Roger *Clausewitz: A Biography*, Wayland Publishers, London, 1970.

Perlmutter, Amos 'Carl von Clausewitz, Enlightenment Philosopher: A Comparative Analysis', *Journal of Strategic Studies*, vol. 11, no. 1 (March 1988).

Porter, Bruce D. *War and the Rise of the State*, Free Press, New York, 1994.

Posen, Barry R. 'Nationalism, the Mass Army and Military Power', *International Security*, vol. 18, no. 2 (Fall 1993).

Rapoport, Anatol 'Introduction' in Clausewitz, *On War*, Penguin Books, Harmondsworth, 1968.

Reynolds, Charles 'Carl von Clausewitz and strategic theory', *British Journal of International Studies*, vol. 4, no. 2 (July 1978).

Ritter, Gerhard 'Die Lehre Carls von Clausewitz vom politischen Sinn des Krieges', *Historische Zeitschrift*, vol. 167 (1943).

Ritter, Gerhard *The Sword and the Scepter* (vol. I, *The Prussian Tradition*), University of Miami Press, Florida, 1969.

Ropp, Theodore *War in the Modern World*, Duke University Press, Durham, NC, 1959.

Rosello, Victor M. 'Clausewitz's Contempt for Intelligence', *Parameters*, vol. XXI, no. 1 (Spring 1991).

Rosinski, Herbert 'Die Entwicklung von Clausewitz' Werk "Vom Kriege" im Lichte seiner "Vorreden" und "Nachreden"', *Historische Zeitschrift*, vol. 151 (1935).

Rothenberg, Gunther E. *The Art of Warfare in the Age of Napoleon*, Indiana University Press, Bloomington, 1980.

Rothenberg, Gunther E 'The Age of Napoleon' in Michael Howard, George J. Andreopoulos, and Mark R. Shulman (eds), *The Laws of War: Constraints on Warfare in the Western World*, Yale University Press, 1994.

Rothfels, Hans *Carl von Clausewitz Politik und Krieg: Eine ideengeschichtliche Studie*, Dümmler, Berlin, 1920 [reprinted Dümmler, Bonn, 1980].

Rothfels, Hans (ed.) *Carl von Clausewitz: Politische Schriften und Briefe*, Drei Masken Verlag, Munich, 1922.

Rothfels, Hans 'Clausewitz' in E.M. Earle (ed.), *Makers of Modern Strategy*, Princeton University Press, 1943.

Roxborough, Ian 'Clausewitz and the sociology of war', *British Journal of Sociology*, vol. 45, no. 4 (December 1994).

Scarry, Elaine *The Body in Pain: The Making and Unmaking of the World*, Oxford University Press, New York, 1985.

Schelling, Thomas C. *The Strategy of Conflict*, Oxford University Press, New York, 1963.

Scheuner, Ulrich 'Krieg als Mittel der Politik im Lichte des Völkerrechts' in Wagemann and Niemeyer (eds), *Freiheit ohne Krieg?*, 1980.

Schmitt 'Clausewitz als politischer Denker. Bemerkungen und Hinweise' in Dill (ed.), *Clausewitz in Perspektive*, 1980.

Schössler, Dietmar *Carl von Clausewitz*, Rowohlt, Reinbeck bei Hamburg, 1991.

Schramm, Wilhelm von 'Clausewitz und die politische Philosophie', *Aussenpolitik*, vol. 9, no. 11 (November 1958).

Schramm, Wilhelm von *Clausewitz: Leben und Werk*, Bechtle Verlag, Esslingen am Neckar, 1976.

Schwartz, Karl *Leben des Generals Carl von Clausewitz und der Frau Marie von Clausewitz* (2 vols), Dümmlers, Berlin, 1878.

Shy, John 'Jomini' in Paret (ed.), *Makers of Modern Strategy*, 1986.

Skinner, Quentin 'Meaning and Understanding in the History of Ideas', *History and Theory*, vol. 8 (1969).

Smith, Hugh 'The womb of war: Clausewitz and international politics', *Review of International Studies*, vol. 16, no. 1 (January 1990).

Starkey, David J. 'A Restless Spirit: British Privateering Enterprise, 1739–1815' in David J. Starkey, E.S. van Eyck van Heslinga, and J.A. de Moor (eds), *Privates and Privateers*, University of Exeter Press, 1997.

Steiner, Barry H. *Bernard Brodie and the Foundations of Nuclear Strategy*, University Press of Kansas, Lawrence, Kansas, 1991.

Strachan, Hew *European Armies and the Conduct of War*, Allen & Unwin, London, 1983.

Strachan, Hew 'Essay and Reflection: On Total War and Modern War', *The International History Review*, vol. XXII, no. 2 (June 2000).

Strachey, John *On the Prevention of War*, Macmillan, London, 1967.

Suganami, Hidemi 'Stories of war origins: a narrativist theory of the causes of war', *Review of International Studies*, vol. 23, no. 4 (October 1997).

Sumida, Jon Tetsuro *Inventing grand strategy and teaching command: the classic works of Alfred Thayer Mahan reconsidered*, Woodrow Wilson Center Press, Washington, 1997.

Sumida, Jon Tetsuro 'History and Theory: the Clausewitzian Ideal and Its Implications' *Journal of the Royal United Services Institute of Australia*, vol. 21 (June 2000).

Sumida, Jon Tetsuro 'The Relationship of History and Theory in *On War*: The Clausewitzian Ideal and Its Implications', *Journal of Military History*, vol. 65, no. 2 (April 2001).

Summers, Harry *On Strategy: A Critical Analysis of the Vietnam War*, Presidio Press, Novato, CA, 1982.

Tashjean, John E. 'Pious Arms: Clausewitz and the Right of War', *Military Affairs*, vol. 44, no. 2 (April 1980).

Tashjean, John E. 'The Translatlantic Clausewitz, 1952–1982', *Naval War College Review*, vol. 35, no. 6 (November–December 1982).

Tashjean, John E. 'The Cannon in the Swimming Pool: Clausewitzian Studies and Strategic Ethnocentrism', *Journal of the Royal United Services Institute* (June 1983).

Tashjean, John E. 'Clausewitz: Naval War and Other Considerations', *Naval War College Review*, vol. 39, no. 3 (May–June 1986).

Tashjean, John E. 'The Short-War Antinomy Resolved: or, From Homer to Clausewitz', *Defense Analysis*, vol. 8, no. 2 (August 1992).

Thibault, Edward 'War as a Collapse of Policy: A Critical Evaluation of Clausewitz', *Naval War College Review*, vol. 25, no. 5 (May–June 1973).

Toffler, Alvin & Heidi *War and Anti-War: Survival at the Dawn of the 21st Century*, Little, Brown & Company, Boston, 1993.

Türpe, Andrée 'Carl von Clausewitz' Verhältnis zur Philosophie seiner Zeit', *Militärgeschichte*, vol. 18, no. 5 (1979).

van Creveld, Martin *Supplying War: Logistics from Wallenstein to Patton*, Cambridge University Press, New York, 1977.

van Creveld, Martin *Command in War*, Harvard University Press, Cambridge, Mass., 1985.

van Creveld, Martin 'The Eternal Clausewitz' in Handel (ed.), *Clausewitz and Modern Strategy*, 1986.

van Creveld, Martin *The Transformation of War*, Free Press, New York, 1991.

van Creveld, Martin *Technology and War: From 2000 B.C. to the Present* (revised ed.), Free Press, New York, 1991a.

van Creveld, Martin 'The Clausewitzian Universe and the Law of War', *Journal of Contemporary History*, vol. 26 nos 3/4 (1991b).

van Creveld, Martin 'The Structure of Strategic Studies' in D. Ball, D. Horner (eds), *Strategic Studies in a Changing World*, Strategic and Defence Studies Centre, Australian National University, Canberra, 1992.

van Creveld, Martin 'What is Wrong with Clausewitz?' in Gert de Nooy (ed.), *The Clausewitzian Dictum and the Future of Western Military Strategy*, Kluwer Law International, The Hague, 1997.

van Creveld, Martin *The Rise and Decline of the State*, Cambridge University Press, Cambridge, 1999.

van Creveld, Martin *Men, Women and War*, Cassell & Co., London, 2001.

Villacres, Edward J. and Christopher Bassford 'Reclaiming the Clausewitzian Trinity', *Parameters*, vol. XXV, no. 3 (Autumn 1995).

von Caemmerer, Rudolf *The Development of Strategical Science during the 19th Century* (trans. Karl von Donat), Rees, London, 1905.

Wagemann, E., Niemeyer, J. (eds) *Freiheit ohne Krieg? Beiträge zur Strategie-Diskussion der Gegenwart im Spiegel der Theorie von Carl von Clausewitz*, Dümmler, Bonn, 1980.

Wallach, Jehuda L. 'Misperceptions of Clausewitz' On War by the German Military' in Handel (ed.), *Clausewitz and Modern Strategy*, 1986.

Walzer, Michael *Just and Unjust Wars*, Allen Lane, London, 1978.

Weigley, Russell F. *The Age of Battles: The Quest for Decisive Warfare from Breitenfeld to Waterloo*, Pimlico, London, 1993.

Weil, Eric 'Guerre et Politique selon Clausewitz', *Révue Française de Science Politique*, vol. 5, no. 2 (April–June 1955).

White, Charles E. *The Enlightened Soldier: Scharnhorst and the Militärische Gesellschaft in Berlin, 1801–1805*, Praeger, New York, 1989.

Wilkinson, Spenser *War and Policy: Essays*, Constable & Co., London, 1900.

Wilkinson, Spenser *The Brain of an Army*, Gregg Revivals, Aldershot, Hampshire, 1992.

Windsor, Philip 'The Clock, the Context and Clausewitz', *Millennium*, vol. 6, no. 2 (Autumn 1977).

Index